THE BOSS OF BOSSES

THE BOSS OF BOSSES

THE LIFE OF THE INFAMOUS TOTÒ RIINA, DREADED HEAD OF THE SICILIAN MAFIA

Attilio Bolzoni and
Giuseppe D'Avanzo

Translated by Shaun Whiteside

An Orion paperback

First published in Great Britain in 2015
by Orion Books Ltd.
This paperback edition published in 2016
by Orion Books Ltd,
Carmelite House, 50 Victoria Embankment,
London EC4Y 0DZ

An Hachette UK company

7 9 10 8 6

Copyright © 2007 – 2011 RCS Libri SpA
English translation © Shaun Whiteside 2015

A CIP catalogue record for this book is available
from the British Library.

Trade Paperback ISBN: 978 1 4091 6098 4
Mass Market Paperback ISBN: 978 1 4091 5380 1

Printed and bound in Great Britain by Clays Ltd, Elcograf S.p.A.

MIX
Paper from
responsible sources
FSC® C104740

www.orionbooks.co.uk

FIFTEEN YEARS ON

It's almost fifteen years since Totò Riina was arrested. If, in the event of a new edition of *Boss of Bosses*, the threads of his criminal history are picked up once more, it will be apparent that the scene has changed only superficially.

As Tommaso Buscetta warned at the time, the Mafia has scattered bombs all over the continent. It was the final step in the terrorist strategy of the peasants of Corleone. What has followed since 1993 has been a season of invisibility. Of men, methods and wealth. A return to the past, to a non-aggressive accommodation with the state and a complicit embrace with Sicilian society. The apparent calm has allowed the elites – political and administrative – to wipe the Mafia question from public debate. It has allowed the bosses of Cosa Nostra to put the organisation back in order under the 'wise' guidance of Bernardo Provenzano.

And then the other *viddano*[1] in Corleone was captured at last after forty-three years on the run, on 11 April 2006.

---

1   Italian *villano*, a coarse-mannered peasant.

Attilio Bolzoni and Giuseppe D'Avanzo

The fall of Totò Riina might lead one to believe that an adventure had come to an end once and for all. It's a mistake to think such a thing. Nothing ever really changes in Cosa Nostra. Nothing has changed today. The fathers, reduced to impotence, are followed by sons already brought up for the Mafia life that awaits them.

After almost fifteen years, the canvas is new only in this respect: where once there were old men, there are now new ones. The surnames remain the same: Riina, Provenzano, Bagarella, Inzerillo and Bontate, Gambino and Di Maggio. They are all seeking reasonable compromises to ensure that they don't start killing each other again. Will the families make peace, or will they wage war on each other as they did two decades ago?

Attilio Bolzoni and Giuseppe D'Avanzo
October 2007

FOREWORD

We got the idea of writing the story of Totò Riina after seeing him. He's a peasant. Modest appearance, roughly spoken, the simplicity of his thoughts and his lies don't correspond, in any apparent respect, to the refinement of the strategies of Cosa Nostra, the organisation that he conquered through bloodshed and ruled with terror for over a decade.

The question of why Cosa Nostra abandoned its traditional and cautious camouflage in the shadow of legality to unleash a terrorist war against the state, which saw the fall of magistrates, policemen and politicians, shady or not, is still open. We believe that many of the reasons lie in Salvatore Riina's will to power. We are convinced, at the end of our work, that the force of this pack leader lies in his peasant nature, and that the reasons for his choices and his appetite for danger lie in his having lived at least half of his life on the run, pursued more by his enemies in the Mafia than his enemies in the state. It was his life as a hunted animal that made him alert, astute, paranoid and – above all – cruel.

To talk about Totò Riina, in the first year of his visibility, we need to rely on scraps and fragments of the truth. We have tried to reconstruct his criminal story by relying where possible on direct testimonies.

The first part of the book describes a Sicilian world that has now disappeared: life in Corleone immediately after the war, Riina's family, his friendships, the escapades of the Liggio gang and the arrival of the Contadini clan in Palermo. A story that has been possible thanks to the courage and generosity of half a dozen residents of Corleone who agreed to meet us under very risky circumstances.

The second part of the book, which concerns Riina's rise to the upper echelons of Cosa Nostra, is also based on other eye-witness accounts – seven in particular. It deals with his 'politics', his network of connections, the style with which he governed the organisation, his clash with the state. A universe revealed by the confessions of Tommaso Buscetta, Salvatore Contorno, Antonino Calderone, Francesco Marino Mannoia, Gaspare Mutolo, Giuseppe Marchese and Baldassare Di Maggio.

We have also, as will become apparent, studied court files, police reports, parliamentary documents. And here – although we cannot name any individuals – we want to thank the magistrates, the policemen, the civil servants within the Ministry of the Interior who facilitated our task by giving us precious and useful evidence. The facts, the dialogues and situations reported in this book have all been painstakingly obtained from the declarations of witnesses or legal documents.

We think we have fulfilled our rights and duties as chroniclers in recording the facts that we have received from various sources. Let us remind both ourselves and our readers that only the judiciary will be able to write the last word on the events related in these pages.

Special thanks to Eugenio Cirese, Claudio Giua and Enzo Mignosi.

Attilio Bolzoni and Giuseppe D'Avanzo

PART ONE

THE PEASANT OF CORLEONE

THE *MASCULIDDU* OF PIAZZA SOPRANA

THEY WERE ALL IN SINGLE FILE

The Batticano River had been dry for six months. The air was sticky and the flies buzzed around the animals, thin cows, mangy dogs. The smells of dry countryside were scattered on the sirocco wind. The summer of 1943 had been extremely hot. It was the eleventh of September. The sky was still high, the fields scorched. They were coming down from the Frattina vines, through the hills of Venere del Poggio. They were in single file. The father, Giovanni Riina, the first male child, Salvatore or 'Totò' for short, the second male child Gaetano. Last came Francesco, the youngest brother. Francesco was seven years old, swaying back and forth on top of a mule. It was the end of a hard day's work like so many for a peasant family.

Giovanni Riina had inherited a bit of land from his father, who had inherited it from his father's father: two hills in Marabino, four hills in Frattina, three hills in San Cristoforo, another four hills in Mazzadiana. That made almost three hectares of land. Enough land to eat at least once a day. To make bread, pick beans, barter a sack of grain for some bales of raw wool, or leather to mend shoes, or iron and copper to repair tools. They were hard times, times of war. Just before the big crossing there was a bridge that

9

passed over a dry riverbed. Then the path climbed to the mountain that had adopted the name of the village: Corleone.

In the first seven months of the year the fear always arrived from above, in the 'planes with two tails'. That was what they called the Lightning bombers with their double fuselage, dual-propellor planes with four machine guns and a light gun. They appeared suddenly from north-north-east. People said they were coming from Monreale. There were so many of them that they darkened the sky like swarms of locusts. Then they dropped their loads and disappeared towards the south, behind the hills of Lercara Friddi. The most terrifying bombing raid was the one on 9 May. The aerial incursions by the Allies on the Sicilian cities ended on the last day of June. An unexploded bomb was found by Giovanni Riina in the fields at Venere del Poggio on the afternoon of 11 September 1943. The Americans had already disembarked nine weeks previously, and the bomb was now 'war surplus'.

It gleamed in the sun. It was the colour of bronze. Giovanni Riina absolutely had to bring that bomb home. It was precious. Gunpowder for the cartridges of the *scupetta* and iron to reinforce the ploughshare. Among the sods of earth there was also a grey cylinder. It was a cannon shell, about forty centimetres long. It was broken at the top. The Germans had left it there when they fled the area on 10 July. The peasant told his son Francesco to jump down from the mule, because they had to load on the bomb and also the shell. He asked Totò, the stronger of the other two boys, to help him. They delicately lifted up the devices, then slipped them into a jute bag. And they set off back towards the village.

An hour later they reached the gates of Corleone. It was still seriously hot, an oppressive sultriness. It was six o'clock in the evening, and the children were playing in the area around Piazza Soprana. They were running down the alleyways barefoot, hiding behind the trees, slipping underneath the carts.

The Riinas' house was on Via Rua del Piano. It was a poor peasant house, with grey stone walls and loose tiles. There was a big room which, on one side, also became a stable. On the other side were the beds, the big wooden table and the chairs. And lined up on the ground the *quartare*, terracotta jugs used for keeping fresh water. They were also used for oil when the harvest was good. The father and his three sons stopped in Via Rua del Piano, on the corner with Via Ravenna, at around seven. It was still very light. Giovanni Riina decided to defuse the American bomb in the alley, right outside his own house. Totò stood silent in a corner and Francesco stood and watched him. Gaetano was sitting on a low wall near the mule. Then they carried the cannon shell into the house.

It seemed empty, with no more than a gram of gunpowder. He started banging it with a stone. The shell slipped from the hands of Giovanni Riina, class of 1897, a peasant from Corleone listed by the Royal Carabinieri as a 'subject capable of doing damage to people and the property of others'. There was a great bang and a flash of flames. There were shouts and screams after the explosion. Giovanni Riina died, disembowelled. Little Francesco died too. The shrapnel from the shell entered Gaetano's right leg, injured his neck and shredded his cheeks. Even the mule was lying on the ground and wasn't moving. The mule had died too. There wasn't a scratch on it.

The funeral took place in the church of Santa Rosalia two days later. It was 13 September. There was a big crowd in the streets of Corleone. A woman dressed in black dragged herself dry-eyed to the cemetery; she had no tears left to weep for her husband and son. She was desperate. She was pregnant, Maria Concetta Rizzo, the widow Riina. Twenty-six days later she would give birth to Giovanna Francesca. Her oldest daughter was close to her. She was fifteen at the time, Caterina. And she was holding Arcangela, the other sister, the last to be born, by the hand. Her son Gaetano was still in a hospital bed. He was alive, he had been saved by a miracle. The only male in the family to accompany his father and his brother Francesco's coffin was Salvatore. Totò.

Now he was the new head of the family. Salvatore Riina was the man who had to run the house and the land. He was thirteen years old. He still wore short flannel trousers like all the other boys his age, shoes that had been mended top and bottom, socks made of black cotton that could be darned. He had chestnut hair, the thin face of the teenagers of those years, the strong, callused hands of people who worked in the fields. His arms were long, too long. Or perhaps they were normal and he was short, even for his age. They already called him *u Curtu*, Shorty, but they never said it to his face. Never when he was close enough to hear, when he happened to be passing through the square on his way back from the field.

He was a boy who didn't say much, little Totò Riina. And when he spoke he always stared hard at you with those black eyes of his, which studied you, drained you, intimidated you. As if he could read other people's thoughts. They were frightening, those eyes of his. But not that day, the afternoon of the funeral. He kept them low on the ground. Every now and again he looked at his mother, then he bent his head again and stared at his broken shoes. From the house in Via Rua del Piano to the cemetery he said only four words: *'Murìu frati Cicciu.'* My brother Ciccio died.

In Corleone today they swear that he wiped away a single tear, hugged his mother and the little women in his family. It was the last time anyone saw him cry.

It was almost sunset when the cortège left the church of Santa Rosalia and passed slowly down the streets of the village. The steep slope of Via Roma was swathed in silence. The coffins carried on the backs of the bearers stopped in front of the parish church on Piazza Garibaldi, then disappeared down Corso Bentivegna. The wind rose up. The weeping of the women became heart-rending in the dusty little street leading down to the graveyard.

Giovanni Riina and his son Francesco were buried in the earth. Two wooden crosses amidst a hundred wooden crosses. Only eighteen years later – on 26 February 1961 – their remains were transferred to a little niche on Via dei Cipressi. The grave had a number, 20, fourth on the left from the beginning of the avenue.

Giovanni Riina and Francesco, d. 12.9.1943.

Someone mistranscribed the day of their death on the marble. An anonymous niche among the family chapels of Corleone. A white slab and three photographs. The faces of Giovanni Riina and two nameless women.

On the morning of 18 January 1993 two little boys went into the graveyard of Corleone. It was a Monday. The previous Saturday Francesco and Giuseppe Salvatore had come back to the village with their mother Ninetta and their two sisters. Their father had been arrested in Palermo after twenty-four years on the run. Totò Riina's two sons – half a century after the bomb went off – were clutching a bunch of flowers. They knelt down and prayed on their grandfather's grave.

WHEN THE BARBER WAS ALSO A DENTIST

The barber always knew everything. He knew because he could know. In Corleone the barber was worth a good six inches more than the mayor and a couple of inches less than the parish priest of the Matrice, the main church in the village. The barber was a barber and also a dentist. But above all he was a confessor. He had the privilege of guarding other people's secrets, sins and sufferings. Someone who did the job he did inevitably inspired trust:

13

after all, it wasn't a small thing to entrust your own throat to a stranger.

The barber in Corleone was called Giovannino. His barber's salon faced out on to Piazza Garibaldi, between the Alaimo Café and the Ospedale dei Bianchi (the Hospital of the White Fathers). Also passing his days in the small shop was a little boy who spent hour after hour listening to what the grown-ups were saying. '*Vituzzu, facci na bedda sapunata o cavaleri.*' Vituzzu, give the knight a good soaping. Vito – Vituzzu – was an alert child who would become the mayor of Palermo twenty years later. The powerful Vito Ciancimino. At the time he was only a boy. The son of the barber of Corleone.

Salvatore Riina didn't go to Giovannino's barber shop. It was a place only the important people of the village could go to: the landowners, the chemist, the *sensali*[1], the lawyer, the dean, the three doctors from the hospital. And the Mafiosi. People like Salvatore Riina went to a different barber shop. It was also on Piazza Garibaldi, but fifteen metres from Giovannino's; he was the barber for the peasants. You paid him once a year. Fifty-two beards and twelve haircuts in exchange for wheat – between fourteen and sixteen kilos – from one mound of earth.

Totò Riina's world was the countryside. He left the house on Via Rua del Piano at dawn and walked down to Marabino. He left in darkness, he came home in darkness. There was no Christmas and there was no Easter; the days were all the same. The aroma of chicken soup was smelled in the alleyways only on two occasions: a birth or an illness, when a child had to be fed or an old person cured. Life in Sicily in the years immediately after the war was grim, and Corleone was not spared poverty.

---

1   Commercial agents or brokers.

But the soil in the fields was rich and fragrant. Even malaria had gone with the DDT brought by the Americans. There was talk of agricultural reform. But meanwhile, at sunset, the country-folk looked out on barren wastelands, yellow hills that turned dark brown when the stubble was burned. The water came down in abundance from the Belice, but never reached the valley. The livestock wandered in search of grazing. There was always the spectre of hunger and famine. These were days that prepared for the occupation of the big estates. The conquest of the land.

The masters and ancient names. Cammarata, Valenti, De Cordova. Barons, counts, marquises. And the sons of barons, counts and marquises passed through the estates from time to time. There were the *campieri*, the stewards who looked after the interests of their estates. Stewards on horseback in big leather boots. They clutched whips, and had hunting rifles over their shoulders. In the estates of Corleone there were two who commanded 're-spect'. One was known as 'Borbone' (Bourbon) because he was at La Ficuzza, between the woods and the hunting lodge that Ferdinand IV had had built a century and a half before. Borbone's name was Vincenzo Catanzaro. He was a *maffioso* and the son of a *maffioso*. The other was Salvatore Cascone. Because of his reputation as a wise man he was known as 'Salomone' (Solomon). Evidently he only had the gift of the gab. He bled to death after being shot in the face. Salomone had persistently wooed the wife of a very jealous shepherd.

The farmer Salvatore Riina saw the *campieri* passing through the estates, surrounded by their men. Ugly thugs. Cowards who were prepared to fire their shotguns at any poor wretch for the slightest thing. He saw them on horseback and greeted them with a nod of his head, but only when they had glanced in his direction. Only after they had given him permission to greet them. Salvatore knew how to behave, he knew the law of the estates.

During those months he had also heard about what was happening beyond the mountains of Monreale. In Borgetto, in Giardinello, in Montelepre. The bandit Giuliano had become a 'colonel'. A colonel of Evis, the Voluntary Army for the Independence of Sicily. Everyone said *Turiddu*[1] wanted to give land to the peasants. But meanwhile he was killing the peasants. As at Portella della Ginestra. Salvatore Giuliano also killed policemen; he had finished off a hundred and five of them since his headquarters had been in the hills of Sàgana. He killed for the utopia of a 'Sicily for the Sicilians'. And he also wrote to Harry Truman, the President of the United States of America. But such matters weren't of much interest to a boy from Corleone who hadn't yet turned eighteen. A boy who was condemned to live between Marabino and Frattina with his little piece of land. In the countryside with the cold in winter and the heat in summer. With a fatherless family, three sisters and a younger brother to feed. For Totò, *Turiddu* Giuliano was a *pupo* – a puppet. Someone called the shots, and the bandit of Montelepre fired the gun.

It was during these difficult years that Salvatore Riina met another boy like himself. He was one of the lads from the village who he passed at least once a day in those parts. He was three years younger than Totò. He was big, thickset, tough. He never said a word. His name was *Binnu*, Bernardo. At dawn Totò Riina saw him coming down from Corleone with his father Angelo and his brother Salvatore. His father had no land, and worked as a day labourer. His sons followed him like shadows. They followed him everywhere, until he found a *campiere* who 'did him the courtesy' of letting him bend over his hoe for twelve hours at a time. Meanwhile Binnu and Salvatore weeded the wheat fields.

---

1   Nickname for Salvatore Giuliano.

THE BOSS OF BOSSES

Every morning on every day of the year they took the same steep path. Angelo, the father, walked ahead of the mule and his sons Salvatore and Binnu walked behind, close to the animal's tail. For almost fifty years Totò would share his life with that little boy, strong as an ox, who he saw passing by his lands at dawn. And soon he would call him Binnu. His Binnu. Bernardo Provenzano.

THE DOCTOR'S FATHER WAS A SPY

Even on summer evenings, a fresh breeze blew down from the Montagna dei Cavalli towards Corleone. It was pleasant to be out in the streets. People strolled back and forth along Corso Bentivegna. Giovannino's barber shop was closed. At that time of day everyone went to the club for a game of cards and a glass of wine. There were three clubs in the village. The *Burgisi*, the *Mastri* and the *Buoni Amici*. They talked about everything and nothing, and they always ended up talking about the land. About *tumuli*, barrels of wine, vines, olives. There was always a *sensale* listening. The *sensali* were the middlemen who bought and sold land. They were *intesi* – insiders – and all the villagers knew they had to treat them with respect.

In the streets every evening people complained about sheaves of grain that had disappeared between sunset and dawn.

'Last night they stole about forty around Manganelli.'

'Who was that?'

'Pff, passing outsiders . . .'

'Bastards! I hope their balls fall off . . .'

Rumours of those thefts reached the ears of the boys who walked in the fields, like Binnu Provenzano or Salvatore Riina. Then Totò was in the square closest to his house, in Piazza Soprana, in the upper part of the village, although he had also been seen a few times near the Saracen Tower. Totò was never alone, he was always with other boys. And with them was an 'important' person.

The local doctor of Corleone took long walks around the Saracen Tower. He was a short, fat, bald man. He had graduated from Palermo University in 1929. His clothes were shabby. He had lots of friends. Michele Navarra was doing 'very well' in the village. It was whispered that *u dutturi* (the doctor) had replaced Borbone, the old *campiere* of the Ficuzza forest, as Mafia boss. On the little street that passed below the Saracen Tower, for some time the doctor had been seen in the company of tenant farmers who would never have been seen in Piazza Garibaldi during the day. They were young, some of them very young. One of them was delicate and sickly, with a limp. His spinal column had been damaged by Pott's disease. He was the son of tenant farmers, but he had never gone to work in the fields. His name was Luciano Liggio. And with him there was another, stouter boy, although he was really small. Totò Riina was barely five foot four.

The sickly boy was said to steal livestock. He carried out raids on cattle and horses in the valleys around Corleone. The breeders didn't react and didn't protest. Nor did they ever think of revenge. Not least because Dr Navarra had put it around that *Lucianeddu* had become the *campiere* of Strasatto, a big estate between Corleone and Roccamena. The owner was a man from Palermo called Caruso. Dr Navarra had also made it known that Lucianeddu was 'his personal matter'. In the village they had understood. The old *campiere* was dead. Murdered. 'Homicide by persons unknown', it said on the judicial report on the killing of Stanslao Punzo.

At around this time the young farmer Salvatore Riina stopped seeing the glorious sunrises of Corleone. He no longer went to the fields of Frattina as he had once done. He stayed in the village, going no further than Piazza Garibaldi. He strolled along Via

Firmaturi, near the Ospedale dei Bianchi. Some time previously Michele Navarra had become head of the medical department at the hospital. Salvatore went down the alleyways and spent whole mornings at the Alaimo Café. He was no longer 'Totò, son of Giovanni, the one who was killed by the bomb'.

He had become a *masculiddu*, a real man. He knew when to speak and when to shut up. Being a *masculiddu* meant above all being *sperto*, shrewd. And acting consistently. Knowing you were being observed by more important people, people who could make you into either a 'man of respect' or a 'useless object'. It was all about looks, gestures, carefully judged words. Of calculated gestures and silences. Some of the old people of Corleone still remember them today. They remember Totò Riina first appearing in Piazza Garibaldi. And they also remember the words he used to say over and over again, with rage and despair. It wasn't a lament, it was a promise: 'I don't intend to stay in Corleone all my life. I don't want to die poor. I don't want to live like a beggar.'

It was around this time that Totò Riina first went to Giovannino's barber shop. He was with Michele Navarra and Lucianeddu, the *campiere* from Strasatto. The doctor was welcomed with a bow, and then a kiss to the hand. A hundred lips a day brushed the ring that gleamed on Don Michele's finger. Lucianeddu was chatty. He was constantly joking and telling stories. Totò was silent, introverted and diffident. He spent most of his time sitting in a corner and listening. He leapt to his feet obediently only when the doctor said his name. Then he went back into the corner and listened again, as motionless as a marble statue.

There was only one story that was never heard in the barber shop of the eminent people of Corleone. And it concerned his godfather, Dr Michele Navarra. But the barber Giovannino couldn't have known that particular detail. It was jealously guarded in an old safe in the office of the chief of police of Corleone.

It was a secret stored in a file of classified papers concerning Giuseppe Navarra, the father of the village's new Mafia boss.

It was just a few lines written on a sheet of vellum paper, stamped and signed. 'Giuseppe Navarra son of Giuseppe and Giuffrida Maria enjoys a good reputation, employed as a teacher at Corleone Agricultural College, belongs to the so-called middle class [. . .]. He has no criminal record, and the only things recorded against him are: a) alleged administrative irregularities claimed by the managers of the Bernardino Verro Agricultural Cooperative; b) and having presented himself during the time of Prefect of Police Cesare Mori, collaborating with the local authorities to suppress the Mafia.' The father of the new boss of Corleone was a *muffuttu*. He was an informer who had passed information to the 'Iron Prefect'. To help him catch, one by one, the Mafiosi of Marineo and Godrano.

THE COOKING OF ITALIA

In Piazza Garibaldi in Corleone the men were divided into two categories. Those who strolled and those *sciusciavano*. *Sciusciare* in Sicilian means to blow. In Corleone more than anything else it meant to create a wind without lifting a finger. Moving air while staying where you were. It was a privilege exclusive to the Mafiosi.

One day Salvatore Riina himself had begun to *sciusciare* between the square and Corso Bentivegna. Totò had changed. He was a different person now from the time when he had met Dr Navarra and the *campiere* of Strasatto. He passed in front of the clubs and smiled at the old people who had watched him growing up. And he looked up, towards the sky. He looked at the four black stone houses built below a mountain crag. Above it was 'the castle': Corleone prison. A flight of steps carved into the rock ran about sixty metres up the slope. There was an iron gate. And behind the walls an orange grove, a vegetable garden and bougain-villea climbing the walls. There were also the rows of prickly pines that hid a pigsty and a rabbit hutch. Totò had heard the old people say: 'Any real man will finish up there at least once in his life.'

The village was dominated by the castle. Corleone jail was a famous one. The fugitives in the area who had one or at most two years of their sentences to serve climbed those seventy metres of rock and knocked on the iron gate. They knew it was a 'comfortable' prison. There was only one prison warder, the council employee Calogero Listi. In the morning Don Calogero went to the council offices, then he dropped in at the 'castle' to visit his inmates. Don Calogero was a clerk and a rural policeman. He also had the keys to the prison. The food for the prisoners was brought twice a day by his wife, Italia. She was from northern Italy – Venice, to be precise. In spite of what the old people in the village said, Totò Riina never spent a single night in his life in the 'castle'. Nor did he ever sample Italia's cooking.

Totò Riina lived in the countryside as he had always done. But he was no longer a farmer who counted the bags of grain at the end of harvest. And his land was no longer the land between Marabino and Frattina. Now he was in Strasatto. With Luciano Liggio, with Calogero Bagarella, with Bernardo Provenzano. With another twenty or so *masculiddi* recruited by Dr Navarra between Piazza Garibaldi and Corso Bentivegna. They were a gang. Raids on fields, thefts of livestock, clandestine butchery. Lives cut short, farms burnt. A gang of young Mafiosi. On the Sicilian estate the Corleonesi were being born, the thoroughbreds of the criminal species, the most accursed of the *cosche*[1] that would spread hatred

---

1   Gangs.

for another half-century. The scorched lands of Strasatto were producing the peasants who would conquer Palermo and, with Palermo, Cosa Nostra.

Chief among the thugs who served Dr Navarra at the time was Lucianeddu. Totò was not one of the many. He was the most astute. The cruellest, the coldest, the most devilish. He was the most Corleonese of the Corleonesi. His instinct drove him far. Outside the country. Beyond the estate. Even then he knew already what his strength was, and the strength of people like him. The desire to possess Sicily was in his blood.

They were always seen in a group of three. Totò, Calò and Binnu. Totò Riina, Calogero Bagarella and Bernardo Provenzano. They were inseparable. All three 'the same thing'. Together in the fields, at the Alaimo bar, together on the low wall of Piazza Garibaldi. When they met, they kissed each other on the cheek. They spent whole days without speaking. They didn't need words to understand one another. A look was enough, or a silence, or a nod of the head. They were born within five years of each other. Totò was born in 1930, Binnu in 1933, Calogero in 1935. They seemed so different from their boss. They seemed to come from another world. They weren't brazen and insolent like Lucianeddu. None of them ever opened his mouth if he didn't have something to say. And particularly if that something wasn't strictly necessary. They were very young, but already they knew what they wanted. They were ready for anything. At their head was Luciano. He was above all a friend, a protector, the leader of the pack.

But he wasn't like them. That was why they worshipped him, and why they didn't trust him. He had never been a country boy. They had never seen him lying on summer nights on the damp grass that grew along the streams between Corleone and Contesa Entellina. Lucianeddu had never gone fishing for eels, he had never soaked baskets made of bulrushes in the water.

Lucianeddu had never struggled through the fields behind a mule or a jennet.

THE COURAGE OF PLACIDO

What happened in Corleone on the evening of 10 March 1948 unleashed a political storm over the next few weeks. The secretary of Corleone Trade Union Headquarters had disappeared. Disappeared meant dead. Kidnapped, murdered, his corpse fed to the animals. The trade unionist was Placido Rizzotto. He was a socialist. He was twenty-four. Three times Luciano Liggio was accused of murder, three times he was acquitted for lack of evidence. In the thousands of pages and files of the three trials, the name of Totò Riina always appeared in the vague background of the raids by the *campiere* of Strasatto. But in a psychobiography of 'Salvatore Riina of Corleone, the first son of Giovanni [. . .] who was the first and only son of Salvatore Riina and Caterina Orlando', the secret services dedicated a passage to him assigning him a prominent role: 'The first major crime that the young Riina was known to be involved in was in 1948, when Placido Rizzotto was killed. [. . .] The deed was carried out by Luciano Liggio with the collaboration of the young Riina . . .'

The death of the secretary of Corleone Trade Union Head-quarters must have occurred on the night of 10 to 11 March. A few months previously Rizzotto refused to allow Dr Navarra to join the section of 'Combatants and Ex-Servicemen' of which he was secretary. He had asked the doctor to provide evidence. He said his 'papers as combatant and ex-serviceman' were in order. He had been a deputy second lieutenant in the 10th Trieste Heavy Artillery. He had been discharged a year later and called up again on the brink of the war. He had immediately been declared unfit for military service and sent home. Placido Rizzotto didn't want to have someone like him 'among the combatants or the ex-servicemen'. With Luciano Liggio the trade unionist did something even worse. About three weeks before the murder some ex-partisans from Catania passed through Corleone. They were travelling in two military-style trucks. They were on their way from Agrigento to Palermo. Crossing the island from the Sicilian Channel to the Tyrrhenian Sea was a considerable enterprise in those days. Beaten earth road, mountains to climb, at least seven hours in the dust. The ex-partisans stopped in Corleone.

A pause to grab a piece of bread. The trucks were in front of *u funnacu*, the place where the carters had once tied their mules and horses. The ex-partisans were having a rest, and a group of little Mafiosi was walking around the trucks. Liggio was one of them. He mocked and insulted them. That was the start of the fight. Someone went to call the man who could calm those hotheads down, Placido Rizzotto. The trade unionist came running to the *funnacu* but even he couldn't manage to put a stop to the brawl. Then he took the side of the outsiders. He supported them, against Lucianeddu and his companions. Eye witnesses say that Luciano Liggio was lifted up in the air by Placido, and then thrown against a wall and pinned up by his jacket on the bars of the town-hall gate. Leonardo La Torre, the nephew of another Mafioso, was also injured in the pandemonium. That day Placido signed his own death warrant. First he had 'offended' Dr Navarra, then he had humiliated the *campiere* of Strasatto. Those were two good reasons to kill him, even though Placido would die for another, more serious reason: he had set the peasants against the *campieri*.

For three years the trade unionist walked around the estates putting up banners. He talked at rallies, he argued with the barons, and with the excise men, and with the Mafiosi. People like Rizzotto were dangerous. Eight months before, the socialists and communists had triumphed in the regional elections. The People's Block had won twenty-nine seats in the assembly, nine more than the Christian Democrats, and thirty per cent of the vote. The fight at the carters' post was only the last incident. In fact, rather than an incident, it was an opportunity to present the excitable trade unionist as 'a spy', 'a traitor' who was picking arguments with his fellow villagers. To use a term from Corleone, a *tragediatore*, someone who plots behind your back and is never straight with you. His goal is to spread poison, to sow suspicion. Warning others about non-existent dangers and unlikely intentions. Telling lies all over the place. The *tragediatore* doesn't even spare his closest friends, he lives to harm his neighbours. To create tragedies, in fact.

On the evening of 10 March, Placido Rizzotto was the victim of a tragedy of his own. He was walking along the street. Then he stopped outside the Alaimo Café. He was with two colleagues from Trade Union Headquarters. Pasquale approached the three men. He was a peasant, a colleague of Rizzotto's, even though at night he associated with Michele Navarra's gang. It was Criscione who drew Placido into the trap, following an order from Luciano Liggio. And it was Criscione who confessed the crime to Captain Carlo Alberto Dalla Chiesa, Brigadier Capizzi and Police Officer Ribezzo, and then retracted his confession before the magistrates. The 'extra-judicial' depositions of Pasquale Coricione were not enough to sentence Luciano Liggio. Not in the first instance, on appeal, or in the Court of Cassation.

The whole village knew how Placido had died. And a witness also had the courage to write it in an anonymous letter, sent just seven days after the kidnapping of the trade unionist to the police and the Communist MP Girolamo Li Causi.

'Allow me to tell you who it was that killed Placito [sic] *. . . first both the Crisciuna brothers, Luciano Liggio . . .'*

In the world of *omertà*[1], the anonymous letter was the only dialogue possible with the cops, the only possible form of collaboration between a Sicilian and the Italian state represented by men in uniform.

A week after the disappearance of the trade unionist in Corleone a shepherd-boy died. He was thirteen, and his name was Giuseppe Letizia. 'Death by toxicosis' was the diagnosis in the medical report by the director of the Ospedale dei Bianchi. Legend has it that it was Dr Michele Navarra who killed the shepherd-boy – witness to the kidnapping of Placido Rizzotto – by injecting poison into his veins. But the investigations of Captain Dalla Chiesa in fact excluded the Mafia boss of Corleone from investigations.

'The truth is that no connection,' the young police officer wrote to the public prosecutor's office in Palermo, 'has ever existed between the disappearance of Rizzotto and the death of Letizia. [. . .] It has also been ascertained that there are doubts concerning the intervention of the Mafia, and particularly of Navarra, in the shepherd's death.'

Placido's corpse was found 644 days later. It was a Wednesday, 14 December 1949. His father Carmelo recognised it by its shoes. They pulled the skeleton up from a sinkhole in Rocca Busambra, the high crag that rises out of the Ficuzza forest. It was Police Officer Orlando Notari who climbed down on a rope into the *ciacca*, the crack in the mountain. In a big basket he brought up a wallet, a belt, sheep carcases. And also an old unloaded pistol, a model from 1899. Four families were summoned to identify the body. The Rizzottos, the Crapas, the Strevas and the Culottas. Each of them had a son who had

---

1   Mafia code of silence.

disappeared. Then Carmelo Rizzotto saw those shoes. Among the trees on the Rocca Busambra that day was Leoluchina Sorisi, Placido's fiancée. The girl said: 'I will eat the heart of whoever killed him.'

The official identification of the corpse of the trade unionist was carried out in front of the man who represented the law in Corleone. It was the honorary assistant magistrate Bernardo Di Miceli. He was the first cousin of the Mafia boss Michele Navarra.

TWICE HE BORE FALSE WITNESS

On the day when Placido's body was discovered in the sinkhole of Rocca Busambra, Salvatore Riina was almost nineteen years old. He had been in jail for seven months. He wasn't locked up in the 'castle' of Corleone, he was detained in the Ucciardone in Palermo on charges of homicide. In May, on the afternoon of the 13th, he had killed Menicu.

Domenico Di Matteo, Menicu, was a boy from the village, another country boy. They were talking on the hill of San Giovanni, having met on an area of beaten ground once used for playing bowls. It was a little flattened hill on the edge of the village. There were a few trees around it and, behind it, there was an abandoned military warehouse. Ten days before 13 May there had been a punch-up in the alleys above Piazza Garibaldi with sticks and knuckle-dusters. A brawl immediately after the church procession. On one side were Totò Riina and his friends; on the other were Menicu Di Matteo and his cousins. They met up again on the hill of San Giovanni to 'have satisfaction'. And on the hill of San Giovanni blood was shed once more, when the two groups clashed again. First insults, then punches and kicks. And then at a certain moment a boy by the name of Labbita drew a revolver. He was scared.

'Stop it all of you or I'll shoot,' he shouted.

He didn't shoot, at least not straight away. A few days later, the commissioner of public safety for Corleone presented the police report to the state prosecutor's office. It said: 'It was Riina who drew from his pocket an automatic pistol that he always carried with him and fired a shot at Labbita but struck his cousin Di Matteo in the right thigh. [. . .] Di Matteo, finding that he was injured, incited his cousin to fire [. . .]. Riina began firing all the shots he had in the gun he was clutching . . .'

After the gun-fight on the bowling ground, Menicu Di Matteo was taken to hospital. Totò Riina took refuge in the house of his uncle Francesco Di Frisco.

Totò had been injured as well, in both legs. A single bullet passed 'first through the right calf and then through the left calf'. His uncle treated his wounds as best he could. He tied him to a chair and carried him to the Ospedale dei Bianchi, a former convent just around the corner from Piazza Garibaldi. The door was rust red, with an eagle painted at the top. The blocks were arranged in a semi-circle around a garden of palm trees and magnolias. The Ospedale dei Bianchi owed its name to a religious movement of penitents who had over the centuries travelled the length and breadth of Italy wearing only a white linen tunic. Totò Riina was questioned twice at the Ospedale dei Bianchi, and twice he bore false witness.

'It was Di Matteo who wounded me first, then I . . .'

Only at his third interrogation – in Ucciardone prison – did he admit that Menicu Di Matteo wasn't armed. Totò Riina didn't add much to that. 'A friend of his who was standing next to him had the pistol, someone I couldn't recognise because I only saw him for a moment.' In the end Totò Riina supplied his own version, and said that he had fired only one shot, but in self-defence. The witnesses denied it.

'Riina fired several shots in sequence, between five and seven . . .'

On the beaten earth of the hill of San Giovanni the police found three spent cartridges from an automatic calibre-9 pistol. The gun was never discovered 'in spite of the most meticulous searches'. Domenico Di Matteo died at the Ospedale dei Bianchi that same night, 13 May 1949. He had been injured in one leg, and the bullet had lacerated his femoral artery. The cause of death was attributed to 'major haemorrhage'. The motive for the crime was attributed to the brawl, and the clash between two local gangs. No one ever inquired into what had happened on 3 May, immediately after the church procession.

It was the first time that Totò Riina landed in prison. For a few days he was guarded by two *carabinieri*[1] at the Ospedale della Feliciuzza in Palermo. Then the Corleone peasant was transferred to the Ucciardone. His fingerprints were taken, and his first mug shot. A tuft of dark chestnut hair, icy eyes. Thin, well-kept moustache. The prisoner Salvatore Riina was assigned to the 'young adults' section in prison. It was a damp room with bunk beds. A little light came in from a small window from which the prison vegetable garden could be seen.

The trial was held in the deconsecrated church of Montevergini, very close to the baroque squares of Palermo. On the day of sentencing, Totò Riina stood handcuffed in front of the judges. Among the public, behind the transept, was his mother, along with his three sisters and his brother Gaetano. When he heard the first words of the president of the court, Totò Riina

---

1   Policemen.

growled. Later the people in the village said what he had whispered in his rage.

'Lawyers and bloody judges never tell the truth.'

Palermo Court of Assizes sentenced him to twelve years and four months' imprisonment to be served in the prisons of Termini Imerese and Milazzo. But his detention did not last as long as that. After six years he was out on probation. It was 19 September 1955 when Totò Riina returned to Corleone.

He was back at home. And he had met up with his old friends: Luciano Liggio, Calogero Bagarella and Binnu Provenzano. Those Corleonesi had become powerful people. And they weren't as hungry as they had been immediately after the war. Six years had passed. Only six years. Many things had changed. Dr Navarra was even fatter, and increasingly suspicious. The estate of Strasatto was not the place it had once been, where stolen livestock had been hidden, and the sheaves of grain piled up behind the stable. Binnu Provenzano seemed different too. Still silent, always apart from the rest, but with a different gleam in his eyes. The old gang had become a band of bosses. They no longer seemed like inferiors. They were no longer Dr Navarra's guard dogs.

THE *PICCIOTTO* FROM STRASATTO

THE HONOUR OF THE BAGARELLAS

Totò first saw Ninetta on Vicolo Scorsone. She was still a little girl, the youngest sister of his friend Calogero Bagarella. Vicolo Scorsone was long and narrow, and climbed sluggishly from the lower part of the village. The alleyway crossed another alleyway, and then another. It was a labyrinth, a tangle of little streets between the tufa houses built around the square. Ninetta was a quick and cheerful girl. She used to play in a courtyard with a *gebbia* in the middle, a big stone basin where the shepherds stopped at sunset when they came down from the hills. Behind an ivy-covered wall was the church of Santa Rosalia. Above it ran the path leading to the ice factory.

On the day when Salvatore Riina came back to Corleone – after his six years of detention – he noticed that little Antonina had grown up. She was serving her father Salvatore and her three brothers at the table. Then she had disappeared behind a curtain and sat down in a corner. She was reading a book. Ninetta had the beautiful, sly face of Sicilian girls, a perfect oval, tanned by the sun. Her hair was black and gathered at the back. She had shining brown eyes. Totò resolved that she would be his wife.

Totò was twenty-six, he was already a man. And he felt like

one, because he had been in prison. He was semi-illiterate, he could barely spell his name. For the second class of primary school he had attended Camillo Finocchiaro Aprile in Corleone on the threshold of the Second World War. Analysts of the Department of Public Safety thirty years later also dug around in his distant past and compiled a list. 'At the scholastic level he is remembered as a subject who showed an ability to learn quickly . . .'

Totò had immediately left school, and his father had taken him with him to work in the fields. But he managed to pass his primary school exams 'inside', in jail, two lessons a week with twelve other inmates of the prison of Cavallacci di Termini Imerese. Third, fourth and fifth classes in a single exam. What the director of the prison handed him was a useless piece of paper as far as he was concerned.

This uneducated man, who had grown up in the fields and could already slaughter human beings as if they were goats, was enchanted by the little girl. Ninetta had just finished middle school, and signed up for 'Baccelli', the local grammar school. Her family had decided that she was to study, the only member of the Bagarella family who might get a degree. She wasn't yet fourteen.

The love between Totò and Ninetta was born in Vicolo Scorsone with the *impustata alla cantunera*, an ambush on the corner of the street before eight o'clock in the morning, before she left home with her books under her arms. Totò followed her along the labyrinth of alleyways, all the way down to the town hall and 'Baccelli' grammar school. It was a discreet and silent courtship.

'I followed her with my eyes for years, for years I wouldn't let her breathe until she decided to marry me,' Salvatore Riina once admitted.

U Curtu – The Short One – wanted to marry Ninetta, and he had 'promised' his sister Arcangela to his friend Calogero

Bagarella in exchange for this. Two crossed marriages to unite, with a link as sacred as an oath, the link between the two families, blood of the same blood that ran between Riina and Bagarella, to mingle for ever. The brothers and sisters of the one uniting with the brothers and sisters of the other. It was something stronger than love, it was a pact for life. Two families became one big family. It was a seal of the greatest possible loyalty, it was an eternal commitment.

In Vicolo Scorsone during those few months, marriages were made and star-crossed loves perished. Like an engagement that had lasted too long even for those days. She was one of Ninetta's sisters, Maria Matilde, the seamstress. He was a sheep farmer by the name of Ambrogio Miceli. He was an exuberant lad of twenty-eight, who led the animals to pasture behind the mountains of Roccamena. The Bagarellas weren't very keen on him, since Ambrogio Miceli wasn't made of the same stuff as they were. He was a chatterbox, he drank and said things he should never have said. He never bonded with those tight-lipped peasants who lived in the estates of Strasatto.

One day the young sheep farmer went to Vicolo Scorsone to ask for the hand of Maria Matilde. Ambrogio Miceli found her family gathered waiting for him, men and women sitting behind a table and looking him up and down.

The father, Salvatore, spoke first. And he said: 'I have no daughters to marry to a fellow like you.'

'Don Salvatore, I promise you . . .'

'Don't promise, Ambrogio, don't do it! I don't believe your words; how on earth can I believe your promises?'

'But Don Salvatore . . .'

Old Bagarella looked at the sheep farmer with blazing eyes. Ambrogio stammered again, but without any conviction: 'I promise you . . .'

'Go,' ordered Don Salvatore.

Ambrogio was rooted to the spot. He hadn't expected a welcome like this. As he approached the door, his fear and embarrassment made way for blind rage.

'Ambrogio,' Bagarella called after him, 'I never want to see you on this street again.'

Six months passed and Miceli got engaged to another girl, the youngest daughter of a rich cattle trader. There was relief in the Bagarella household; it felt like a liberation. But Ambrogio Miceli couldn't forget the offence done to him in Vicolo Scorsone. He was still blinded with rage at the memory. And he behaved in a very thoughtless way. As no one would ever have dared to do during those years, in a Sicilian village. Especially a village like Corleone.

The sheep farmer casually related intimate details about his relationship with Maria Matilde the seamstress, one of the daughters of Salvatore Bagarella. He talked to everyone about it, even in the village square. The rumours reached Vicolo Scorsone. It was a tragedy that had entered the house of the Bagarella family. A tragedy that was worse, much worse, than an illness. One evening Ambrogio Miceli was confronted by two of Ninetta's brothers. There was Giuseppe, waiting for him at the end of Via Streva, and Calogero, who had followed him from Corso Bentivegna. The first to say anything was Giuseppe. He turned to Maria Matilde's former suitor calmly, weighing his words: 'Ambrogio, now that you're engaged, you've got to stop mouthing off about my sister.'

The sheep farmer pretended not to understand. Then Giuseppe Bagarella came over. He was furious, trembling with rage. And he threatened him: 'Leave my Maria Matilde in peace. You are never to utter her name again . . .'

Ambrogio Miceli burst out laughing, then made some crude

remarks about the girl's honour. His voice could be heard in the last houses on Via Streva.

His body was found at midnight. Ambrogio Miceli was dragged along the alleys pleading for help; no one opened a door, no one called the police. The sheep farmer was left to die in a pool of blood. In the darkness of Via Streva he had taken five pistol-shots to the spine.

The following day Giuseppe Bagarella was arrested for murder. At first he admitted killing Ambrogio Miceli, then he said it was his brother Calogero. In the end he confessed that 'that wretch' had had the end he deserved. They had both killed him, he and his brother. The *carabinieri* looked in vain for Calogero. He had already fled, he had become a fugitive. He was in hiding in the '*case di Drago*', beyond the stone bridge over the Casale River, in the fields that ran along the SS118.

In Vicolo Scorsone honour was saved, and the Bagarellas could hold their heads high. Even the ones in jail, even the ones wanted by the police. And Totò Riina could still go to their house, without feeling any shame about what would one day be his family as well. Totò could still see his Ninetta every morning, and take up his position above the town hall to see her coming out of school.

Ninetta had already finished the first class of high school. She was always good-humoured, curious to know and understand. She had lots of friends. All she did was read. Her teachers followed her studies very carefully. Top marks in Latin, top marks in Italian, never a day's absence.

But there was another Ninetta as well. The lively little girl of the 'Baccelli' turned into a serious, thoughtful woman when she came back to Vicolo Scorsoni. If there were men in the house she never opened her mouth. They were the only ones who were allowed speak. Ninetta didn't ask why Calogero only came home at night, or where Giuseppe had got to.

LONG LIVE THE PRINCE OF GIARDINELLI

Towards the end of 1957, on the estate of Piano della Scala, a sheep- and cattle-breeding company set up. The estate was surrounding by treeless hills. Growing into the valley were vines that produced a sweet wine so dark that it looked like ink. It was Luciano Liggio who collected money from the farmers of the area, persuading them in both good and bad ways. Then he got hold of some names for the breeding society. A few months earlier Lucianeddu had also bought some trucks, to transport the livestock stolen from the markets of Palermo. His associate was Giacomo Riina, Totò's uncle. But the purchase of the trucks was above all an investment, given the huge task they were talking about, the construction of a dam above Corleone, a vast basin that would irrigate a hundred thousand hectares between the provinces of Agrigento and Trapani.

It was a project on a grand scale, and the General Electrics Company had promised to carry the water even beyond the mountains, to Bagheria, Ciaculli and the Conca d'Oro. There was already a consortium, with 37 billion and 854 million lire for the building of roads, aqueducts and farmhouses. The *campieri* of Piano della Scala had caught the scent of money, and discovered public contracts. The *campieri* were about to embark on the first big business deal in their history.

The consortium for the reclamation of the medium and high Belice was presided over by the prince of Giardinelli. In the 1958 election campaign Luciano Liggio, Giacomo Riina and their families campaigned for a candidate member of the Italian Liberal Party in the Senate, the prince of Giardinelli. In May of that year they went around the village every day, district by district, house by house, door by door. But the prince didn't become a senator because the elections were won by the Christian Democrats, who were given twice as many votes in Corleone as they had in 1953. The person who controlled the most votes in that party was Michele Navarra, and he had exerted all his influence to persuade people to vote for a shortlist of three: Bernardo Mattarella, Franco Restivo and Calogero Volpe. His candidates were important politicians, two of whom would become ministers and the third an under-secretary.

Dr Navarra did not appreciate the blow that Luciano Liggio and Giacomo Riina had dealt him in the elections. And everyone in the village knew, among other things, that he was also opposed to the construction of the dam. The doctor had spread the rumour that such a big reservoir was too dangerous, that the dammed water would sooner or later submerge Corleone. In reality Michele Navarra didn't want a single drop of water ever to arrive beyond the mountains. In Ciaculli, in Bagheria, in Villabate, in Misilmeri there was the Mafia of the gardens, which controlled the supply from the wells. Water was like gold for the country-folk, and once distributed to the orange groves it would mean the end of power for the doctor's old friends, the end of centuries of extortion.

But it wasn't only the dam and politics that poisoned relations between Don Michele and the Mafiosi he had trained on the estate. During those weeks something happened in the farmland around Piano della Scala. There was a friend of Michele Navarra, one Angelo Vintaloro, who had bought an area of land adjoining the territory of the animal-breeding company. Vintaloro had bought the land in line with the conventions of the time, after asking 'permission' from the doctor and also the neighbouring landowners, Luciano Liggio and Giacomo Riina. Apparently no questions were asked. But immediately after purchasing the land, Angelo Vintaloro couldn't sleep for a single night on his farm.

One day all the barrels in the cellar were smashed. When the grain ripened, in mid-June, no peasant dared to venture into the new owner's fields. The grain turned black under the scorching sun. It was gathered at night, but the sheaves disappeared. Some people claimed to have seen them being loaded onto Liggio and Riina's trucks.

The 'authority' of Don Michele Navarra had been called into question for the second time in a month. These were dangerous signals, enough to punish the *campieri* who were getting cocky. They urgently needed to be taught a lesson to avoid a loss of face; the whole village had to know who was in charge of the land around Corleone. Dr Michele Navarra spoke to a few of his young right-hand men, and gave the order to kill Luciano Liggio and everyone who was with him in Piano della Scala. Half a dozen thugs armed with shotguns and revolvers hid in Angelo Vintaloro's stable. And at dawn two of them slipped out towards the nearby farm. Then they started shooting. Liggio was accompanied by two other men, and all three were injured but not seriously. Michele Navarra's plan failed.

In Corleone no one knew that there had been a shoot-out on the estate of Piano della Scala. Even the police weren't informed of it. At the end of 1958 officers from the external unit of the Palermo police force wrote in a letter to the chief prosecutor of the Republic: 'News of the attack emerged only subsequently, after the explosion of the armed conflict that followed between the Navarra family, the so-called "old Mafia", and that of Liggio's acolytes, known as the new Mafia recruits.'

Not even then did the police manage to provide precise information about the shooting match. They only knew it had happened in the third ten-day period of the month, 'sometime between the 20th and the 30th of June'.

By the early summer of 1958 Salvatore Riina had paid his dues to the forces of law and order. After six years in jail and three on probation for the murder of Domenico Di Matteo, he had no further obligations to the authorities. At the start of that summer, all of a sudden, Totò disappeared. No one looked for him, no one issued a warrant for his arrest, there were no police on his heels. Just before the August holidays of 1958 a brigadier from the commission of public safety in Corleone updated his file. Among his personal data he found a report a few lines long, a single sheet of paper: 'Riina Salvatore son of the late Giovanni was impossible to trace'. Totò had gone into hiding. His family had decided to erase Dr Michele Navarra from the face of the earth. What was stirring in the estates around Corleone was a revolution, an earthquake that would shake up the Sicilian Mafia for ever.

Totò Riina was twenty-eight. With his friends Binnu Provenzano and Calogero Bagarella he had entered a new life. They told him he had been chosen from among many, and also that 'the family' is worth more than a wife or a child. Totò Riina knew how to kill in cold blood, and he knew how to fire a gun. He was capable of killing even with his bare hands. He knew how to stay silent. He had sworn loyalty until death, and had been initiated just before the war. Totò Riina had joined Cosa Nostra. He was a man of honour.

In the forty-five years that followed, no one ever discovered how Totò had been initiated, who had been present at the ceremony, which Mafia had acted as guarantors for his 'valour' and his 'qualities' as a Mafioso. And no one ever revealed the Corleonese *punciutal*, the puncture that draws blood from the tip of the index finger of the right hand. The hand that shoots the gun, the finger that pulls the trigger. In the Palermo suburb of Altarello di Baida, when initiating a new member they used the thorn of a wild orange tree. In the village of Riesi they pierced the skin with a gold pin. In Torretta they used ordinary sewing needles.

Somewhere in the village of Corleone someone guarded the arcane rules of the ritual that had to be undergone if one was to become a man of honour, and the complete list of family affiliates. The Corleonesi knew all the bosses of the other clan, but only some Corleonesi were known to the rest of Cosa Nostra. They were obsessed with secrecy and mystery. If the Sicilian Mafia had come into being as a secret society, the Corleone *cosca*[1] had remained a sect of invisible men. Only a few could be exposed. Only a few could be given a face and a name.

REQUIEM FOR A BENEFACTOR

One hundred and twenty-four cartridge cases were found on the ground. Ninety-two bullets in the body of Michele Navarra. A total of five guns had been fired. A Thompson-brand American submachine gun, a Breda 6.35 calibre Italian-made rifle, and three automatic pistols. There were no witnesses to the ambush, and at the spot fifteen kilometres along the Prizzi–Corleone road that day there were only killers and victims. It was said that there must have been at least seven killers, five of them carrying the guns and two of them driving the cars. It was also said that the Fiat 1100 in which Navarra was driving with another doctor, Giovanni Russo, was suddenly forced to slow down after a bend to avoid an obstacle, probably a cart or another car.

A week later the *carabinieri* found a small truck, hidden in a stable in Piano della Scala. It was a red Leoncini. The bumper was dented and one of the headlamps was broken. The murder of the powerful Mafia boss of Corleone had taken place in the early

---

1   Gang.

afternoon of 2 August 1958, at about three o'clock, in the district of Portella Imbriaca, in the countryside around Palazzo Adriano. The area was surrounded by dry fields, the ground was scorched and there had been no rain since February.

The first journalist to arrive along the secondary road from Prizzi to Corleone was Nicola Volpes, the crime correspondent of the Palermo daily newspaper *L'Ora*. He reached Portella Imbriaca at about six in the evening. There wasn't so much as a breeze, and the heat was asphyxiating. It was almost a two-hour drive from Palermo; the driver, Saro Mineo, cursing, had stopped at the Ficuzza turn-off to change a flat tyre. In the back seat of the newspaper's car, the photographer Nicola Scafidi bumped every time they went into a pothole. The editors had been alerted by the usual phone call from their contact in Corleone: 'Get a move on, there's a job for you.'

The old informant never wanted anything in return for the information he passed on. He liked to keep the journalists on their toes, curious people who brought confusion to the village and plagued the police with their naïve questions. It was very amusing at the club the following day to read stories that were always a little approximate but always curious. With the full names and addresses of Mafia bosses who thought they ruled the world. But that afternoon was different from the other times, and the voice of the Corleone contact was quavering.

The photographer, Nicola Scafidi, only had time to approach the roadside, and then he had just a second to capture the crime scene. It was the first and only photograph of the murder of Michele Navarra. The *carabinieri* roughly manoeuvred Scafidi away; they were nervous, they couldn't work out or even imagine who could have carried out such an act of war, who would have been brave enough to bump off the doctor of Corleone. The dark blue Fiat 1100 was riddled with holes, almost all of them in the right-hand side of the vehicle, the side on which Navarra had been sitting. Dr Giovanni Russo was still clutching the wheel, his head dangling towards the side window, blood dripping from his forehead. The body of the Mafia boss could not be seen from outside, as it had slipped from the seat after the first spray of bullets from the Thompson gun.

The information collected that afternoon by the reporters of *L'Ora* was sparse and rather vague. The paper informed its readers that the young doctor had died in a 'tragic misadventure'. By chance he had been carrying Michele Navarra as a passenger in his Fiat 1100. In reality the doctor Giovanni Russo had been killed only because he had seen the faces of the murderers.

The funeral of Michele Navarra was held on 4 August in the parish church of San Martino, the main church in Corleone. The crowd filled Piazza Garibaldi and all the neighbouring streets, hundreds of wreaths of flowers commemorated 'the benefactor' for the last time. Civic mourning was declared, the flag flew at half-mast from the balcony of the town hall, and delegations of Mafiosi had arrived from all the villages in the four provinces of western Sicily. For the first time in ten years Corleone didn't have a district doctor. It didn't have an inspector of the Mutual Sickness Fund, or a medical director of the Ospedale dei Bianchi. It had lost the president of the Small Farmers' Association, and the trustee of the Agricultural Consortium. Corleone no longer had a Mafia boss.

In the two nights that followed the terrible bloodbath in Portella Imbriaca, the *carabinieri* launched inquiries in the farms of Strasatto, Torrazza and the Via Rua del Piano and Vicolo Scorsone, and searched stables and barns. A big manhunt was on for about fifty Mafiosi, all the friends and enemies of Michele Navarra. In the houses the *carabinieri* found women, children and old people, but none of the men they were looking for. The Riinas and the Liggios were gone, and so were the Provenzanos, the Bagarellas, the Ruffinos and the Vintaloros.

Corleone was like a ghost town. The men from the two *cosche* had gone into the hills, hidden in safe houses. They were preparing for a war that would decide the survival of only one of the two factions. A fratricidal war, Corleonesi against Corleonesi. Thirty-four days passed and thirty-four nights after the murder of Dr Michele Navarra. No one moved until 6 September, when the first shotgun blast went off. What followed was to have echoes even on the other side of the ocean, in New York, in Chicago, in Detroit. The Sicilian-American bosses of Cosa Nostra started to call Corleone 'Tombstone'.

I WANT NO WITNESSES . . .

It was almost dusk on another scorching day, and it seemed as if summer would never end. The sirocco wind had started blowing again during the night. It was the eve of a party in the village, a Saturday. The only respite to be found was beneath the trees of the San Rocco fortress. Planes and pines shaded the old people of the village, sitting around the dry fountain. Even the grass in the flowerbeds was scorched. Three or four little boys were coming up the steep street; it was a dusty alley, Via della Consolazione. On one side three men were walking slowly down the street, on the other a man stood waiting for them with his back to the wall. He had no gun, he was on his own, just looking around. Totò Riina was impatient. Beneath the trees of the San Rocco fortress, at dusk on 6 September, the two Mafias of Corleone had arranged a meeting. It was the *paciata* – the formal reconciliation – after the killing of Michele Navarra.

Friends of friends had made it known that the doctor's lieutenants didn't want war, but preferred to discuss what had happened. And above all what still might happen. Totò Riina was the first to speak.

'The dead are dead, their souls have passed away, let's think about the living.'

U Curtu made the sign of the cross.

The little boys had disappeared around the corner, the old men, enjoying the cool of the evening around the fountain, strolled off one by one towards the village square. Only stray dogs lay stretched in the shade of the planes and pines.

Few witnesses observed the scene, and did so from a distance. They said the meeting lasted at least half an hour, and they also said that Pietro Maiuri and the brothers Giovanni and Marco Marino listened to Totò Riina's words without saying a word. In the end only Maiuri whispered something and held out a hand. But it was too early for Totò Riina, who hadn't finished the discussion.

'There's just one small matter: you have to surrender those bastards who tried to kill Liggio at Piano della Scala.'

The evening was still light, the barber shops were open, the villagers were strolling past the clubs when they heard the first shots ring out from up by the fortress of San Rocco. Suddenly Binnu Provenzano and Calogero Bagarella appeared from among the trees, wielding sawn-off shotguns, firing, reloading and firing again. Pietro Maiuri was the first to die, with a blast to the face. His two friends darted off down Via Puccio. They were slaughtered like sheep.

Another three or four armed Mafiosi came running from the square and started firing at Totò Riina. The shoot-out lasted between seven and ten minutes. The thugs ran down the alleys, bullets flying like punches, and in the end a two-year-old child was among the injured. Sixteen people had witnessed the slaughter:

44

seven women and nine men. There were also one *carabiniere* and two agents of public safety who saw Totò Riina 'among the hit-men giving chase and fleeing'.

At nine o'clock in the evening Binnu Provenzano went into a room in the Ospedale dei Bianchi, his shirt drenched in blood. He had been wounded in the head. He told the duty doctor that he had fallen on a pavement in Corso Bentivegna.

'I was walking along, I felt an intense pain in my head, I lost my senses and wasn't aware of anything.'

The doctor asked no further questions.

On the evening of 6 September the new Mafia of Corleone had found a man who spoke words of peace while clutching weapons in his fist. Totò Riina was a master of the double game. He was ruthless. He was a skilful conjuror who always bet on the lives and deaths of other people. The peasant from Via Rua del Piano was about to become the implacable murderer of the Liggio gang. On the evening of the massacre at San Rocco fortress he began his takeover bid within Cosa Nostra, murder after murder, massacre after massacre, *tragedia* after *tragedia*. For the time being he was just behind Lucianeddu.

Luciano Liggio and Totò Riina began to win their reputation as invincible figures that winter, in the last few weeks of 1958. With a strategy – both elemental and free of any rules – that Luciano had come up with. Killing all their enemies, never leaving a single enemy behind them. But first they had to dig them out, the men loyal to Dr Navarra; they had to be brought out into the open. That was how the 'player' Totò Riina persuaded old Mafiosi to act as mediators between the two groups, their own and Navarra's. It was the only way to confront the men who needed to be wiped out. There were secret negotiations, and some accepted while others died only because they refused to trust Totò Riina.

One of those Mafiosi was called Carmelo Lo Bue. He was a

landowner who had lands all the way to Campofiorito. He had olive groves, vines and herds. His sons had emigrated to America, and he wanted to join them and leave Corleone and Sicily for ever; for six months he had been applying for a visa from the consulate. Carmelo Lo Bue was out of the fight – he wasn't with Liggio or the others. He was an old man, almost eighty. He had only been in jail once, in the days of Mori, the same prefect of police who had forced him, one night, onto the ferry to Ustica. Carmelo Lo Bue never managed to see his sons again, or escape to America. He was killed one evening in November. He was coming from the fields, on horseback, along Via del Calvario. Totò Riina shot him once in the back and then again in the mouth.

One evening that same winter Vincenzo Cortimiglia was killed, the most dangerous hitman in the rival gang. The ambush was reconstructed in a police statement: 'Cortimiglia was walking along with his hands in his pockets, in which he carried two big revolvers . . . Forewarned as he was, Cortimiglia sensed betrayal when he met Calogero Bagarella and Giovanni Provenzano, the cousin of Bernardo . . .'

Vincenzo Cortimiglia took out one of the two pistols and shot Giovanni Provenzano in the face. Then he fled, hiding in a grocery shop. The shopkeeper was a first cousin of Luciano Liggio, and Totò Riina was in the shop. A shotgun blast ripped open Cortimiglia's chest, blood poured from his mouth, and he was dying on the ground when Police Officer Augusto Giannasi came into the shop. The policeman told his superiors what he had seen: 'Totò Riina was in the shop. He fired and then fled, leaving the weapons there, a 12-calibre sawn-off shotgun and a 45-calibre Colt pistol.'

Totò Riina was now the chief killer in the Liggio gang, its 'bravest' thug. He was forever repeating to Lucianeddu, Binnu Provenzano and Calogero Bagarella: 'We must never leave jobs unfinished, witnesses are always dangerous . . .'

A 'trustworthy source' then told the *carabinieri* of Corleone about the death of a local shopkeeper. He sold fruit and oil, and his name was Paolo Riina but he wasn't related to Totò U Curtu. He was killed with three blasts from a shotgun. One in the back, one in the heart and the last in the mouth. The trustworthy source said that the hitman was Totò Riina, and the *carabinieri* recorded the motive for the killing in a report: 'Shopkeeper Paolo Riina was a talkative and cowardly figure who had made only one mistake: he had watched every stage in the shoot-out at the San Rocco fortress and in Via Puccio from the front door of his house . . .'

DANGEROUS!

The first coach from Palermo arrived in Corleone at about four o'clock in the afternoon. It stopped at the last turning of the main road, and then went back a few metres, scrapping the stone post and then set off again belching clouds of black smoke. The first to get off the coach were the vendors of *L'Ora*, who unloaded hundreds of copies of the freshly printed newspaper on the pavement of Corso Bentivegna. The newsvendors started shouting, walking up and down Piazza Garibaldi: 'Dead, dead and injured . . .'

After a few minutes their shouts became a lament, an obsessive dirge that spread through the narrow alleys leading up to the church of Santa Rosalia. '*Quanti ne muriru, quanti ne cadiru . . .*' Some have died, some have fallen.

It was the war report, the gruesome story of the previous twenty-four hours.

At four o'clock on one of those afternoons a huge man was one of the people to get off the coach. He had a square face and a goatee. His hair was grizzled, his eyes blue. The giant picked up his suitcase and walked resolutely towards the nearest bar. He went into the café opposite the church of San Martino, nodded at the regulars and ordered a glass of milk. Then he introduced himself: 'I am the new commissioner of public security in Corleone, Dr Angelo Mangano.'

It was four hundred metres from the bar on Piazza Garibaldi to the old commissariat, and the policeman went there on foot. A thousand eyes followed him from behind the curtains. The commissioner was very elegant; he wore an immaculate grey linen jacket, he had a white silk handkerchief in his pocket and had a large ring on the little finger of his right hand. As he passed no one raised their hat or deigned to greet him in any way.

In Corleone that afternoon they didn't yet know that they would curse the name of Angelo Mangano. And soon Luciano Liggio would have more cause to curse it than anyone else. Only a few days had passed since his arrival, and already Angelo Mangano had made a name for himself. The commissioner appeared in the square early in the morning or late in the evening. He arrived on his own, went into the usual bar, ordered his glass of milk and began talking in a loud voice. He told everyone that to capture Lucianeddu 'you had to follow his trail of gold and blood'. It was a way of telling them that he – the commissioner of public safety – represented the law in Corleone.

In the last few weeks of 1962 the sawn-off shotguns stopped firing in the streets of the village. But there hadn't been a signal to announce the end of the war. So why, after so much noise, had the shotguns fallen silent? People began to understand when women dressed in black appeared processing down the street, women in mourning. Their husbands had disappeared, had been swallowed up by the void. It was the 'white shotgun', the cruel and refined death that left no traces. It was the death reserved for those who didn't deserve the honour of a bullet. The death of spies, of informers, of traitors. Their wives wouldn't even find their bodies; they would have no graves to mourn their loved ones.

'They set fire to evildoers, and not even the ashes are ever found,' people whispered in the village when they saw the widows of the vanished men passing by. It was the Corleonesi, at the end of the 1940s, who invented the vicious technique of the white shotgun. They would kidnap a man, interrogate and torture him, and feed him to the pigs or the crows of Rocca Busambra. If no body was found there was no physical evidence, and if there was no physical evidence then there was no crime.

Six black-clad women came out of their houses during the last few days of 1962. Their husbands had all been friends of Michele Navarra. In his monthly report to the captain, the marshal of the Criminal Investigation Department of Corleone noted: 'At a certain point, when the Navarra *cosca* tried to recruit new forces or win new members in the political arena, the others decided to put them down, not with the traditional method, in ways reminiscent, however vaguely, of those used in Russia by the communists: disappearance.'

The style was unmistakable, and always the same. They would be approached by a trusted friend, someone who didn't arouse any suspicions, who hugged them, invited them to eat in his house, with his children, with his wife. And then they disappeared. It was a terrible, silent slaughter.

'Some died, some fell,' the newsvendors went on calling, even though the blasts from the sawn-off shotguns had ceased to ring out in Via Puccio, at the fortress of San Rocco, in Via del Calvario. The newspaper *L'Ora*, a lone voice in the mire of Sicilian journalism, decided to carry out an investigation into the new breed of Mafiosi that had devastated Corleone. The front page carried a banner headline: 'DANGEROUS!'

Underneath was a picture of Luciano Liggio, 'a rich, feared and fearful man, a man capable of riding with a sawn-off shotgun, a cross between an old Mafioso and a modern gangster.' It was the portrait of the Corleonese. On the inside pages much space was devoted to his lieutenants, 'the peasants Salvatore Riina and Bernardo Provenzano'. The investigation was printed on Thursday afternoon; during the night from Saturday to Sunday a kilo of dynamite destroyed *L'Ora*'s presses.

THE VICTORS OF CORLEONE

They were all wanted men. They were known to be up there, beyond the mountains. In Corleone the fugitives came down every night to embrace the mothers of their children, to eat and sleep in their houses. Then they left the village at dawn. They headed for the Rocca dei Maschi, an area normally frequented only by rabbit hunters.

The Rocca dei Maschi was the mountain of the *mascara*, the man whose job it was to light the fireworks for St Leoluca, the patron saint of Corleone, on the first of March every year. Behind the crag there was a road that climbed to Prizzi, forty-seven bends and eleven hairpins. After a few kilometres there was an area of ground, unmarked on any map, by a stone drinking trough; leading from there were seven paths that disappeared into the fields. From the Rocca dei Maschi you could get to half of Sicily. To the Belice Valley, among the vines of Partinico, towards Agrigento. There were three paths to Palermo. The most northerly passed through Piana degli Albanesi, the one to the south via San Giuseppe Jato. The other led through the park of Altofonte. There was also a dusty track that emerged among the hills further away. On the edges of the Vallone, in the province of Caltanissetta.

Everyone said that Corleone was an isolated village, locked away among the mountains, inaccessible. In fact Corleone was the heart of Sicily.

The fugitives won their Mafia war. It had lasted for five years. Dr Navarra's friends had ceased to exist, and were all under the ground. Luciano Liggio, but above all Totò Riina, Binnu Provenzano and Calogero Bagarella had become the bosses of Corleone, and with the shrewdness and ferocity that only peasants who have grown up between Marabino and the Strasatto estate can have. They were used to living in solitude in the fields, people who had spent their lives in the pastures, closer to animals than to men. Their secret weapon was their instinct. They struck first and thought afterwards; they killed first and then reflected on their actions. Instinct now led them to lay down their weapons, to put by the shotguns that had already made too much noise, that had irritated the big bosses of Cosa Nostra in Palermo, in Trapani, in Castellammare del Golfo, in Mussomeli.

There was a need for peace in Sicily, for silence, for calm. There was a tacit agreement that had prevailed on the island for almost twenty years, since the end of the war, when the Allies had landed. No one had ever explained to these peasants that there was an unwritten pact between the Mafia and certain sectors of the Italian state. Whether they were to ignore or help one another depended entirely on the moment or the circumstances. A fatal embrace in the name of freedom, of anti-communism, of progress. It was a pact that had survived superbly before, during and after the upheavals of the independence movement and the mysterious death of Salvatore Giuliano. Over the previous few years no one had been shocked or concerned or surprised by the desperate words uttered in court by Gaspare Pisciotta, the cousin who handed the corpse of the bandit of Montelepre to the Mafia and the state.

'We are all one thing, we are all one body, Mafia bandits and police, like the Father, the Son and the Holy Ghost', Pisciotta had shouted at the judges of the Court of Assizes in Viterbo. His cries had sounded like the ravings of a man torn apart by grief and driven insane by remorse. Then the traitor Gaspare Pisciotta died of poisoning, one morning when he was served coffee with strychnine in a cell in the Ucciardone. The day after that murder another Sicilian, Mario Scelba, became president of the council. He had been the last minister of the interior, and his police force had distinguished itself almost as much as the Mafia in quelling the revolts of the peasants on the estates.

Many years had passed since those days. The Giuliano gang was a distant memory, like the massacre in Porta della Ginestra, the anti-bandit units, the sheep-rustling raids in Strasatto. The world no longer revolved around Vinaloro's stable in Piano della Scala, his sheaves of grain and his barrels of wine. 'Benefactors' like Michele Navarra had had their day. The terrible story of Sicily had turned yet another page. And even for the fierce peasants of Corleone, the time had come to leave their fields and look to the city and future; and try to think on a larger scale, to find money, lots of money. To inveigle their friends, children, cousins and nephews into town halls, administrative offices, local councils, consortiums, the oil business and the agricultural sector. They also needed to have friends in the rooms of the Sicilian Regional Assembly, among the police, in the courts, in the political parties. They needed to dig themselves a niche in that burgeoning rabbit warren that was the state. Those peasants couldn't stop at the village boundaries. Men like Totò Riina or Binnu Provenzano couldn't stay in Corleone.

THE PRISONER OF THE UCCIARDONE

SUNBURNT FACES

Seen from the summit of Gibilrossa it was extremely beautiful: the sea a deep blue, the houses immersed in the green of the gardens. The streets were wide and lined with trees, luminescent. The beautiful art nouveau houses were hidden by tall ficus and magnolia trees, and the buildings on Via Maqueda were luxurious. The ice cream parlours in the Foro Italico served coffee granitas with cream from February to November: winter never came to Palermo. It was the city that once appeared like a mirage at the end of the wheat fields of the estates, it was the city they wanted to conquer. And now there it was, magnificent at the feet of its bare hill, Montepellegrino.

The Contadini of Corleone reached the gates of the Sicilian capital at a very difficult time: the days of the raids of the new viceroys of Palermo. It was the war of concrete; the Regional Assembly had made funds available for the reconstruction of the four districts, and the city council was drawing up the development plan.

They were all fugitives, Totò Riina and Luciano Liggio, Binnu Provenzano and Calogero Bagarella. They were all Mafiosi in the same gang that had taken command of Corleone and grabbed every hectare of land between Misilmeri and Chiusa Sclafani. They landed in Palermo to go into hiding there, and to cut themselves a slice of business in the city, to introduce themselves as bosses of the provincial villages to the big Cosa Nostra families. To the La Barbera brothers, to Don Pietro Torretta, to the Grecos of Ciaculli and their cousins of the same name in Croceverde. The Corleonesi came down from the hills and timidly entered the city in their suits of black flannel or wide-fitting corduroy suits, their muddy shoes, their flat caps.

Their faces were sunburnt and their hands callused. They were humble, respectful, sometimes even servile. The viceroys looked at them and laughed: the people who came from the countryside were *viddani*, coarse peasants. They were silent, the short, stocky men who lived around La Rocca Busambra. They were as obedient as dogs to their masters; they knew the rules, they wanted to do things but not overdo them. Some people started to call them, with a mixture of irony and contempt, *picciuttunazzi*, the little thugs of Corleone.

The first to receive them at his court was Salvatore La Barbera, a representative of the family of Palermo-Centre. Salvatore and his brother Angelo were high-standing Mafiosi. They had discovered the world of construction, they had become entrepreneurs, and had opened a building site in every part of town. They were said to have privileged relations with the council administration, and it was even said, in hushed voices, that the mayor was a friend of theirs. Their associate, in fact.

The first citizen of Palermo at the time was a man who, along with an ex-barber from Corleone, had taken charge of the Christian Democrats in Palermo. Salvo Lima and Vito Ciancimino, the 'young Turks': they were the new masters of the party. There was talk of infiltration of organised crime in the council, of exchanges of favours, electoral pacts, of 'friends' who came into the damasked rooms of the Palazzo delle Aquile to decide where to knock down a hovel and where to erect a building.

These were rumours, whispers; no one knew at the time that Don Vincenzo, the father of Salvino Lima, was a man of honour of the Palermo-Centre *cosca*. And his son Salvino went around the city with the tricolour badge of mayor, talking with ministers from Rome, dining in the Curia with cardinals and monsignors, meeting state prosecutors, magistrates, prefects of the Republic, choosing administrators and general secretaries, handing out contracts and billions of lire.

The new life of the *picciuttunazzi* of Corleone was lived out quietly in a city that had not yet emerged from a state of indolence. In Palermo Totò Riina was a foot soldier, but he had a brain, sangfroid and patience. He knew he had to wait in silence. He was the one who brought the orders of Luciano Liggio to his Corleonesi. It was he who first came into certain secrets, the offers that the Palermo Mafiosi made to Lucianeddu. Totò knew at once which tasks should be accepted with a bow and which refused, but always with a good excuse. His friends Binnu Provenzano and Calogero Bagarella were simple gunmen; they were still the murderers of the old days. And they still always walked as a group of three, as they had done fifteen years before, in the paths through the fields of Marabino and Frattina.

One day their boss, Liggio, had suddenly disappeared. He had gone to the north, where he stayed in big hotels in Rome and Milan, surrounding himself with beautiful women. He had luxury cars and a lot of money in his pocket. The newspapers published photographs of him and wrote that he was trafficking drugs with a Sicilian-American originally from Partinico whose name was Frank 'Tre Dita' – Three Fingers. Every now and again Lucianeddu went back to Sicily, to Palermo, to Corleone. He hid in safe houses, or else recovered in hospital under a false

name, immobilised by that damned pain in his vertebral column. Only Totò Riina and his two inseparable friends had kept
their *peri incritati*, the dirty, soil-covered feet of peasants. They
looked like yokels amidst so many bosses who put on a new suit
every day, silk shirts and a shiny ring on their little finger. The
others spent money on prostitutes (*'buttane'*) and champagne,
Alfa Spiders and parties. For them, on the other hand, the city
was like the country, Palermo was like Corleone, Salvatore La
Barbera was like the late lamented Michele Navarra when all three
'were still in his heart'. Don Salvatore had hidden them and tak-
en care of them, the *viddani* of Corleone, and all he asked for in
return was that jobs should be done precisely, discreetly, silently.
They were jobs suited to *picciuttunazzi* who came from outside.
No one knew them, they were trusted, they could always come
in useful. Not least because an ill wind was blowing in Palermo.

BOMBS AMONG THE MANDARINS

One morning in January 1963, Salvatore La Barbera disappeared.
His grey Giulietta was found six days later in fields in the province
of Agrigento: the keys were in the ignition, the doors were open,
there wasn't a scratch on the paintwork. It was the ritual of the
white shotgun. His brother, Angelo La Barbera, set off to find the
murderers, calling the bosses of Cosa Nostra to account and threatening reprisals. All the representatives of the Palermo families
insisted that they didn't know anything about the disappearance of
Don Salvatore. And that was really true, they were telling the truth.

But inside Cosa Nostra there was a man who was cheating,
someone who had infiltrated his men into all the other *cosche*
to control the movement of his adversaries. To spy on them, to
make mischief. It was Michele Cavataio – a Mafioso who was also

involved in the construction industry – who had La Barbera kidnapped. It was also Cavataio who had stuffed dynamite into a Fiat 1100 that then blew up outside the house of the Greco family of Ciaculli. The heads of the families, during those few months, didn't understand that someone was playing them off against each other. And for fear of losing power they killed each other like animals.

This went down in history as the 'first Mafia war' in Palermo. There were hundreds of deaths, and gangs of murderers filled the streets of the city with blood. There were shoot-outs in fishmongers' shops, ambushes at the fruit and vegetable market, attacks on building sites. Totò Riina's Corleonesi prudently stayed out of this conflict. The *viddani* witnessed an unprecedented massacre, they saw the Mafiosi of Palermo self-destruct within a few months, eliminating each other without really knowing why. Some of them tried to get rid of Angelo La Barbera, then the vendettas struck in the other direction. These forays continued until the night of 29 June, when a Giulietta filled with explosives was taken to Ciaculli.

The hitmen wanted to park it outside the home of Totò Greco again, but on the way there they had a blow-out. The car was abandoned on the road to Villa Serena. It stayed there for a whole night. The next morning someone noticed the Giulietta abandoned among the mandarin trees, and alerted the police. A tangle of electric wires could be seen through an open door, and there was a tank of liquid gas on the back seat. An army anti-explosives expert arrived in Ciaculli, and deactivated the bomb in a few minutes. All danger seemed to have been removed. But when the boot of the car was opened there was a terrible explosion. Men and trees went up in the air, and on that suburban path four *carabinieri*, two soldiers and a police officer died. It was the afternoon of 30 June 1963.

In the six months after the Ciaculli massacre the state discovered the Sicilian massacre. For the first time since the war, Rome showed its fierce face to the bosses. The pact of peaceful cohabitation had been violated; dynamite and shotguns had unsettled public opinion in Italy and unleashed opposition in parliament. People started talking about scandalous political protection, about collusion, about conspiracies between Sicilian Christian Democracy and the men of the Mafia families. There were also clashes and incidents at the Regional Assembly. One day the Christian Democrat deputy Dino Canzoneri was attacked in the house by communists. He was the member of parliament with the most votes in the area around Corleone. But he was also Luciano Liggio's defence barrister.

The spectre of Prefect Mori returned to Sicily. Spectacular raids in the suburbs. Round-ups at night. Whole districts were surrounded, cut off and searched inch by inch. Early in the autumn, Mariano Rumor, the minister of the interior, addressed the Italians on television: 'The Sicilians and the country must be sure that the police has decided to persecute organised crime, and those involved in criminal activity must be under no illusions: in the challenge between themselves and the state, the state will not be the first to give in.'

At the end of the year the minister also supplied the figures for Mafia suppression in Sicily: '89 individuals were reported to the forces of law and order, 455 were under suspicion, 222 proposed for internal exile, 84 rifles and 60 pistols confiscated, the 192 driving licences and 124 gun licences were revoked and suspended.

A total of 855 suspected Mafiosi were arrested in the four provinces of western Sicily. One of them was a short Corleonesi, who was with Luciano Liggio but seemed to have come from another world, and had a reputation for cruelty. Even then it was said that he was the most ruthless of them all. Totò Riina had been a refugee for five years and three months. He was a hitman, he was wanted for murders 'committed between September 1958 and July 1962 along with Bernardo Provenzano, Calogero Bagarella and other person unknown . . .'

SOONER DEAD THAN A COP

The tunnel was 428 metres long and crossed the mountain above the power station. It was always very quiet in those parts. Only every now and again – and only at night – did one hear the distant sound of an engine. Headlights illuminating the rocky walls, shadows moving in the eucalyptus forest. That evening too there was someone at the end of the tunnel. It was nearly nine o'clock, it was very cold, and a few snowflakes had fallen during the day.

The squadron was commanded by a marshal from Calabria, two brigadiers were Sicilian, the other six officers were all '*continentali*', from the mainland. The taupe-coloured Fiat 1100 was parked in the middle of the tunnel. The driver was smoking one cigarette after another, and waiting. A quarter of an hour later, the 1100 started coming down towards the village, at a walking pace and with its lights turned out. The marshal was positioned behind a concrete pillar; it was only a matter of seconds and the car would pass by at any moment. But things didn't go exactly as the officers from the commissariat of public safety of Corleone, third external service patrol, had predicted they would between 20.00 and 24.00 hours on 15 December 1963.

The road block had been planned to surprise some robbers, a gang who had struck three branches of the Bank of Sicily in Palermo. In the tunnel a shout suddenly rang out, then a burst of machine-gun fire. The driver had realised that they were lying in wait for him. The Fiat 1100 reversed the whole length of the tunnel and disappeared at full speed down the other side of the mountain. The policemen didn't see the driver's face or the car registration.

Meanwhile a man had slipped to the bottom of the slope and run among the bushes before rolling all the way to the riverbed of the dry San Leonardo River. They chased after him in the darkness, and he was caught by the officers who pointed their pistols at him. The man didn't open his mouth, he had dark eyes that glared with hatred at those uniformed boys. He was short and stocky, with the modest appearance of a peasant. He was wrapped in an overcoat, he wasn't armed, and he said his name was Giovanni Grande, a small farmer from San Giuseppe Jato. He had an ID in his pocket, which seemed authentic. He was taken in handcuffs to the village commissariat, and they began to question him.

At two o'clock in the morning Commissioner Angelo Mangano offered him a glass of milk, which he refused. At three o'clock Mangano went on the attack: 'What's your name, what do you do?'

The answer didn't change: 'I am Giovanni Grande, I am a tenant farmer in San Giuseppe Jato.'

In the interrogation room at the commissariat, Angelo Mangano drank down his glasses of milk. He was tired. He was irritated by the prospect of staying up asking questions of a man who wasn't going to add anything to what he had already said. He had a futile sleepless night ahead of him. Sitting in a corner was Brigadier Biagio Melita, the commander of the small criminal investigation unit of the Corleone commissariat. Brigadier Melita had said nothing until then, but at four o'clock in the morning he walked over to the farmer, who was handcuffed and motionless on a chair. He looked at him and said: 'I know who you are . . .'

The man looked up and held the policeman's gaze.

'. . . you're Totò Riina.'

The farmer's face didn't twitch, it was a mask. Commissioner Mangano was losing patience; he walked back and forth in the room, daring the occasional reproachful glance at his brigadier: 'Totò Riina?' he fumed. 'Please, don't talk nonsense, Biagio.' The handcuffed man kept his silence for another hour. Then the inspector took from an envelope the identification photographs of a thin young man with a tuft of hair coming down his forehead. They were photographs from 1949, the year of Totò's first arrest for the murder of Domenico Di Matteo on the bowls ground in the district of San Giovanni. Commissioner Mangano was now thinking out loud. 'He looks nothing like Totò Riina.'

At dawn on 16 December the farmer from San Giuseppe Jato confessed. It was him, Riina Salvatore, son of the late Giovanni and Rizzo Maria Concetta, born in Corleone on 16 November 1930. He was that skinny boy in the photograph taken almost fifteen years before. He had become a man, Totò Riina. He had been through a Mafia war, there had been dozens of killings since the day he had disappeared without a trace. Commissioner Mangano went back to his room and started to dictate a telephone message to police headquarters in Palermo: 'At 21.15 last night on the Palermo–Agrigento road, near San Michele Arcangelo, police arrested an individual who had got out of an unidentified vehicle and was running at speed towards the inhabited centre. Police had received information that the fugitive Riina Salvatore was due to arrive near the tunnel to visit his family . . .'

At seven o'clock in the morning Brigadier Biagio Melita allowed himself the first coffee of the day and then strolled around the deserted streets of the village. He wanted to be on his own and think peacefully about the long night he had just been through. A policeman like him couldn't fail to recognise someone like Totò Riina. He remembered him, Totò, when he had started 'blowing' between Piazza Garibaldi and Corso Bentivegna. The old brigadier had seen him grown up, he had told him not to be seen going around with Luciano Liggio, the *campiere* of Strasatto. He found himself remembering the words the young peasant from Via Rua del Piano had used in response to his warnings.

'You people from the state feed off us, you give us grief, you have us arrested, you send us to jail and you put us under house arrest. Sooner dead than a cop.'

The small tenant farmer had already chosen which side he was on.

The news of the 'alleged capture of farmer Salvatore Riina' was reported on the inside pages of a Sicilian daily newspaper only six days after 15 December. It was an article without many details, and the journalist wasn't sure that the man arrested near the tunnel really was the Mafioso from Corleone. Strangely, there was no official confirmation. The article mentioned 'a rumour spread yesterday in Corleone about the arrest of the fugitive [. . .] but we haven't had an official communication, the chief of police has refused to hold a press conference on the outcome of the investigation, and the conclusion of the inquiry is under strict embargo.'

WOMEN ONLY CAUSE TROUBLE

The detention room at Corleone police station measured three metres by four. There was a bed, a sink, and an air-vent window with no glass. Totò Riina hadn't slept, he was tired and he wasn't hungry. The plate of pasta that a policeman had brought him at midday was still on the floor beside two apples. It was cold in the cell. Outside the sky was black, preparing to rain. Totò Riina saw Inspector Mangano through the spyhole in the iron door. He called out, 'Inspector, are you still here?'

Mangano jerked around, then approached the cell. He said, 'If I'm still here, it's because of the work given to me by people like you.'

The Mafioso wanted to talk, and he chose to ignore the inspector's brusque tone. He smiled.

'We both have our job to do; you're the policeman and I'm the defendant . . .'

Mangano didn't smile.

'There is a difference, my dear Totò. I am on the law's side, I am the law. You don't even know where the law lives.'

'That's not true, Inspector,' Totò immediately interrupted. 'Yes, you are about to go home, and I can only dream about my home, but that doesn't make me a *malacarne* (a dyed-in-the-wool criminal) . . . In my life I've always tilled the earth to put bread on the table . . .'

'Bread . . . and a bit more besides, eh, Totò? A big slice of ham or a nice round lump of meat. Don't act the idiot to stay out of conflict, Totò. We know you're making money (*piccioli*).'

'*Piccioli, ne*! I live my life, Inspector. I keep myself busy, that's hardly against the law. I've become a businessman, I've been around . . . even outside Sicily.'

Mangano understood what he had to understand. If Totò Riina was talking to him here, at this time of day, it could mean only one thing: he would answer a few questions when he was put on record. 'Fine, fine,' the inspector thought.

The first official questioning of the Mafioso Salvatore Riina took place at 18.30 on 16 December 1963 at the commissariat of public safety in Corleone. He was interrogated for two hours. Mangano wanted to start with the last crime the prisoner was accused of, the murder of Paolo Riina, the trader killed in Corleone a year and a half before.

'So, Totò, what do you know about this man Riina?'

'I know what I've read in the papers, Inspector.'

'Great, and what have you read in the papers? Tell me . . .'

'That they killed him. I was shocked . . . such a good, honest, hard-working fellow. Who could wish him any harm?'

'Who indeed?' said Mangano, staring coldly into Riina's eyes.

'Women, Inspector, women only cause trouble. I don't know anything, but I've heard it said . . .'

'Tell me . . .'

'*U trunzu* [the cabbage stalk], you know that – don't you? – that they called him *u trunzu*, he was a bit too involved with certain women. Only women go to that shop, and the men are in the fields and Paolo *u trunzu* must have had some unsavoury thoughts. He will have paid some sort of compliment that he shouldn't have or, worse, put his hands where they shouldn't have gone. And in the evening the woman complained to her husband and the husband didn't complain to anyone . . . He took his shotgun and he fired . . . That's what I've heard, but I don't know anything.'

'You don't even know that you're accused of murder?'

'I read in the paper that they wanted to get hold of me. Me, Calogero Bagarella and a few others . . .'

Salvatore Riina was calm. He answered Commissioner Mangano's questions without ever raising his voice. He spoke in a whisper.

Mangano asked him: 'And where were you when he was killed?'

'Who knows, Inspector, so much time has passed. I hadn't seen him – Paolo Riina, I mean – for years. Perhaps not since 1958. Who knows where I was when they killed him . . . perhaps in Palermo at the home of my uncle, Giacomo Riina; I was always there during that time.'

Commissioner Mangano didn't lose patience, and didn't press Totò on the murder of the shopkeeper. He was sure that this would be Totò Riina's first and last version, even if he put the thumbscrews on him. The policeman was more curious about the papers he had found in the pockets of the fugitive's overcoat. Mangano wanted to know what Totò Riina had been doing during the five years and three months that he had spent on the run.

The story that the Corleone peasant had to tell was very unlikely, but the questioning was still a long way from the information that the inspector wanted. Meanwhile the Mafioso was becoming nervous; he was irritated by the explanations he had to give about the papers that had been found on him. They were pieces of paper covered with names, with numbers, with bank accounts. There was information about two companies, one set up years before with Luciano Liggio, Binnu Provenzano and Calogero Bagarella. There were also movements of money leading to two savings books, the first in the name of his brother Gaetano and the other in that of his cousin Giuseppe.

'Good business, Totò, well done,' Mangano said ironically as he looked through the papers with the figures in a column. 'You say you're a farmer. For a farmer you're doing a lot of trading . . .'

'What sort of trading, Inspector? I have lived my life. What you're forgetting is that I was forced to go into hiding in 1958. The state forced me into a nomadic life, always moving . . . first in the fields of Corleone . . . then I went to Palermo, to Rome, to Milan, but never being a *malacarne*: I traded in livestock, cattle and sheep . . .' His voice had changed. Riina seemed to be getting more and more nervous, for some reason that the inspector couldn't guess. U Curtu was nervous because he had to give explanations. He was forced to give them about those two pieces of paper that police had found on him. He promised himself once again that he would never again write down a bank account number or name.

To remember them he would use those coded scribbles that Binnu knew how to do . . .

'In 1962 I went into business . . . yes, into business . . . with Luciano Liggio, Calogero Bagarella and Bernardo Provenzano. We set up a livestock-breeding company. We bought 440 sheep, 30 goats, 21 cattle and a mare . . . in all we had 7 million 500,000 . . .'

He had set up another company with his uncle Giacomo and his cousin Giuseppe. They had bought jukeboxes and pinball machines to put in bars and gaming arcades. Salvatore Riina said he had earned 350,000 lire in the last four months, and also that his associates had chosen him as administrator.

'Inspector, I know how to do accounts . . .'

The questioning was coming to an end. Totò Riina spoke knowledgeably about cows, goats and beasts for the slaughter. And also about the jukeboxes he had bought in Milan. Inspector Angelo Mangano suddenly asked him: 'So, do you know Bernardo Provenzano and Calogero Bagarella well?'

'Yes, I know both of them.'

'When did you last see them?'

'I last saw Binnu Provenzano last June. Let me think . . . I saw him in Prizzi . . . So, on 2 June, that's right . . . at the cattle market. I saw Calogero Bagarella four months ago, however, on 28 August this year . . .'

The inspector left the room. He was smiling, and satisfied with his questioning. For the first time since he had been in Corleone he had signed a report longer than two pages.

That evening the inspector also questioned Maria Concetta Rizzo, the Mafioso's mother, who was accompanied by her daughter Arcangela. Totò Riina's mother talked about her persecuted son.

'Salvatore left home in 1958 because you were looking at him; he didn't wanted to be arrested under any circumstances. During those years he never came back to Corleone, and he only wrote to me once. It was a postcard.'

The woman didn't remember when and particularly from where that postcard had been sent. The next morning Angelo Mangano called someone else to the station. At ten o'clock in the morning a pretty dark girl came into his room. She nodded and stood in front of the inspector and didn't say anything. And she didn't ask why the police wanted to see her. The inspector started talking about what had happened the previous night at the tunnel above the power station, and the girl said nothing. Every now and again she glanced at the clock, to indicate to the inspector that she was in a hurry.

Antonina Bagarella was twenty years old. Her face was still that beautiful dark colour, she had big eyes and her hair was blacker and blacker. The summer before she had graduated from the Baccelli grammar school. In November she had enrolled for university, in Palermo, in the faculty of jurisprudence. The inspector asked the girl to sign a piece of paper, walked her to the door, and looked into her eyes for a moment. Mangano shook his head and left. Everyone in Corleone knew that Ninetta was Totò Riina's fiancée.

THE LUXURIES OF THE GRAND HOTEL

The prisoner Salvatore Riina spent the whole of Christmas Day 1963 in his cell. In the morning he had exercised in the courtyard of the Ucciardone prison, and after that he lay down on his bed to think, about Corleone, about the treeless fields around Mazzadiana, the vast pastures of tender grass. And above all he thought about his friends Binnu Provenzano and Calogero Bagarella, who were luckily still at liberty and able to guide the family. Totò Riina was thirty-three, and didn't know how long he would still be spending in the eighth section of the prison in Palermo.

The Ucciardone was completely full – all the men of honour had ended up in there after the Alfa Giulietta had been blown up in Ciaculli. Cosa Nostra was like a house that had just been in an earthquake. Some charismatic bosses had left Sicily for ever. Totò Greco, *Chicchiteddu*, had emigrated to South America with all his children. He no longer wanted to know about people like the La Barbera family who only thought about money, or about killers like the Corleonesi who wouldn't listen to reason. And Palermo wasn't what it had once been. The government had sent a parliamentary inquiry commission. For good or ill, that dynamited Giulietta marked the end of an era.

It was commonly said that 'you were almost better off inside than out', and the Ucciardone was compared to the Grand Hotel. Lobster and champagne came in every day via the register office, and ended up in the cells of the big guns. There was Pietro Torretta from Uditore, there was Masino Buscetta from Porta Nuova, the Di Peris from Villabate, and Tano Badalamenti from Cinisi, Gerlando Alberti from the suburb of Danisinni, Paolino Bontate from Santa Maria del Gesù, and the Matrangas, the Chiaracanes, the Nicolettis. The exclusive circles of the Mafia were locked up in the fortress that the Bourbons had built in the heart of Palermo.

Every boss had a mania, a habit, a vice. Gerlando Alberti was famous for his pinstripe silk suits. U zu Tanu (Uncle Tano) Badalamenti for his massive gold watches. Pietro Torretta for his cigarette holders: Don Pietrino couldn't smoke without his gem-incrusted silver cigarette holder. Only Totò Riina seemed like a starving man in there. He dressed as he had always dressed: the big, creased jackets that farmers wear. He had remained the same person as ever, a man with *peri incritati* – dirty feet. But Totò

Riina had a secret, burning ambition. One day the Corleonese confided in a cellmate: 'When I get out of here I want to walk on a carpet of 100,000 lira notes.'

His cellmate thought that, like everyone else, U Curtu had a lot of illusions.

Before Totò Riina could regain his freedom, the iron gate opened to admit his old boss, whom he hadn't seen for many months, Luciano Liggio. He had been arrested in Corleone, in the first house on the left after the new bridge, a two-storey house where Leoluchina Sorisi lived, the girl who had been engaged to the trade unionist Placido Rizzotto. During those tragic weeks in 1948 the girl had sworn revenge on Placido's murderers, and shouted in the village square that she would eat their hearts. But many years later Luciano Liggio, Placido's murderer, found refuge at Leoluchina's house, of all places. He was hiding in the girl's bedroom when Commissioner Angelo Mangano burst in. Leoluchina Sorisi didn't say anything, just lowered her eyes with shame. It was a warm evening in May 1964, and Luciano Liggio was in the Ucciardone for the first time in his life.

Over the next few months, the trial of Lucianeddu's so-called 'favourites' opened at the Palace of Justice in Palermo. There were twenty-two men and women who had protected and hidden him for years. They were doctors, professional people, shopkeepers, all with clean records, all citizens above all suspicion except one: Salvatore Riina from Corleone. In the court of the first penal session, Totò appeared one winter morning, with handcuffs around his wrists and two *carabinieri* behind him. He was sitting on the defendants' bench, wearing a black woollen jacket. He no longer had that thin moustache on his upper lip, and he had put on weight in prison.

The hearing hadn't yet begun when two journalists approached the defendants' bench. The first was Mario Francese, the crime correspondent of the *Giornale di Sicilia*. The other was Aurelio Bruno, an old court reporter who worked for RAI (Italy's equivalent of the BBC). It was Francese who spoke, while a little way away Aurelio Bruno listened and smiled. Mario Francese was a curious journalist who wanted to see face to face the men whose names ended up in his articles every day. They swapped jokes for ten minutes or so; Totò Riina asked him for a cigarette, and Francese got hold of one for him. The Mafioso only had time to take a few puffs before the judges came in.

Life at the Ucciardone was spent waiting for an event that the VIP prisoners considered important, even crucial for their own survival. The bosses were waiting for the ruling of the Court of Assizes in Catanzaro about the trial into the Ciaculli massacre, and which was being held in Calabria *per legittima suspicione* [meaning that the trial and the venue had been challenged on grounds of lack of impartiality]. It had always been called, no one quite knew why, 'the trial of the 114'. In fact there were 113 accused, all members of the old, the new and the very new Palermo Mafia. The trial closed with a shameful list of acquittals. Only a few thugs and a number of second-ranking bosses were sentenced to a few years in jail, but they were already free, having served their jail terms on remand. Cosa Nostra had absorbed the blow, which could have been fatal, of the aftermath of Ciaculli; they had demonstrated that even the most difficult trials could be 'adjusted'. In the streets of Palermo, Angelo La Barbera, the Greco cousins, the Fidanzatis of l'Arenella and that fierce, diabolical man who was Michele Cavataio started acting like godfathers again.

The Ucciardone prison was emptied within three weeks, and few Mafiosi were left in the seventh and eighth blocks, those who hadn't been accused in Catanzaro. One day they brought a thug from the suburb of Pallavicino into Totò Riina's cell, a man with a big, black, drooping moustache. His name was Gaspare Mutolo,

Asparino. He was a disenchanted, intelligent and experienced guy. He wasn't a 'made man' – or not yet. Salvatore Riina liked the fellow. He kept him cheerful, and was a good cellmate. Not least because – it was discovered much later, along with many other things – Asparino had taught him to play draughts.

HE REVEALED PEOPLE'S SOULS

The rumour had passed from mouth to mouth towards evening, when the cells were in darkness and silence reigned in the blocks. It was a Monday, and a long day of visits and meetings with family had just come to an end. The news spread by prison radio in sections three, four and six and mentioned a mysterious singing 'nightingale' (*cantante*). Prison radio was seldom wrong: there was an inmate who had met up with the cops or, more probably, intended to do so. No one knew his name or his face. No one knew anything, except for one small detail that had trickled out of the interview room thanks to a prison warder. The *cantante* was from a village in the Palermo provinces.

Everyone started to suspect everyone. That Monday stripped away the peace of the people of the Ucciardone – 327 ordinary prisoners and 41 on police files as Mafiosi. Only one of them seemed calm and indifferent to the rumours and the fear running through the prison corridors. Rumours and fear made him smile, he said they were 'all nonsense . . .' But that wasn't exactly what Totò Riina thought. It was just what he wanted to make the others believe.

The Mafioso Salvatore Riina had won himself a place in the sun within the Palermo prison. He was listened to, his words carried weight. This was partly down to his old Corleonese friend Luciano Liggio, who was already a myth. For years the newspapers on the mainland had called him 'the scarlet pimpernel' because he was impossible to catch. Not a week went by without his face appearing on the front page, with a cigar between his teeth and the confident, arrogant air of someone who could challenge the whole world. But within the walls of the Ucciardone Salvatore Riina owed it mostly to himself if he had become a respected man, an *inteso*, someone who distributed advice, who had a wise answer to every question, a solution to every problem. Totò Riina's appearance was still that of a coarse peasant, but his mind was refined, his reasoning subtle, his observations sharp, precise and always convincing. Totò Riina had grown, he had learned how to enter other people's minds. He was a confessor, the confessor of the Ucciardone. He was becoming a boss.

The line formed down in the courtyard, during exercises. The prisoners silently lined up one behind the other and waited their turn. To talk to him, to ask a favour, to tell him what had happened the previous night in a cell or in the sick bay or the register office. Totò Riina had a thought for each of them, a word for everyone. The *viddano* was revered; he had charisma, with his keen black eyes he revealed people's souls.

They greeted him deferentially and didn't approach without a bow. And they feared him. They all knew what Totò Riina had done in Corleone in the five years of war against Michele Navarra. What they didn't know was how he had managed – him with dirt on his feet – to accumulate so much information about Cosa Nostra in Palermo. About the men of honour in every family, about the practices of the *capidecina* (lower-ranking bosses), about the rancour stored up in Ciaculli, about the demands being made in San Lorenzo, the weaknesses of the old bosses in Uditore, the clashes in the suburbs of Passo di Rigano and Cruilas.

One day when Totò Riina was in confidential mood, he even

recommended to his cellmate Gaspare Mutolo who he should go and see once he got out of jail.

'If you live in Pallavicino, always stay close to Saro Riccobono and don't do anything to harm him . . . all the others will be in heaven soon . . .'

It was a bit more than advice for Asparino. It was a secret, a 'present' that the little suburban *picciotto*[1] had shown he deserved. Totò Riina had also recommended a book for the young Asparino to read, one of the books from the prison library. It was the story of a secret seventeenth-century sect, men with their heads covered by hoods who moved at night in the underground of Palermo. Totò Riina knew by heart the story and the deeds of the *Blessed Pauls* in the popular novel by William Galt, alias Luigi Nàtoli. For the men of honour it was a bible.

The years in the Ucciardone were important for U Curtu and his peasants. The world was going their way, in spite of jail and the arrest warrants, police roundups and ministerial announcements. The wind was turning once again in Sicily; the memory of the massacre of Ciaculli had faded with time. Palermo was Palermo again. It was a special city, a continent. It was capable of forgetting immediately or never. Capable of swallowing up and hiding in its guts even the most recent, painful past. Even the dead of the city, especially the dead. It was a saying that the Sicilians of the times liked to repeat to explain that, in the end, what had happened was never irreparable. 'If the water bathes you, the wind will dry you . . .' That was how it was in Sicily: everything worked as it always had.

Meanwhile the rumour going around the prison about the mysterious *cantante* disturbed the sleep of many prisoners. A spy

---

1   Small one or young one, commonly used when referring to young mafiosi.

in the Ucciardone meant life sentences. It also meant the loss of security and power in a prison where the Mafiosi had always been secure and powerful. So the boss Gaetano Badalamenti had the idea of infiltrating one of his men, a member of his family, into the parliament. One Sunday he called half a dozen bosses into his country house three kilometres from Cinisi, talked about the pros and cons, then said that one of them would be more use to him in the Ucciardone than in parliament. The man he was talking about was an MP. But he was also a very well-known doctor in Palermo, an ear, nose and throat specialist. His name was Franco Barbaccia, he was originally from Godrano, a country boy from the interior. For two legislatures he had been elected in the territory of Western Sicily, winning a high share of the votes for the Christian Democrats.

Franco Barbaccia had never been to a political meeting in his life, and at the parliament in Montecitorio he hadn't spoken once. In ten years in the Chamber he had never signed a bill or presented an intervention. A ghost MP at the service of Cosa Nostra. His new job wasn't all that bad: a job working in the Ucciardone, visiting two days a week, on Mondays and Thursdays. During those months Sicilian politics lost a Mafioso, but in compensation a man of honour of the Cinisi family became part of the organic structure of the prison of Palermo. But before the ex-MP set foot in the Ucciardone sick bay, something happened. And that something could have done damage to Totò Riina and his Corleonesi. Damage that could have changed their entire story.

A FUGITIVE IN PALERMO

THE DOTS OF *MALAVITA*

Water dirty with sand had been coming down for three days. The cars were covered with a yellowish dust, the asphalt in the streets of Palermo was slippery. Between the Four Corners of the city and Porta Nuova, on the morning of 11 January 1966, the traffic was paralysed, the deafening noise of the klaxons had broken the silence of the gardens of Villa d'Orléans. There was a procession moving towards Palazzo dei Normanni: a few thousand construction workers and dockers were protesting at the gates of the Regional Assembly. A little way off there was a flying squad unit in a semi-circle, and a small crowd was waiting in front of a stage for the trade unionists who were supposed to be giving a rally. Alone among the palms of Piazza della Vittoria, far from the noises of the strike, there stood three women dressed in black.

They were speaking under their breath, heedless of the rain. One of the three – the oldest – had suddenly started shouting incomprehensible words. The other two tried to calm her down, holding her by an arm and shouting in their turn. Then they started ed running. They pursued each other among the plants and the stone benches, they stopped and ran again. They started talking quietly before walking in silence towards a corner of the Piazza della Vittoria. There was an iron gate there, and a marble plaque. On it was written: 'Palermo police headquarters'.

The older woman walked towards the uniformed sentry and, weeping, whispered something. The sentry understood only her name – Biagia Lanza – and then the last of her sobbed words: '. . . because there was a prisoner from Corleone who had some important revelations to make . . .' The woman had asked to speak to Deputy Superintendent Angelo Mangano. She knew he worked at Palermo police headquarters, in the heart of the criminal investigation department. Commissioner Mangano had been transferred and promoted to Palermo after the arrest of Luciano Liggio. He had left Corleone as he had arrived, on the coach, in the afternoon, clutching his suitcase. There were no official ceremonies to accompany his transfer. And no mayoral leaving ceremony for the policeman as he left Corleone. Now Angelo Mangano was here, on the second floor, standing motionless at the window. Behind the glass he saw the rain falling into the garden, then close to the door of the police station he recognised the wife of a man he had known a long time ago, in the fields around Corleone. He phoned the sentry and ordered him to let the black-clad woman in straight away.

On the morning of 12 January it was still raining in Palermo when a state police van passed through the gate of the Ucciardone. The director of the prison held a sheet of paper, which he was reading with some perplexity: there was an investigating magistrate wanted to question 'the prisoner Raia Luciano, son of the late Carmelo, accused of extortion and aggravated criminal association'. Deputy Superintendent Mangano loaded Luciano Raia onto the van. They only greeted one another later, when they found themselves face to face.

'Hello, Chief Inspector . . .'

'Hi Raia, we meet again . . . I hope you haven't come here to waste my time.

Luciano Raia was thin and quite tall. He wasn't yet fifty, but he looked at least ten years older. He was an agricultural labourer, and Mangano remembered him as a violent character, suspected of having killed on more than one occasion. His face was hollow, and at least three days' growth of beard made him look ill. His eyes were small, black and bright. He was almost bald, and there was a small scar on his neck. On the inside of his right hand, between his thumb and index finger, he had a tattoo, five tiny greenish marks, and the dots of *malavita*[1].

Between the Ucciardone and the court, Luciano Raia didn't say a word. He was sitting in a corner of the van, with his head between his legs, and stayed in that position until the door opened and he was lifted by the arms of two policemen. Luciano Raia was shaking. He knew that the big step had been taken, and if he got out of that van there would be no turning back. The corridor was deserted, there were no lawyers or magistrates. A stout man with glasses appeared from a doorway. Luciano Raia recognised him. He was Judge Terranova.

At about ten o'clock in the morning Deputy Superintendent Angelo Mangano, the investigating magistrate Cesare Terranova and the Mafioso Luciano Raia studied one another in silence for a few minutes. It was the tall, thin man with the long beard who started to talk in a faint voice. He was scared, confused, he said over and over again that he had got everything wrong and committed terrible crimes. He wanted to ask forgiveness of God and men. He said he hadn't slept for many months, and remorse was destroying him day after day. He said he had seen too many deaths,

---

1 Organized crime; underworld.

and that he wanted to confess all his sins. He too had killed, one, two, three, four times . . . He described in detail the murder of a shepherd who brought his flock to his lands. He remembered the terror he had seen in that man's eyes when he had strangled him near the Batticano River.

Luciano Raia spoke and wiped his brow with a handkerchief. He fiddled with his left earlobe, then folded his hands, straightening his trousers every now and again. He was drenched in sweat when he took the final decision. He said that he wasn't an informer like the others, and asked to put in writing everything he knew about the Mafia and the killings in Corleone. Luciano Raia was a turncoat criminal, a *pentito*.

THE END OF TEPISTO

Judge Terranova's room was small and dark. There were files and papers on his desk, piles of books, a stack of old newspapers, three or four pipes. Deputy Superintendent Mangano locked the door and started pacing nervously back and forth. The Corleonese Mafioso Luciano Raia's lips were dry, and he was starting to shake again.

He asked after his wife Biagia, and Mangano told him about the meeting he had had with her at police headquarters the day before. Judge Terranova looked at the prisoner in front of him. Then he got up and walked around the armchair in whose depths Raia was sitting.

'Don't be scared. No one's going to do anything to you. In fact I promise . . . no one's going to harm you . . .'

Luciano Raia kept his chin pressed close to his chest and didn't even look up. Terranova towered over him. The judge went on: 'But take care that if you are really sure about delivering this testimony, you have to tell us everything, really everything, from start to finish.'

Raia nodded.

The magistrate put some blank sheets of paper down on the desk and handed a pen to 'Raia Luciano, son of the late Carmelo'. The confession was long and very detailed, and for many months only two men – Deputy Superintendent Angelo Mangano and Investigating Magistrate Cesare Terranova – knew the secrets revealed by the Corleonese.

'So, Raia, shall we get started?'

A shiver ran through Luciano Raia. He looked around. He looked at the books, the yellowed newspapers, the legal files and finally the round, fatherly face of Cesare Terranova. The judge encouraged him with his eyes. Raia began his story, stumbling over his words and leaving long pauses.

'I was in the fifth section of the Ucciardone. I don't remember when it was . . . It was hot, but not very hot . . . maybe the beginning of June, maybe September. More likely September than June. It was exercise hour. The others were walking under a wall, around the football field. I was on my own, sweeping the courtyard. Eventually I heard loud laughter. I turned round and saw a little group walking towards a corner of the courtyard. I didn't recognise all of them. One of them was definitely Vincenzo Liggio, who thinks he's such a big shot because he's a friend of Lucianeddu, and Gaetano Riina, who's the brother of Salvatore Riina. They're a little apart from the others, then Liggio and Riina go off to talk about their own matters, right to the end of the courtyard. They're whispering, but you can see they're talking about something important. They're waving their hands about, looking around . . . I walk over, with the excuse that I'm sweeping the courtyard and I hear . . .'

From his pocket Luciano took a grey, red and blue handkerchief and wiped away the sweat that was now flowing down his face. He went on: 'Gaetano Riina said they'd been keeping an eye on Francesco Paolo Streva, Biagio Pomilla and Antonino Piraino. I couldn't hear what Gaetano was saying. I had to keep my distance, or they'd have noticed that I was listening to them . . . Gaetano was explaining that in the end they'd managed to surprise them and kill them. One of the three – I couldn't make out who – had put up some resistance, and I also heard that they'd set fire to the weeds to destroy the three corpses.'

Luciano sweated as he remembered. He asked for a drop of water, and Deputy Superintendent Mangano also set down a pack of cigarettes on the table and offered him a light. The Mafioso was cold, so they closed the window. Someone knocked at the door. A clerk came in with a tray of coffee. The prisoner took a breath, looked at the judge like a whipped dog and started again.

'They also talked about another murder. The man was nicknamed *Tepisto*, he was a night watchman, his name was Pietro Splendido. He guarded the wood store at Corleone near San Michele Arcangelo where the tunnel's being built. Tepisto often saw Luciano Liggio, Salvatore Riina, Binnu Provenzano and Calogero Bagarella, all of them fugitives, around those parts. They didn't trust him to keep his mouth shut, so they killed him.'

The memories of Luciano Raia slowly emerged, with references and names. He talked for an hour about that man Tepisto and how he had died. Judge Terranova wrote in a notebook and looked up only to meet the witness's eyes. The magistrate interrupted him and asked, 'You talked about three murders, but who really killed them? Who burned the corpses?'

Raia reached out his hand, took another cigarette from the pack and slipped it into his mouth. Then he said: 'It was them, them, who else? They did it. Salvatore and Gaetano Riina, Luciano Liggio, Bernardo Provenzano, Calogero Bagarella.'

Inspector Mangano also recorded another crime in Corleone, the murder of Paolo Riina. And coming right up to Raia he asked him: 'Did you also know a certain Paolo *u trunzu*?'

A half-smile appeared on the prisoner's lips. Yes, he remembered Paolo Riina. He was a dick – a *minchione* – and deserved his nickname, Paolo *u trunzu*. Luciano Raia started talking again, but addressed the judge and not the policeman who had asked the question.

'If you want to know who killed Paolo Riina, you'll have to ask his wife. She knows where her husband went the day before he was killed . . . I know too . . . I saw him in Bisacquino, at the livestock market, then I noticed that Salvatore Riina was there too. He was sitting on the trunk of a tree. Hmmm, I thought, what's he doing there . . .? Riina was a fugitive, and everybody knew he was always out in the mountains . . . then I saw him following Paolo Riina and I knew something bad was going to happen to him. The next day Paolo *u trunzu* was murdered.'

Luciano Raia's revelations went on for days and days, and were personally checked by Deputy Superintendent Mangano. Their investigation wasn't easy; the policeman believed every word Raia said, but for a few murders he could find no cross-checks nor other witness statements. There was no evidence, for example, about the involvement of Gaetano Riina (*Tanuzzu*), Totò's brother, in any crime. Gaetano was never brought before the courts for the murders revealed by Raia.

After Luciano Raia's confessions the deputy inspector and the magistrate decided to question U Curtu again. Perhaps the time had come to trap that bloodthirsty Corleonese. There was a man making accusations about him, and who wanted to give evidence against him in court. The committal proceedings hadn't yet finished. Judge Cesare Terranova wanted to talk to Totò Riina again.

They arranged to question him on the afternoon of 24 March

1966 in the interview room in Ucciardone prison. Totò Riina was accompanied to a little windowless room. When the Corleonese saw the face of Angelo Mangano for the first time in three years, he grimaced, first with surprise and then with disgust. And when Judge Terranova appeared behind the policeman, Totò Riina asked the policemen to go back to the seventh block straight away. The peasant refused to answer any questions – he said he was the victim of persecution. But before disappearing behind the door of the interview room he glanced at the magistrate and told him in a sarcastic voice why he would never talk to him. 'With you, you end up like the Jews: you're always after me, every five minutes there's an arrest warrant. From now on I'll only answer the president of the court; I refuse to sign a single one of your pieces of paper. You and I, Judge Terranova, won't see each other again until the trial.'

THE MAFIA EXISTS BUT . . .

There were sixty-four accused at the bar, all of them born in Corleone. The trial of the five-year Mafia war was held, once again, '*per legittima suspicione*', outside of Sicily – in Bari this time. The big Cosa Nostra trials were held far away for reasons of expediency, since there was a suspicion that the Palermo law courts might be corruptible in some way. In Bari the state was represented by the deputy prosecutor of the Republic, Domenico Zaccaria. It was a difficult trial, and the air was electric. And some strange things happened. One day the public minister's gun was stolen, a revolver kept in the drawer of a desk in his office. The magistrate had just asked for three life sentences and three hundred years in prison for the Corleonesi.

Totò Riina was in the dock for all forty-seven of the Bari

hearings. He sat in the corner nearest the court, and never missed a line. He never took his eyes off the judges and the jury who were trying him and all his friends from the village. There were about thirty accused, including Luciano Liggio.

The Contadini were all there waiting for the verdict. The only ones missing were Binnu Provenzano and Calogero Bagarella. The trial was to finish early in the summer of 1969. The judges were going into the council chamber, and the sentence seemed to be a foregone conclusion. The evidence against the Corleonesi was damning. But on the morning of the last hearing a postman arrived at the Palace of Justice. He had a letter to deliver to Vincenzo Stea, the president of the first session of the Court of Assizes in Bari.

It was an express delivery, postmarked Palermo. It was a letter full of mistakes, written in black ink and signed with a cross. The president of the court read it in silence, turned pale, took out a handkerchief and wiped his forehead, which was pearled with sweat. Then he hurriedly passed on the message to all the judges and jury members. The letter that had come from Sicily was very eloquent.

'You people in Bari have not understood, or rather, don't want to understand what Corleone means. You are judging honest men denounced by the *carabinieri* and the police on a whim. We want to warn you that if an honest man from Corleone is sentenced you will go up in the air, you will be destroyed, you will be slaughtered as will your families. All you have to do now is show sound judgement.'

On 10 June 1969 the court left the council chamber and President Stea read out sixty-four names and sixty-four declarations of innocence. The charges of criminal association were dropped, as were the accusations of murder. Salvatore Riina, Luciano Liggio, Binnu Provenzano, Calogero Bagarella and all the other

Corleonesi who had laid waste to their village were acquitted for insufficient evidence. The sentence was scandalous, much more so than anyone had predicted, but no one could ever have imagined the reason for the mass-acquittal of the Corleone.

To demolish the prosecutor's case the evidence of the facts was denied, and the judges and the jury were so 'judicious' that they even argued with the police and magistrates who had prepared the case for the 'reprehensible thoughtlessness with which the charges had been brought against the defendant.' The sentence was a reproach levelled at the state, or at least that part of the state that had tried to halt the dramatic advance of the Corleonesi.

The surprising reasons for the sentence delivered in Bari were summed up in 307 pages; each page dripped with contempt for the criminal investigation department, each step contested the circumstances set out in dozens of reports. The court couldn't help recognising the existence of the Mafia, 'because it cannot help but take account of it', but ruled that 'the equation Mafia equals criminal association on which investigators have for so long insisted and to which the investigating magistrate has devoted such argumentation, is without appreciable consequences at the level of the trial.' It was an important precedent, and the Bari sentence would continue to make history over the next ten years.

These legal acrobatics swept away evidence and clues, and Luciano Raia, the criminal who had turned state evidence, was held to be 'mentally unstable'. Dozens of certificates came in from all over Italy, from asylums and psychiatric hospitals, attesting to his 'frequent epileptic seizures', diagnoses were dredged up of 'obsessive symptomatology with a confused drug-induced state in a depressed subject', old neurological examinations were discovered which revealed 'his periodic emotional and volitional instability'. The key witness in the Bari trial was a lunatic.

The judges had no doubts, these were lies put about by a

warped mind. 'Because of the above we may reasonably affirm that the misgivings which have arisen concerning Raia's dependability are aggravated when we come to assess the personality of the witness from the moral point of view . . .' A witness statement arrived from Corleone, which even told the court about Luciano Raia's sexual habits. One Arcangelo Li Causi informed the Bari tribunal: 'He is a homosexual, but not only that, he is truly depraved . . . Having examined many men, I may say that I have never known a man so depraved in the sexual sphere.'

The court's final ruling on the *pentito* was clear and pointed the way towards many other sentences over the years to come.

'It is entirely legitimate to conclude that Raia Luciano is without the moral judgement that would have led him to divulge to the investigating authorities the facts of which he was aware, obeying his urgent civic duty to assist the course of justice.' Once again, the judges were quick to rebuke the policemen and magistrates who had believed him: 'The court is obliged to mark as absolutely unreliable all the content of Raia's depositions for which, without deserving it in any way, he has been identified as a key witness.'

The two chief-accused, Luciano Liggio and Salvatore Riina, had been brought before the court 'without a scintilla of evidence, however circumstantial, solely because of their alleged membership of a Mafia *cosca*, even though their physical presence at the crime scene has never been proven . . .' The sentence also mentioned the secret confidences and public rumours which 'had created a psychological and suggestive situation from which it was not easy to extricate oneself, and that is the only possible explanation for their being summoned before the court . . .'

The judges devoted a few pages of the sentence exclusively to Lucianeddu and his Pott's disease: 'Liggio certainly suffers from ambulatory difficulties which are far from negligible, and which make it extremely unlikely that he was involved in the material perpetration of the crimes.' Then they struggled to find a clue linking him to a criminal association: 'There is some identifiable evidence involving the illegal slaughter of animals, evidence proven beyond a reasonable doubt, since this a recognised offence.'

They were all acquitted, hitmen and instigators, bosses and accessories. Totò Riina was found guilty of the theft of a driving licence, the identification document found in his pocket when he was arrested near the tunnel in Corleone. A sentence of a year and six months' imprisonment plus an 80,000 lire fine. In the Court of Assizes in Bari, Totò Riina smiled as he read the sentence: he smiled because he was finally going to be a free man again after so many years on the run and five in the Ucciardone. On 10 June 1969 an Italian court had ruled, beyond reasonable doubt, that he was neither a Mafioso nor a murderer.

ROOM 11

The fresh air of freedom had left him slightly dazed; he looked around, holding his suitcase in one hand and with the other pointing out the approaching car to Liggio. The man in the car was their lawyer. Donato Mitolo opened the car door and started laughing. 'I've come to get you, I promised I would . . .'

A few hours before, a court official had delivered an envelope to the register office. It was the order from the Court of Assizes for the release from prison of Salvatore Riina and the other sixty-three 'honest men from Corleone'. Evening had not yet fallen, there was a cool wind coming from the sea, the sky was pink and the *viddani* were all free. Totò Riina and Luciano spent their first night as ex-prisoners seventeen kilometres from Bari, in the town of Bitonto. Their lawyer, Donato Mitolo, went with them to the lobby of the Hotel Nuovo, where they presented their identification papers, took two rooms, and told the manager of the hotel that they would be staying there for a few days.

In the rooms of the Hotel Nuovo, Luciano Liggio and Totò Riina spent three days, locked away, studying a plan to delay their return to Sicily, to Corleone, straight away. On the morning of the fourth day, on 14 June, Salvatore Riina left the hotel and presented himself at the register office of the town of Bitonto. He was holding a request for a resident's permit, and wanted to stay in Puglia. In the request presented to the town council he also maintained that he had already found a job as a clerk in the legal chambers of Donato Mitolo. He also informed them of his temporary residence: 3 Via Anita Garibaldi, the address of his lawyer's father. That morning Salvatore Riina handed in his request to the register office and returned to his hotel. He waited another three days and three nights until two policemen from the office of public safety in Bitonto knocked at the doors of rooms 11 and 12 of the Hotel Nuovo.

It was about eight o'clock on the morning of 17 June, and Salvatore Riina and Luciano Liggio were to leave the town of Bitonto by the evening of the following day. The police had a mandatory expulsion order to issue to the two Corleone Mafiosi. They were not to return to the area for three years. They were 'socially dangerous', and were not permitted to stay in Puglia. The notice was signed by the police superintendent of Bari, Girolamo Lacquaniti. The policemen delivered the mandatory expulsion order to the hands of Totò Riina and Luciano Liggio, who signed the papers; they didn't say a word, they were furious. Then they immediately called their lawyer. There was no time to lose; they had to do something to stop the expulsion order. Again it was their friend the lawyer Donato Mitolo who tried to find a way. First he called the chief prosecutor of the Republic in Bari and then he presented a petition to the prefect. It was the first attempt to block the police chief's order.

The letter was dated 19 June, the day before the deadline for Police Chief Lacquaniti's expulsion order. It consisted of four pages, written in perfect Italian and full of technical references to the acquittal pronounced just a week before by the Court of Assizes in Bari. Also attached to the letter were the copies of two statements, one sent directly to the chief of police and the other to the general prosecutor of the Court of Appeal. All the letters were signed by Salvatore Riina.

'I am one of the sixty-four defendants in the trial recently held before the most excellent Court of Assizes in Bari, and I was acquitted of the most serious crimes of bloodshed because I did not commit the crimes and was also acquitted of criminal association for lack of evidence. When I was released from prison I decided, for reasons there is no point listing here, not to return to Sicily and to look for work and decent accommodation in this province. I had expressed this intention to my trusted defence lawyer Donato Mitolo, whom I had also requested, aware of his keen sense of humanity, to help me make my wish reality. Donato Mitolo offered me the opportunity to work for him as an office clerk in Bitonto, but the Chief of Police of Bari issued an expulsion order according to which I am socially dangerous [. . .] It is plainly evident, Illustrious Prefect, that such an order is absolutely illegitimate and arbitrary [. . .] the Bari sentence has confirmed, in a clear and unequivocal manner, that I am absolutely innocent, and that I have the sacrosanct right to live in the part of the state in which I consider it most opportune to reside . . .'

On the evening of 20 June the lawyer Donato Mitolo took Luciano Liggio in his car to the Ospedale della Santissima Annunziata in Taranto. Liggio was admitted to a ward in the infectious diseases ward where a friend was working, a Sicilian, a doctor originally from the province of Palermo. It was almost night by the time Mitolo returned to the Hotel Nuovo in Bitonto, climbed to the first floor and went into room number 11. He spoke for a moment to Salvatore Riina, explaining to him that there was nothing to be done, and the shouts of the peasant from Corleone could be heard all the way down to the lobby. Totò Riina was furious: the petition to the prefect in Bari had been useless. He had to leave Bitonto at midnight on the dot.

And at midnight two policemen came to take him from the hotel, put him in a green Alfa Giulietta and drove him to Bari station. Then they put him on the express train for Calabria. The Mafioso who wanted to be a clerk in Bitonto was going back to Sicily; Totò U Curtu was going back to Corleone.

AND HE BECAME A GHOST

The train journey to Sicily was endless, and that night Totò Riina couldn't sleep. He was obsessed by the trick the cops had played on him. Even though he had been acquitted, he wasn't free, he still had the police breathing down his neck. He reached Palermo station the following day, late in the afternoon. There were black clouds in the sky, announcing a storm, and on platform four there were three friends waiting to take him back to Corleone. Almost two hours on the road, twisting roads, and hairpin bends, uphill and down; it was dark by the time they reached the village. The car transporting him passed by the town hall and turned into Corso Bentivegna. After the square it continued up the alleys that climbed to Via Rua del Piano. Totò Riina hugged his mother and sisters. He only just had time for dinner. It was ten to midnight when ten of the inspector's officers entered the house at number 13 Via Rua del Piano.

'You have to come with us, we have an order for you to be remanded in custody.' It was from the Palermo state prosecutor's office, and the magistrates had requested the arrest of Salvatore Riina 'for reasons of justice'. It was a strategy designed to lock him up in a cell for a few days. That night the Mafioso went back to Palermo under escort and in handcuffs. From the coast road he saw the unmistakable black outline of the Ucciardone. He recognised the familiar face of a guard who opened the iron gate. They were taking him back to prison, to the eighth wing. Police headquarters had suggested his imprisonment, since he was also socially dangerous in Sicily 'because his return might unleash struggles for a settling of scores between the Mafia clans'. The internal exile order for Totò Riina had been issued to the court by Pietro Giammanco, a young magistrate who became chief prosecutor in Palermo twenty years later.

On the morning of 5 July Salvatore Riina was brought into the courtroom for the first section of the tribunal in Palermo, where the hearing to rule on his internal exile was to be held. Totò Riina was flabbergasted. He had been put in prison, put on trial and acquitted, and his lawyers couldn't explain to him what was happening. After being acquitted at the Court of Assizes he couldn't believe they wanted to send him to prison. He had gone back to the Ucciardone, and he was still in a court facing judges and *carabinieri*. The hearing lasted only a few hours; the magistrates quickly decided on the fate of Totò Riina. For four years he was obliged to stay within the boundaries of San Giovanni in Persiceto, a village just outside Bologna.

His Palermo lawyer – Giuseppe Savagnone – asked the court for 'three to four days' leave so that Riina Salvatore, before leaving Palermo, could go to Corleone to resolve the needs of his mother (widow) and his two sisters (unmarried) who were his responsibility'.

Leave was granted, and Salvatore Riina returned to the village. No one saw him around during those three days; no one ever met him for as much as a moment in Piazza Garibaldi. On 8 July his lawyer Savagnone went back to the court and lodged an appeal against the four years of confinement. In his petition he reconstructed the life of Totò 'since he had the misfortune at the age of eighteen and a half [. . .] to be in a bowling ground in Corleone and in the course of a game, over a banal challenge, an individual by the name of Di Matteo, more adult than him, and violent and impulsive of character, fired a pistol-shot at him which hit him in one thigh'. The version of the 'misfortune' in the district of San Giovanni supplied by the lawyer was very different from the one recorded in the police report. Savagnone write: 'Riina, who was armed like any other farmer in the years immediately after the war, drew his pistol in turn and fired a shot at Di Matteo, killing him.'

The rest of the statement depicted Totò Riina as an honest man, a victim of circumstances.

'In December 1953 he was arrested again, but acquitted after five and a half years of harsh, cruel and unfair imprisonment [. . .] today, even if we admit that in his past Riina may have committed certain acts of stupidity, it is not legitimate to claim that he is a perverse and dangerous individual simply for that reason. Five years of jail can radically transform a thoughtless boy into a thoughtful, responsible man.

The judges didn't have time to read the report by the lawyer Giuseppe Savagnone. Totò Riina had already disappeared. He wasn't at 13 Via Rua del Piano. And neither was he at the home of his uncle Giacomo in Palermo. He had never reached the village of San Giovanni in Persiceto. Totò Riina had disappeared. It was a day in the third week of July, 1969. The longest and most mysterious absence in history of a Cosa Nostra boss began on the

Friday. From that moment Salvatore Riina became a ghost. For twenty-four hours.

At around this time the prosecutor's office in Palermo also issued a custody order for Luciano Liggio. Lucianeddu was followed from one central-Italian hospital to another by very discreet and equally listless police. He fled in the autumn of that year. Some people cried scandal, there was an inquiry, and the parliamentary anti-Mafia commission denounced 'a series of incorrect and objectively illegal behaviours' in the state apparatus. The chief prosecutor of Palermo, Pietro Scaglione, and his deputy, Pietro Giammanco, were questioned, as were the chief of police of Palermo, Paolo Zamparelli, and his deputy, Emanuele De Francesco, plus Colonel Alberto Dalla Chiesa, who was in charge of the legion of *carabineri*, and Deputy Superintendent Angelo Mangano, who was the head of the crime squad.

In the end it was Chief of Police Zamparelli who paid for everything by being fired. Chief Prosecutor Scaglione was demoted in the Higher Council of the Magistracy. Then Pietro Scaglione was suddenly promoted. And transferred to the general prosecutor's office in Lecce.

THE PIGEONS IN ST MARK'S SQUARE

The raid took place, as always, at dawn. The streets were deserted, at five in the morning, and the houses seemed to be clinging to the black mountain. There was only one far-away light, and sometimes the plaster Madonna lit up below the Saracen Tower. Vicolo Scorsone was blocked at the top by a jeep, and at the bottom by a small army of police. It was a raid, a fugitive-hunting operation. In Corleone they were looking for Totò Riina, the boss who had disappeared after the Bari trial. Someone claimed to have seen him in the village and among the vines of the Rocche di Rao, on the boundary with the lands of the sanctuary of Tagliavia. Informers swore that he was hiding in the fields during the day, and then coming up to Corleone at night.

They didn't find him: there was no one there but his old mother and his sister Arcangela. The 'flying squads' were rerouted in a few minutes to 24 Vicolo Scorsone, Bagarella's house. The policemen entered the little old cuboid building by breaking the door down. They broke everything, looking for weapons that they couldn't find; they cut up mattresses and even disembowelled the cushions. They emptied wardrobes and sideboards, they took apart furniture and bathroom fittings. There was nothing. In Bagarella's house there wasn't even a man. Not even Leoluca, Luchino, the youngest of the boys. They were all on the run. Or in jail. Or under internal exile. There were only the women of the family. His mother, Lucia, and four daughters, Maria Matilde, Angela, Emanuela and Antonina.

The three rooms on the ground floor and the four others on the first floor had been turned upside down, but Totò Riina wasn't there. The women had been awoken in the middle of the night; they were still in their dressing gowns, sitting silently around the kitchen table. The police were forever opening and closing drawers, asking questions, demanding to know, every moment, 'Where is he? Where is he? It'll be better for everybody if you tell us . . .'

Then a shout was heard from a bedroom, followed by the sound of two men whispering. One of the policemen came downstairs, holding a vase. It was made of china, it was white with a gilded decoration that climbed from the pedestal. The vase was empty: there was no water and there were no flowers. He slipped a hand inside the vase. He struggled to take it out. He was clutching something in his fingers.

It was a rolled-up photograph, and the picture was unmistakable: Venice, St Mark's Square. In the foreground there was a smiling man. He was quite plump, with a round face and curly hair. He was wearing trousers and a short-sleeved shirt. His feet couldn't be seen, covered as they were with pigeons. And two pigeons had settled on his right hand. The man was Totò Riina. The photograph was hidden in the bedroom where Antonina Bagarella slept. The policeman started plaguing her with questions. She didn't say a word. Before they left they approached Antonina again, and asked her about Totò.

'Who knows? Who knows where he is?' she replied.

In the village they called her 'the little schoolmistress' because she taught PE to the children of the Sacred Heart school in Corleone. She had given up university after the first year 'for serious family reasons'. She had moved to Campania for a few months, helping her father, Salvatore, and her brother Giuseppe, who were in internal exile in Frattaminore, a small village in the province of Naples. She had come back to Sicily at the end of the Bari trial, had taken a master's degree and wanted to live for ever in her Corleone.

Ninetta Bagarella wasn't just a pretty girl of twenty-six, Ninetta was, above all, Totò Riina's woman.

'Other women don't want me, only Ninetta . . . aren't they going to make me marry her? And I kill people,' Totò once confided to the Catanese man of honour Nino Calderone.

Ninetta had grown up in a Mafia village, her family was Mafia, and she had fallen in love with a Mafioso. And she was a Mafiosa herself. Or at least that was what the *carabinieri* and police of Corleone thought. They were sure that Ninetta had maintained her links with Totò Riina and all the fugitives in his *cosca*. She was a kind of messenger, an outrider with freedom of movement.

And she was sly, alert and intelligent. Above all she was extremely reliable.

The trips outside Corleone always to Palermo, and always to Monreale. Ninetta went to the city once a week with Emanuela. Always with her, the sister who never left her on her own. Emanuela was four years older than Ninetta, and she was a very religious woman. Even as a little girl she had taught Sunday school to the children of Santa Rosalia, the little church built on a hill between Via Rua del Piano and Vicolo Scorsone. The parish priest was Don Girolamo Liggio, a cousin of Lucianeddu. There were and had been other priests and other nuns among Luciano Liggio's uncles, cousins and close and distant relations. The members of his family had also acquired the nickname of '*Cattoliti*', Catholics. A family extremely devoted to the patron saint Leoluca and all the other saints in the calendar – like the Bagarellas and Totò Riina's sisters.

Ninetta and Emanuela arrived in the morning, visiting day for the inmates of the Ucciardone. They brought laundry and food to the men of their family in jail. Then in the afternoon they went up to Monreale. The outing ended up in the square in front of the Norman cathedral. The two women disappeared inside the church and slipped into the rooms of the archiepiscopal curia. They talked to the priests about money and papers; for decades the Bagarella family had been lease-holders of the Pirrello plot, an area of land between Corleone and Monreale owned by the curia. Then the two women retraced their steps. From Monreale to Palermo, from Palermo to Corleone. Nothing ever came of these meetings: Ninetta and Emanuela never made a false move. Not even a few years later when the police were given a truly unique opportunity.

All the women in the Bagarella family were about to leave for Campania, to say their last goodbyes to Giuseppe, who was dying in Frattaminore. Ninetta and her sisters boarded the *Canguro Azzurro*, the Tyrrhenian ferry, in Palermo. The police found out, and put two tiny hidden cameras in the cabins occupied by the women. They were sure they could catch Totò Riina or at least pick up some secrets about where he was hiding. During the crossing from Palermo to Naples they didn't hear a single word. Ninetta and her sisters didn't speak all night, they didn't say a word for ten long hours.

THE COSA NOSTRA TRIUMVIRATE

THE MAN IN THE BLACK TIE

The black tie was a sign of mourning, it was worn whenever someone in the family died and it was kept on, out of respect for the deceased, for at least a year. Just before New Year's Eve, Totò Riina walked around in black tie. In Via Rua del Piano everyone was still alive; the mourning was for his brother-in-law, Ninetta's brother. Calogero Bagarella had died one rainy evening that winter on a pavement in Palermo, cut down by a shotgun blast. And he had been loaded like a sack into the boot of an Alfa Giulia, wearing a bloody policeman's uniform. For many years his death had been a mystery, even within Cosa Nostra. It was a secret known only to the select few.

The first few months that Totò Riina spent in hiding hurried by. From the last days of July until December Totò Riina had been hidden between Palermo and Corleone. He was waiting for a nod from *zu Tanu*, Gaetano Badalamenti. Now Totò was taking his orders from Cinisi's boss. Only from him. U Curtu had acquired a certain gravitas. He was famous as an infallible hitman. Luciano Liggio was hardly ever in Palermo. He was in Milan, in Rome, in Catania, in Switzerland. All the while Totò was growing in power . . .

The Ucciardone had recognised the man of honour and his charisma. Then there had been the outcome of the Bari trial, the acquittal of all those hitmen on grounds of insufficient evidence, which had enhanced his status still further. Who better than Totò Riina – the Palermo Mafiosi wondered – to solve 'the big problem' that no one in Palermo was willing or able to confront? Who better than him to kill 'that lunatic Cavataio'? Michele Cavataio was a businessman in the suburb of Acquasanta who had turned all the rules of Cosa Nostra upside down. With double games, with deception, with betrayal. His strategy was destabilising the Mafia system. The man was a loose cannon. And he was still crashing dangerously around the streets of Palermo.

All the bosses of the Sicilian families met up in Switzerland, in a hotel in Zurich. The summit had been organised to decide whether Michele Cavataio should live or die. In the end they voted to let him live, and told him about it. But some families didn't agree. They bowed to the wishes of the majority and kept their side of the bargain. Then they met again, this time in secret. They made their bravest men available to get rid of the 'lunatic'. The last word went to the representatives from Ciaculli. They said: 'He's a beast who has no honour and doesn't keep his word. Sooner or later he'll bring about the ruin of Cosa Nostra.'

The execution of the sentence was entrusted to Totò Riina, the fugitive *viddano*, the peasant who would, only a few years later, inherit from Michele Cavataio not only the hint of madness but also the nickname of 'Belva', the beast. To kill the Mafioso of Acquasanta six of them would set off in two Alfa Giulia cars – one light-coloured, the other dark. One of the murderers wore the uniform of a traffic police captain, another four looked like real policemen. Also present was Totò Riina, who was driving around in another car. He was checking the movements along the tree-lined avenue leading up to a pink building covered with climbing plants. Then Riina got out of the car and walked quickly along the avenue.

On the evening of 10 December 1969, the hitmen went into the offices of the Moncada construction company on Viale Lazio. One of them started firing without waiting for the order from Totò Riina. He killed two men sitting behind a desk. They all drew their guns. A third man died as well. Two company employees were wounded. Michele Cavataio was still alive. He was barricaded behind a wardrobe. He was angry and shouting; they heard him swearing as he reloaded his revolver. He replied to the fire with his Colt Cobra and stuck Binnu Provenzano in one hand. Then he picked up a shotgun and fired into Calogero Bagarella's chest. A moment later the story of Michele Cavataio of Acquasanta ended with a hole in the forehead. Right between the eyes.

Totò Riina was furious with one of his thugs, the one who had fired without waiting for his order. His name was Damiano Caruso, and he was part of the Riesi family. It had been Caruso's haste that had caused the death of Calogero Bagarella. When they left the Moncada offices, Totò whispered seven words in Caruso's ear: '*Tu si na minchia china d'acqua*', 'you're a dick full of water'. A useless thing, a man who doesn't deserve respect.

During the escape, the light-coloured car and the dark one bumped into each other at a crossing, then disappeared into the slow traffic of Palermo on a rainy evening.

The corpse of Calogero Bagarella was taken to a mysterious place and buried. Totò Riina didn't want to inform the cops, or even all the Cosa Nostra bosses, that his Contadini had been the murderers on Viale Lazio. Totò Riina didn't want to shoulder the official blame for the massacre. Many years later the remains of his brother-in-law ended up in a grave in Corleone cemetery. But a different name was carved into the white marble stone. Hidden as a living man and hidden as a corpse. That was the fate of Calogero Bagarella. Someone discovered that secret: it was Ciccio Coniglio, the chief undertaker in the village of Corleone. A few months later Ciccio Coniglio was killed. He had been a police informer. During those weeks they also killed a quiet council office worker. Every morning he recorded the burials that had taken place at the cemetery the previous day in a big council record.

The only sign of mourning shown by the Riina and Bagarella families was the black tie worn around Totò's neck. His friend Calogero was not only the brother of his Ninetta, he was also the fiancé of Arcangela Riina, one of his three sisters. From the day of the shooting in the Moncada offices, Arcangela Riina never looked at another man. She was widowed even before her wedding. But the massacre on Viale Lazio brought pain to the heart of more than one woman in Corleone.

The massacre left a permanent stain on the life of Palermo. Nothing that had happened in Cosa Nostra until then applied to the future. The history of the Mafia was divided in two: before and after the massacre on Viale Lazio.

ONCE UPON A TIME THERE WAS THE CONCA D'ORO

'Palermo is beautiful, let's make it more beautiful,' the mayor repeated in his thick-tongued voice. He was a bulky man, with curly hair that was white in spite of his young age. His eyes were those of a tiger. Standing on a stage or sitting in a drawing room, the mayor was always coming out with the phrase. Then a smile appeared on his lips. It was his constant refrain, and spiteful people suspected he didn't know how to say anything else. The mayor of Palermo was Salvo Lima, known inside Cosa Nostra as Salvino. He too – the *pentiti* would say a quarter of a century later – was a man of honour. His family was from Viale Lazio. 'Palermo is beautiful, let's make it more beautiful . . .' And meanwhile the concrete of his friends in the construction industry was erasing the last splendours of one of the most fascinating cities in Europe.

At one time Salvino had had contact with the La Barbera brothers, and then with Don Paolino Bontate, the Mafia boss of the suburb of Santa Maria del Gesù, who went down in history as 'the boss who slapped the politicians'. Don Paolino had publicly come to blows with two or three regional MPs, deputies who had neglected to vote for a law that the boss of Santa Maria del Gesù had wanted them to pass.

The secretary of the Christian Democratic Party at the time was Giovanni Gioia. He was a close friend of the Greco cousins of Croceverde. The communal administrator of public works was 'in the hands of Totò Riina'. His name was Vito Ciancimino, son of Giovannino, the barber of Corleone. All three *did politics*. There were men from the families in every faction of the Christian Democrats, and Mafiosi from various districts had been elected to the city council. Cosa Nostra had representatives in the Regional Parliament, in Montecitorio and also at Palazzo Madama. Old Sicilian ministers like Bernardo Mattarella and Franco Restivo were very 'close'.

In was during these years that the broad, tree-lined streets of Palermo were made narrow and bare. And straight roads curved to avoid trespassing on friends' territory. Night after night the early nineteenth-century buildings on Via Libertà were blown sky-high, dynamite bringing national monuments crashing down. Beautiful palm trees were cut down to create land that could be built on. The Mafiosi did more damage than the Liberators and Lancasters that had bombed the historic centre during the war.

Palermo had turned its back on the sea; it could no longer be seen from the city – it was a long way from the buildings resting on what had once been the Conca d'Oro. Big barracks-like buildings in iron and concrete had invaded the gardens of the Piana dei Colli, in every suburb there was a crane and a building site, and behind every crane and every building site there was a concrete plant. And hastily erected sheet-metal sheds, council surveyors redesigning projects in a night, last-minute businessmen, Mafiosi, technicians and accountants, engineers, ministers opening districts with unpaved roads and tower blocks without balconies. The sack of Palermo bore the mark of Salvino Lima. But the project of mass destruction had been stamped by the former barber's shop assistant in Corleone. Don Vito was the councillor who had planned the new Palermo; the city that was rising up was his doing. In only three years the council released 4,200 building licences, 3,011 of them made out to pensioners who didn't own a thing. They were the bosses' straw men.

The biggest taxpayer of this new Palermo was Francesco Vassallo. He was a cart-driver who had unexpectedly entered the world of public works. The Company Va.Li.Gio. was registered at the Chamber of Commerce. The initials of the names Vassallo, Lima and Gioia. It caused a scandal. Lima and Gioia said it was all 'slander and infamy' and Ciccio Vassallo remained at the top of the class of contributors to Palermo until 1971. His buildings had been selected by the city and provincial councils to house schools of all kinds of levels. The administrations put hundreds of millions into the ex-carter who was 'renting out' six medical schools, three teacher-training institutes, three technical institutes and three scientific secondary schools.

'Sulu grazie a mmia in Palermo si studìa' – It's thanks to me that people study in Palermo – the ex-carter boasted.

The school-building project was a 'personal matter' for Vito Ciancimino.

The ex-barber had turned up in Palermo five or six years before Totò Riina. The Corleonesi had sent him on a reconnaissance mission – they had staked everything on Vituzzo, the smart boy they had known since the days of good old Dr Navarra. And Vito hadn't disappointed them. He was already high up in the Christian Democrats and also a very deft businessman. He was a real Corleonesi, who had managed to set up a faction of his own in the party, and had even placed many of his men in the other Christian Democrat groups. And also among the Republicans and the Social Democrats. In ten years he had worked miracles – real miracles. He had started with a small rail transport company, which had grown until he had won a monopoly in the sector. The under-secretary for transport was Bernardo Mattarella.

Vito Ciancimino wasn't like Salvino Lima or Giovanni Gioia, Don Vito was a politician and also an 'unusual' Mafioso. His position was very particular in the Christian Democrats and also inside Cosa Nostra. In the words of the councillor for public works, Vito Ciancimino went from being a prisoner in the Ucciardone to a fugitive. Totò Riina's authorisation was indispensable. If a Mafioso needed a construction permit, he knew where to go. First a discussion with the Contadino of Corleone, then the rooms of the Palazzo opened up too, the rooms of Ciancimino. Don Vito took his orders only from his Corleonesi, the *viddani* who had brought him to the city and crowned him lord of Palermo. And he would hold that position for at least twenty years. Don Vito was one of the Contadini who had grown up around the Rocca Busambra.

In that captive, dominated Palermo, the Mafia kidnapped a journalist who had become too curious, and had started digging around in the mud of the new buildings and the mysteries of the suburbs. Mauro De Mauro was a sleuth, he worked at *L'Ora*. White shotgun. On a late September evening, with the sirocco blowing, Mauro De Mauro disappeared for ever. He had just left the newspaper office and stopped off in a bar to pick up his usual bottle of bourbon and a pound of ground coffee. The murderers took him away in his midnight-blue BMW, to Via delle Magnolie, a smart street in the upper part of Palermo.

The next day the journalists of *L'Ora* printed a front page with a big headline: MAURO, WHERE ARE YOU? And under another headline with nine columns of blank ink: HELP US. The appeal went unanswered, and the city closed up in silence. Mauro De Mauro was a real journalist, but only a few hours after his disappearance – as always happened in Palermo with Mafia victims – strange rumours began to circulate. They spoke of articles and blackmail. The writer Leonardo Sciascia silenced them all with one of his withering phrases: 'In this city you don't die of blackmail, you live off it.'

The memory of poor Mauro slipped away with the end of the summer.

THE CAPUCHIN MUMMIES

On the desk of the chief prosecutor Pietro Scaglione there were two blank sheets of paper with handwritten notes. One showed the time of Mauro De Mauro's disappearance, the other the time of the discovery of his midnight-blue BMW. A week after the kidnapping of the journalist the results of the inquiry were all on those two pieces of paper. Pietro Scaglione was still on the second floor of the Palace of Justice in Palermo. His transfer to Lecce – they had moved and promoted him there after Luciano Liggio's escape – was still being delayed. For forty-one years Pietro Scaglione had always managed to work as a magistrate in Sicily. He had accumulated promotions and certificates of merit. The day after the first murder of a magistrate of the Italian republic, some people in Palermo were saying that 'he died because he wanted to be both a butcher and a priest'. Others claimed that his filing cabinets were filled with hundreds of files concerning trials that were perennially pending and never closed. Successive legal inquiries concluded that the prosecutor 'had pursued his functions in an impeccable fashion.' Pietro Scaglione was killed on the morning of 5 May 1971 in Via dei Cipressi. As in Viale Lazio, the unit of hitmen was driven by a short Corleonese. And the other men who were following the orders of Totò Riina were from Corleone too.

The road took its name from a row of trees that ran along a wall about five metres high and almost half a kilometre long. Via dei Cipressi crossed the old district of Danisinni, from the square to the first mandarin groves. Opening on to the square were craftsmen's workshops, fishmongers' and butchers' shops, and fried food stalls open from dawn till dusk, offering the specialities that the people of Palermo love: chicken or lamb giblets, bread with spleen, boiled tripe with oil and lemon. Around the 'casbah' the stalls and booths of the vendors of pumpkin seeds and *panelle*, chickpea-flower fritters, came and went. On the other side the alley led to a cemetery that ran along the Capuchin monastery. Lined up in the catacombs of the monastery were almost eight thousand skeletons and several hundred mummies. The mummies of bishops, priests and monks, of Palermo patricians who died between the end of the seventeenth century and the beginning of the nineteenth. That morning Prosecutor Scaglione had gone to the Capuchins to put a flower on the grave of his wife, Concetta.

He was sitting in a black Fiat 1300, a smart car with a Trieste number plate. His driver was the correction officer Antonino Lorusso. The car set off from the Capuchin cemetery towards the court. It turned into Via dei Cipressi, slowing down about two hundred metres from the start of a tight bend. It was the only point in the road where two cars couldn't pass. The Fiat 1300 stopped. At that moment the state prosecutor and his driver were killed.

The first killing of a high-ranking official in Palermo had only one witness, a boy of eleven. He told the *carabinieri* he had seen a white Fiat 850 that had blocked the road for the prosecutor's car. He didn't know anything else, or didn't want to. But the next day the little boy went back to the police station to give a more accurate account of his memories. He was accompanied by his father. The boy swore that the previous morning he had been upset, he was confused, so agitated that he had said the first thing that came into his head.

'The Fiat 850 wasn't white, it was black, definitely black . . .'

The corpse of the state prosecutor was still on the marble table when his sister Rose came into the institute of forensic medicine. The woman stood motionless for two hours, looking at her brother's body. Then she screamed with all her might: 'They've killed the prosecutor, so now they'll be laughing because they'll never catch him.'

The hearse stopped in the Vicolo della Chiesa di Casa Professa. The silent crowd parted to greet the coffin, then closed again and followed the first of Palermo's solemn funerals. In the church of Casa Professa on 8 May they didn't hold a state funeral. Colombo, the prime minister, who was in Sicily for an electoral rally that day, did not attend the funeral of Pietro Scaglione. The minister of justice wasn't there. Neither was the minister of the interior, a Sicilian, Franco Restivo from Palermo. Within a day and a night the state had forgotten about the death of a state prosecutor.

It wasn't until a few months later at the Viminale, the prime minister's office, that they issued a reward, 20 million lire 'to anyone who supplies information useful to bringing the perpetrators and possible instigators to justice ...' No one came forward. Not even the usual fantasists and parasites. Only one voice rose up in the silence that surrounded the death of Pietro Scaglione. It was that of a magistrate, the prosecutor of Enna, Mariano Lombardi.

'How will we ever have the courage to find his murderers if we ourselves are complicit?' he shouted to his fellow judges.

In Palermo and Sicily in May 1971 relations between the Italian state and the organisation called Cosa Nostra had changed for ever. The Mafia had killed a magistrate. It was the first attack on the Republic. It was the sign that the rules were changing, the sign that Cosa Nostra was changing.

After the Ciaculli massacre, the families had reorganised, giving themselves a kind of provisional government which they called the 'triumvirate'. There were three men at its summit: Gaetano Badalamenti, the boss of Cinisi. Stefano Bontate, the son of Don Paolino of the suburb of Santa Maria del Gesù. And Luciano Liggio from Corleone. But Lucianeddu had delegated his power to his loyal *Contadini*, Totò Riina and Binnu Provenzano. The Cosa Nostra triumvirate was supposed to lead the organisation beyond the crisis of the early 1960s, strengthen the bonds with the Palazzo that had weakened after the massacres, pilot the organisation, as in the years immediately after the war, into the heart of the state. But the Corleonesi were part of the triumvirate.

They were a breed apart: they were Mafiosi who were strangers to mediation, accommodations, negotiations. And they had got it into their heads that they were stronger than the Italian state.

It was always them, they were the *viddani*, the same men who had been spreading death since they were born in the Strasatto estate.

Nothing was known about the Scaglione murder in the twenty years that followed, except vague details about the 'involvement of Totò Riina and Luciano Liggio in the material execution'. But even in the first few days of spring 1971, the commander of the legion of *carabinieri* of western Sicily had sent information to the state prosecutor of Palermo.

Colonel Carlo Alberto Dalla Chiesa indicated that 'the Sicilian Mafia was divided in two opposing parts in spite of their apparent peace . . .' But a very small clue about the death of the chief prosecutor had been found. It led to the village of Salemi, to the kidnapping of the first-born son of the wealthy landowner Francesco Caruso. His son Antonino had been kidnapped on Ash Wednesday in 1971 and freed on Easter Sunday. It was the first time in Sicily that someone had been kidnapped with a demand for a financial ransom.

Antonino Caruso wasn't just anybody. The landowner was a close friend of prosecutor Scaglione, and the kidnapped boy was the godson of Bernardo Mattarella. The northern newspapers wrote that 'Pietro Scaglione knew everything about the Caruso kidnapping' and suggested that the prosecutor had been killed for the secrets he was keeping about the kidnapping. On Ash Wednesday in 1971 the news that his godson 'had been loaded by persons unknown into a car in the area of Fontana Grande di Salemi', reached Bernardo Matterella in Montecitorio. The Sicilian MP collapsed. The Sicilian politician, who had been a minister in almost every post-war government, died of a heart attack a few hours later.

DAUGHTERS OF THE MAFIA, DAUGHTERS OF THE CHURCH

Her dress was made of linen and came down to just above her knees. It was very brightly coloured, with yellow and red flowers printed on a pastel-blue background. She was carrying a white handbag. Her shoes were white too, with high, wide heels, in line with the fashion of the time. On her wrist she wore a little gold watch, and around her neck, a cameo on a slender chain. She was tanned, smiling and confident. She walked slowly along the corridor leading to the courts; she never lowered her eyes, challenging the curious eyes of lawyers, flunkeys, *carabinieri* in uniform and plain clothes, errand-boys, idlers, journalists, photographers, clerks of court, document-sellers, defendants on bail and the rest of the motley crowd of humanity that populates the Palace of Justice in Palermo every morning.

Ninetta Bagarella entered the courtroom at nine o'clock on 16 July 1971, the day of her trial. Police headquarters in Palermo had, for the second time, sent a report to the state prosecutors' office. The letters said that she was 'dangerous because of her activity on behalf of the Corleonese *cosca*', and that 'the removal of Bagarella Antonina from Corleone with internal exile in an area of northern Italy' was an absolute necessity. They wanted to place her under arrest too, the school-teacher who was Totò Riina's lover. A year before a similar request had been rejected by prosecutor Pietro Scaglione. The inquiry had been filed by the magistrate who was later killed by those same Corleonesi. But the police and the *carabinieri* had presented the file again, and passed on dozens of new pieces of information about the 'role as contact developed by Bagarella'. There was also a note concerning 'periodic meetings with a man driving a yellow motorcycle'. That was a *picciotto* who accompanied Ninetta to Salvatore Riina's hiding places every week.

The hearing opened an hour late. The president of the first session of the court, Ignazio Alcamo, came breathlessly into the courtroom and immediately called for defendant Antonina Bagarella to give evidence. The girl stood motionless in front of the judges. She greeted him, set her white handbag down on a table, then started to speak, about herself, about her life, her studies, her family and her love of Totò Riina. The reporters recorded all her words, and the following day the journalist with the *Giornale di Sicilia*, Mario Francese, told 'the criminal history of the Mafia schoolmistress'. Ninetta Bagarella spoke good Italian, in spite of the marked inflections of her Corleone accent. She defended herself without fear or difficulty for almost two hours.

'You know, Miss Bagarella, that a warrant of internal exile has been proposed for you . . .' the president of the court said.

'I don't think the court will want to send me into internal exile.' She fell silent, as if thinking. 'If you have a conscience, if you have a heart, you won't do it. The only people left in our family are the women. And we have to work for ourselves and for our men, our fathers and brothers who have fallen into misfortune . . .'

President Alcamo waved a hand to stop her for a moment, and to give time for her words to be recorded. He repeated the essence of Bagarella's words, adding his own bureaucratic formulas. When the clerk had finished, the president looked at her, inviting her to continue. Ninetta went on: 'I am a woman and I am only guilty of loving a man whom I esteem as much as I trust him. I have always loved Totò Riina. I was thirteen years old and he was twenty-six, and he has never left my heart. That is the only thing I am guilty of, your honour.'

'Salvatore Riina isn't naïve; he planned these murders, Miss Bagarella.'

'Machinations. Slander. Salvatore is innocent. He is innocent even for the Court of Assizes in Bari, which acquitted him.'

The schoolmistress fixed her eyes on the face of the president of the curt, and a whisper came from her mouth.

'If this court wishes to send me into internal exile, I have few alternatives. I will have to respect the ruling because, in spite of the prejudices of the people at police headquarters, I am a law-abiding citizen. It means that this will have to be my fate . . .'

'Miss Bagarella, they are accusing you of being part of the Liggio gang.'

'I don't even know this Liggio.'

Antonina Bagarella denied ever having gone to a church in Aversa to meet Monsignor Tommaso Rotunno, a priest who was to have celebrated her marriage to Totò Riina. Ninetta spoke without ever raising her voice. She didn't say a single word too many or too few. Then her lawyer, Nicola Ippolito, entered the scene, and reconstructed 'all the suffering endured by his client only because of the name she bore'. The lawyer remembered the police persecution and the 'absurd accusations'. The note from the local school inspector, against 'a teacher beloved by all', and her immediate dismissal from the religious institution of the Sacred Heart 'because of constant denunciations by police and carabinieri'. From his briefcase the lawyer took hundreds of letters from teachers and former pupils, all messages of solidarity received along with 'attestations of excellent moral and civic behaviour from the population of Corleone'.

The counsel for the prosecution asked the court for Antonina Bagarella to be 'sent into internal exile for a period of no less than four years'. The barrister for the defence requested for the charges to be dismissed, quoting a witness 'who had information about the character of the defendant'. He was a priest, the parish priest of Corleone, Emanuele Catarinicchia. The monsignor, who would a few years later become first bishop of Cefalù and then of Mazara del Vallo, set about collecting signatures among the mothers of the village. Emanuele Catarinicchia was also a colleague of Ninetta's, who taught religion at the Sacred Heart. Hundreds of 'declarations of sympathy for Antonina Bagarella' arrived for the lawyer Ippolito. They were signed by the governors of the school, by the teachers, the parents of the students, the neighbours, the caretakers and the secretaries and the civil servants of every level of seniority in Corleone. At the beginning of that August, Ninetta also appealed to the Commission of Human Rights in The Hague.

The Palermo tribunal made its decision at the end of the summer. And it immediately rejected the prosecution's request to send Antonina Bagarella into internal exile. The magistrates sentenced her to special surveillance in the village of Corleone. From 27 September Ninetta could not leave home before seven o'clock in the morning or after seven in the evening. Once a week she had to go to the office of public safety and sign the 'probation book'. For over two years she served her sentence: the special surveillance came to an end on the last day of February 1974. But a week before then, Brigadier Angelino Notaro called in at Vicolo Scorsone to check up on her. It was evening, just after seven. Ninetta wasn't there.

'She's left, she's gone to work in Germany,' her sister Emanuela said to the policeman.

On the morning of 19 February 1974 Ninetta had suddenly disappeared. Antonina Bagarella was on the run too. Like her Totò. With her Totò.

MARRIED AT LAST

Three priests celebrated the wedding, all from the diocese of Monreale. But no one ever found the church where Antonina Bagarella and Salvatore Riina, on 16 April 1974, became man and wife after a nineteen-year engagement. Informants revealed that the altar was set up in the drawing room of a villa, an ancient construction hidden between the pines and the sea at Cinisi. The identities of two of the three priests who brought them together in holy matrimony remained a mystery. Only much later was it discovered that the couple were certainly blessed by Don Agostino Coppola, the parish priest of Carini, a man of honour dedicated to kidnapping, and the cousin of the better-known Frank 'Three Fingers', one of the chief Sicilian drug traffickers.

The day that Ninetta and Totò got married, the schoolmistress of Corleone had spent nine weeks on the list of wanted people. She had become a fugitive to live with her man. He was forty-four, she, thirty-one.

The marriage of the boss of Corleone remained a secret only for a few months, until the summer. On one of the first days of August a major in the *carabinieri* and his men burst into a flat in a building in Palermo, captured a fugitive and found in a drawer the invitation to a wedding feast. The *carabiniere* major was Giuseppe Russo, the fugitive Leoluca Bagarella, and the invitation was to the wedding of Ninetta and Totò. The flat where Leoluca Bagarella was hiding under a false name with his sister and Salvatore Riina was on the fifth floor of staircase B in a block on Via Largo San Lorenzo. On the fifth floor of staircase A the landlord was Francesco Madonia, a local Mafioso, and a particularly bloodthirsty one. The house of the married couple from Corleone was owned by Zoo Sicula, a company owned by

Giuseppe Mandalari, an ex-employee of the regional council department of public works who was also a financial consultant. Mandalari was a thirty-third-degree mason.

The building on Via Largo San Lorenzo had been built by Giovanni Pilo, a businessman who was married to the sister of a man of honour nicknamed *u tignusu* (baldy). *U tignusu*, whose name was Giuseppe Giacomo Gambino, was in turn related to other bosses from the district of Resuttana and the district of La Noce. It was an endless chain of marriages, all godfathers, godmothers, cousins, uncles, nephews and nieces. It was a network of protection, a closed society that opened up only to let in the *viddani*, the peasant Mafiosi of Corleone. Major Russo knew that new equilibriums were being consolidated within Cosa Nostra and in a confidential report he reconstructed for the first time 'the common interests between the group of the Corleonese and the *cosca* of Palermo San Lorenzo'.

This information was familiar to Angelo Sorino, the retired marshal of public safety. Sorino had worked in the second police district, the station in the territory of Piana dei Colli which included the suburbs of San Lorenzo, Resuttana, Partanna and Mondello. The marshal might have retired, but he went on investigating and passing information to his superiors in police headquarters. One day his investigations led him to a flat on the fifth floor of a building on Via Largo San Lorenzo. And retired marshal Angelo Sorino was murdered.

Nine months after the blessing given by Agostino Coppola, Ninetta gave birth to a little girl. She was named after Totò's mother: Maria Concetta. She was born on 19 December 1974 in the Pasqualino e Noto clinic in Palermo. It was a hospital in the centre of the city, at the end of Via Dante, three hundred metres from the palm trees of Piazza Politeama. The clinic was one of the most exclusive in Palermo. There was a black gate that concealed a small dark courtyard. Magnolias covered the first floors of a small brown building which on one side bordered the green of a nursery, and on the other, a silent street. In front of it was the splendid garden of Villa Malfitano. The fugitive Ninetta Bagarella spent a few days discreetly in a quiet room in the Pasqualino e Noto. Then she registered the birth of Maria Concetta at the register office.

The obstetrician who helped Ninetta was Rosa Gelfo, a woman who conquered the trust of the schoolmistress of Corleone. The same midwife also delivered Ninetta's other three children, always in the muffled silence of the hospital on Via Dante. Giovanni Francesco arrived on 21 February 1976 and took the first name of Totò's father. After a year and two months, on 3 May 1977, Giuseppe Salvatore was born. The name of Ninetta's mother – Lucia – was given to the last daughter, born on 11 November 1980. She too had gone to Palermo, on Via Dante, opposite the gardens of Villa Malfitano. All four of Salvatore Riina's children were vaccinated at local health authority office 58. All the certificates were signed by Antonio Rizzuto, the health officer of the hospital complex.

A ghost family started living in Palermo, that city without eyes or ears. Salvatore Riina walked around escorted by his heavies, and Ninetta accompanied by drivers and right-hand men. She went into shops with her children, strolled freely along the streets, and went shopping. He went to restaurants in Mondello and Monreale, villas in Falsomiele, the countryside around San Giuseppe Jato. A few times he was seen at the bar of the Life discotheque. He often drove along the cul-de-sac that passed through Ciaculli. Totò Riina travelled in a white Mercedes that he drove himself. His wife sat in the front seat, the four children in the back. When the boys started growing up and were old enough to go to school, some policemen tried to find them, rummaging through the archives of the Education Authority, checking the records of private institutions, and even searching some schools run by nuns and priests in eastern Sicily. They never found anything.

Now and again reports came in about the hiding places of the invisible fugitives of Corleone. Rumours that vanished into nothing. Like the one about a patrician villa on the edge of Bagheria, or an attic on Viale Strasburgo. One report was a little more precise than the others. It came from the register office of the City of Palermo. On the registration of the birth of one of Totò Riina's children there was an address: Via Torino. It was the second turning on the right from Via Roma climbing from central station towards Teatro Massimo. The 'Riina house' was at number 22. But when the police broke down doors and windows to get into that house, three rooms plus bath and kitchen, they found a blind old railway worker living there.

AT ROCCA BUSAMBRA

One night Lieutenant Colonel Giuseppe Russo found himself in the woods of Rocca Busambra looking for corpses in the sinkholes. Like the *carabinieri* of Captain Carlo Alberto thirty years before, Russo's policemen were searching the paths of the mountain that loomed menacingly behind the Ficuzza hunting lodge. Spring had already come and gone, but above one thousand metres it was bitingly cold. The night was warmed by a few glasses of wine and reminiscences.

Colonel Russo was a tall, thin man, a bundle of nerves. He had a sharp face and the shrewd eyes of a Saracen. He was known as an intelligent investigator, who had commanded the armed lieutenancy in Castelvetrano before becoming the head of the operations unit in Palermo, the anti-Mafia investigations unit. His friends – only his friends – called him Ninì. The colonel had informants in every province, and he stayed in contact with them year upon year. With all of them: victims, defendants, small-time criminals, thugs, informers, professionals, men of honour and men dishonoured.

On the night of the search for corpses in the darkness of Rocca Busambra, Giuseppe Russo wasn't in a good mood. He climbed nimbly on the rocks, shouting orders that echoed all the way down to the valley. At dawn the colonel had lost patience. He confided in Nino Sofia and Gigi Petix, crime correspondent and photographer of *L'Ora* in Palermo: 'There's no point being out in the woods looking for corpses, we're unlikely to find anything but carrion. If only the magistrates would give me permission to knock down a few buildings in Palermo . . .'

Then he sighed and said: 'I'm the only person who knows how many people ended up in the concrete pillars of this city. I'd go straight there. I'd only need two bulldozers and a team of workmen, because I know where to look for the bodies . . .'

The colonel was furious when his outburst ended up on the front pages of the afternoon paper.

Giuseppe Russo had simply been telling the truth: he knew. He had worked out that the Sicilian Mafia was changing its skin while remaining the same inside. The colonel had discovered who had carried out the kidnappings in the provinces of Palermo, Trapani and Agrigento. He had got there along three or four different trails. They all led to a church in Carini. The parish priest had been an administrator of the archiepiscopal seminary in Monreale, one of the biggest and wealthiest dioceses in Sicily: Father Agostino Coppola. But the priest no longer administrated the money of the curial. In the sacristy of the church they found tens of millions belonging to the sequestration company set up by Luciano Liggio and Salvatore Riina. That money came from the kidnapping of Luciano Cassina, the son of Count Arturo, the king of construction in Palermo.

There was something strange about those kidnappings. In the early 1970s Cosa Nostra had made a decision, and its government, the regional Commission, met specially to forbid kidnappings in Sicily. And yet the abductions – the first was that of the son of the wealthy landowner in Salemi, Francesco Caruso – went on. The lawyer from Sciacca, Nicola Campis, was kidnapped. The collector Luigi Corleo was kidnapped in July 1975, and never freed.

Corleo was a brother-in-law of Nino Salvo, a man of honour linked to the Bontates and the Badalamentis. But Nino Salvo wasn't just any Mafioso; he was a wealthy businessman who had built an empire. Nino Salvo, with his friend Salvo Lima, was one of the three or four godfathers in Sicily. The kidnappers demanded a ransom of 20 billion lire for Luigi Corleo. It wasn't a kidnapping: it was a gauntlet that the *viddani* of Corleone had thrown down to the most powerful Mafia in Palermo. Colonel Russo went into the mysteries of the Corleo kidnapping with his quick temper, his morbid curiosity and his tendency to personalise the investigation to excess. It was during those months that he formed a link with Nino Salvo. And he started to become acquainted with 'the people inside' Cosa Nostra. He understood the game that the Corleonesi were playing. Totò Riina had organised the kidnapping 'campaign' to make a bit of money. Then he had moved on to public construction works. Without the one there would never have been the other.

In the valley of Belice there was a thousand billion lire set aside for reconstruction after the 1968 earthquake. And a river of money was also about to arrive for the building of the Palermo–Sciacca road, something that inland areas called the 'valley floor'. Then 20 billion lire had been allocated for the Garcia dam and another 25 for the expropriation of the lands where it was due to go up. Last of all, the Sicilian Regional Assembly had opened its coffers: 200 billion for the dam project and the roads in Belice.

In Palermo and Trapani numerous companies were set up whose legal representative was Giuseppe Mandalari, the thirty-third-degree freemason, the owner of the fifth-floor apartment of Via Largo San Lorenzo. And, summoned one day to the parliamentary anti-Mafia commission, the colonel said in a statement: 'In too many companies the board is always composed of the same names, all people connected with Mandalari . . . and they are companies set up at the same time as revenue was coming in from the kidnappings carried out in Sicily.'

It was a discovery made by Nini Russo with his trusted adjutant, Marshal Giuliano Guazzelli. The two men were getting perilously close to Totò Riina. They were about to enter the circles of Corleone's hell.

Early in 1977 the colonel suddenly went on leave. He had asked to take command of the *carabinieri* of Palermo. He wasn't given the job. General Rovelli suggested that he take command in Messina because he didn't want him in Palermo. Giuseppe Russo decided to leave the armed division. The men in the operations unit gave him a silver plaque. Carved on it were some words taken from *The Day of the Owl* by Leonardo Sciascia: 'Men, half-men, tiny men, drug traffickers, blablablabla . . .' Colonel Russo was waiting for his leave when he told his wife, Mercedes, he wanted to open a plastics factory with two associates, exploiting the funds allocated by the special laws introduced after the earthquake in the Belice Valley.

On the evening of 20 August 1977, Totò Riina's men killed Nini Russo in the little square in Ficuzza. He was on holiday at the foot of Rocca Busambra. The cottage had been found for him by an acquaintance, Professor Filippo Costa, a man from

Misilmeri with Mafia relations. The thugs drove around the square four times in a car waiting for the right moment to strike. They fired when Ninì Russo lit a cigarette. With his hands occupied he couldn't reach for his gun. The Colonel fell face first. He was still holding a filterless Super in one hand and a book of matches in the other. They also killed the man walking with him, Professor Costa: with those family connections, he wasn't a random witness. In Giuseppe Russo's trouser pockets they found a bunch of keys. One of them opened the gate to La Favarella, the estate of Michele Greco, known at the time only as a little country squire who liked to surround himself with counts, marquises, monsignors, prefects and presidents of the Court of Appeal.

The newspapers of the day wrote that Ninì Russo had discovered a secret that he had kept to himself. Perhaps he had known something about the death of prosecutor Pietro Scaglione, or perhaps about the disappearance of the journalist Mauro De Mauro. Perhaps he had discovered the mysteries of the Corleo kidnapping, or the business deals surrounding the Garcia dam. Among the colonel's papers they also found clues to a company with the initials of the surnames of the three associates: Ruscide – Russo, Sci . . . and De . . . No one found out anything else.

'We're following up every clue,' Antonio Subranni replied angrily to journalists the day after the crime.

Then he brought down a fist on his desk with all his might, breaking the glass desk-top. A year later, Major Subranni presented a report to the magistracy about the death of Ninì Russo. He wrote that 'the colonel had crossed paths once more with that group of Mafiosi from Corleone, against whom he had fought vigorously, but whose death they had finally decreed'. But one day, investigations by other departments led to the 'real guilty party' of the crime. It was a shepherd from Camporeale by the name of Casimiro Russo. He was accused of 'materially killing the colonel'. The shepherd didn't confess, and nor did he protest his innocence. But Casimiro Russo was an amputee, having lost his right arm as a boy.

A policeman with a big moustache and a melancholy impression had also begun to investigate the murder of a *carabinieri* colonel. He had a mournful smile and a pleasant voice. His manners were civil, his words always polite and measured. His name was Boris Giuliano.

PART TWO

THE CONQUEST OF COSA NOSTRA

A 'TRAGEDIAN' AMONG THE *COSCHE*

THAT DAY IN RAMACCA

There were the Palermitans and then there were the rest. The rest were the Trapanesi, the Agrigentini, the Nisseni, the Catanesi. There was only one family in Catania. It had few men and little power. It didn't do much business, and had a boss who didn't fire guns. He did the brain work.

His name was Pippo Calderone. He was known as 'silver windpipe' because he had had an operation on his larynx and his voice was metallic. He spoke through a microphone resting on his throat. Pippo Calderone had a very high opinion of himself. He felt like a balanced, just man, one of the elect. 'A man of honour, not just anybody . . .' For his brother Antonino, known as Nino, it was above all Pippo's wisdom – without armies or big money-bags – that had impelled him into the regional Commission, the government of Cosa Nostra.

In actual fact the *'regionale'* didn't amount to much. More than an organ of command, it was a place where conflicts were resolved between families. It had worked until that moment. The heads of the *cosche* in the three Mafia provinces, apart from Palermo, no longer stood on each other's feet; no one died if an agreement could be reached. Thanks to Pippo Calderone, an agreement was almost always reached. For seven or eight years the regional Commission had guaranteed that the Mafia bosses would sleep soundly at night. Then the Corleonesi came down from the mountains. They had made their way into the Belice Valley, advanced towards Trapani and towards the lands around Agrigento. The Commission had become a sort of hell. Worse than hell.

'The *"regionale"* has become pointless,' Pippo Calderone complained to his brother Nino. 'You spend hours there, you talk and you discuss things, you reach an agreement and then . . .' He waved his open hand in the air. He went on: 'The Corleonesi turn up with those stony, silent, humble faces. They don't say anything and you think they've agreed. As soon as they leave the meeting they do what they like. If they'd got it into their heads not to make a businessman working in the territory of another family pay up, he won't pay a thing. And if that crony turns up one day looking for what he's owed, they'll shoot him down like a dog. Who would ever have imagined that shepherd Totò Riina causing us all this trouble? You remember ten years ago . . .'

Pippo Calderone had met Totò Riina in 1969 when he was just out of prison. U Curtu had been acquitted at the Bari trial and didn't expect that the judges would immediately send him into exile. Totò Riina went on his guard. The Corleonesi all went on their guard together during those few days. Luciano Liggio, Binnu Provenzano, Calogero Bagarella all disappeared from circulation – all wanted men. All hidden in Corleone.

Cannarozzu d'argento, 'silver windpipe', first met Totò Riina in the village of Ramacca, near Catania. U Curtu was in hiding in Cinisi. Gaetano Badalamenti had kept him in a hay-loft for a fortnight. For Totò it was a two-week holiday by the sea, accustomed as he was to the chilly rocks of Corleone. Then Tano Badalamenti called Pippo Calderone and told him to look into a hiding place for Luciano Liggio. So they all met up in Ramacca.

That day the Corleonese was with a priest, Don Agostino Coppola, the cleric who had secretly married Totò and Ninetta Bagarella. Tano Badalamenti introduced the priest according to the ritual: Don Agostino was himself a *combinato*, a man of honour. The Calderone brothers looked at each other. 'Christ, a priest in Cosa Nostra . . .' *cannarozzu d'argento* whispered to his brother, Nino.

The years passed and at last Pippo Calderone worked out what made Totò Riina tick. It had taken him a long time, but now that he had got the measure of him he no longer wanted to put up with the duplicities and lies of U Curtu. Neither did Giuseppe Di Cristina di Riesi, a hereditary Mafioso, the son and grandson of bosses.

Giuseppe Di Cristina had had his moment in the sun just before and just after Ciaculli, before and after the dynamite-filled Giuliettas that had blown up in the orange groves. At that time Cosa Nostra didn't even have a commission in Palermo. Everyone worked as best he could. And Di Cristina had kept himself busy. He had invested his money in trafficking cigarettes with the Palermitan families and the Neapolitans. He was close friends with Paolino Bontate and his son Stefano. He was in business with Totuccio Inzerillo of Passo di Rigano. When he had to settle his scores with Il Cavataio, the Palermitans requested that a man of honour of the Riesi family should also take part in the action. Peppe Di Cristina sent Damiano Caruso to Viale Lazio . . .

All long ago, water under the bridge. Then the Commission had been reorganised, and the boss Di Cristina couldn't set foot in Palermo as he had once done. He could no longer do his business deals when he felt like it. He had to ask permission.

'And it's fine,' he said to Pippo Calderone, 'I only go to Palermo with the agreement of the Palermitans, but in Riesi and Nisseno, in *my* province of Caltanissetta, I don't want to ask permission of anyone. I'm the boss here. We Di Cristinas have been the bosses here for three generations . . . they must never be allowed to forget it . . . The Corleonesi have to get it into their heads that Riesi is Riesi and Corleone is something else . . .'

HE WAS ALL SWEETNESS AND LIGHT

The fields on the slopes of Mount Etna were covered with frost and ice. It was a winter evening, February was drawing to a close. The farm was halfway between Bronte and Maletto. The volcano was roaring and belching smoke from its north-eastern crater. Pippo Calderone and Peppe Di Cristina had been hunting all day, walking miles side by side, forgetting all about the Corleonesi. Sitting by the fire, they started to think about them again. It was starting to become an illness. And once again they began to talk about them.

'Yes, it took me some time to understand U Curtu, but it's not easy to understand straight away just how much of a sly fox Totò Riina really is. When I met him it wasn't easy to see what lay in his heart, if the guy ever had a heart,' said Pippo.

'He was like a little lamb, don't you remember? He was all sweetness and light, respectful, ceremonious, always ready to say yes, biddable. He almost wagged his tail, the bastard . . . Then when Tano Badalamenti asked him something, Totò melted . . . Then U Curtu and his friend Binnu were in Tano's hands, completely. And Totò was gentle, extremely gentle. He always smiled at you. He always had this look of gratitude on his face . . . you know . . . as if he was thanking us for paying him attention, because we let him stay – an ignorant peasant – close to us. He had a sad gleam in his eyes and we, my brother Nino and I, thought, "Shit! The *viddani* have had a really rough time of it. First they had to wage war on Navarra, then they had to go on the run. Always with their eyes open, with a gun in their hands, in the snow and in the sunlight."'

'Luciano Liggio . . . was already somebody, he was already an important person . . .'

'Yes, Lucianeddu was a legend, that much is clear! But those two, Totò and Binnu, weren't. For us they were just two poor souls that Badalamenti had taken under his wing, and hidden in Palermo . . . Then he dumped them on us, in Catania. You remember, Peppe, how they dressed. They looked really funny. We dressed them again from head to foot. We made new men out of them, and while we were spending millions keeping them in hiding, those snakes were already thinking about how to get rid of us.'

For Pippo Calderone it was a point of honour to stay calm and impassive in the face of anything that might happen, anything that might go wrong. Few people, inside and outside Cosa Nostra, could say they'd seen him lose patience. And yet every time he mentioned the Corleonesi he seemed like a different person; he couldn't control himself. His eyes gleamed with hatred. On this particular evening, once again Pippo Calderone couldn't hide his feelings, and Peppe Di Cristina didn't hide his either.

'I remember,' Pippo said, 'that between 1970 and 1971 Badalamenti and I were in the Ucciardone prison. Every week my brother Nino came to Palermo to visit us. Totò Riina collected him and accompanied him to the front of the prison. Nino visited us, and told me and Tano what was happening and we gave him orders to take outside. Totò would be waiting outside and they would go for lunch together. At the Gambero Rosso, almost always. Sometimes at La Stalla, near the Favorita Stadium. If Binnu was there they would go up to Monreale, to the Fattoria. Binnu really liked that place. And at the restaurant they would take stock of the situation. My brother Nino reported on what Tano Badalamenti had said, and Totò set about carrying it out. What can I tell you? Tano had said to Nino: 'Tell Totò to *put the tie* on the Silvestri brothers'. And Totò would get himself ready. A few days later the Silvestri brothers, *carnezzieri* (butchers) from the district of Capo, were gone for good. Totò didn't even ask what they'd done . . . No, he was just a guard dog (*canazzu da catena*). Tano let him off the leash and somewhere or other two eyes closed for ever. Then the dog came back to his kennel to wait for his next orders. That was what U Curtu was like. Then he changed.'

'What did he start doing?' asked Di Cristina.

'He changed, and then . . . Let's say he started to reveal himself as the great bastard (*curnutu*) he had always been. Listen . . . He starts asking questions, more and more questions. He interrogates Nino, in that clever way of his . . . he wants to know how things work in Tano's family. He asks if Stefano Bontate and his brother Giovanni agree. In short, he's someone who gets mixed up in other people's business. In about 1973 he starts talking to Nino about drugs. He suggests that they start trafficking on a small scale, no big deal. Apart from one thing: I wasn't to know anything about it. Me, you understand, his brother! And that's the *tragedia* he starts making: taking advantage of the fact that Tano was at the Ucciardone and he was needed because he was outside. Some people actually thought Tano had made him deputy of the family. Deputy, what crap! He was just a messenger boy; he was just supposed to be a messenger boy. If we have a problem with U Curtu today, pal, it's because during those years we left Totò to his own devices, uncontrolled. He was always going around the place, listening to everybody with that Pope-John face on him. He met everyone, he knew everything about everyone, he knew the secrets, the envies, the ambitions, the weaknesses of every man of honour. He knew how much this *picciotto* earned and how much that one did, and what he was dealing in. He knew the wounds and resentments of all the families. Someone who knew all those things, and he's also – you know – as much of a trouble-maker (*tragediatore*) as they come; all he could do was sow poison and the trouble (*tragedie*) that we're seeing now, and which we'll see more of.'

'That great bastard!' (*'Stu gran curnutu!'*) exclaimed Peppe Di Cristina, his face turning purple with rage.

'Take the game he plays with me and Nino,' Calderone continued. 'He involves Nino in a drug deal, but he tells him to say nothing to me. He starts making Nino keep secrets that had to be secrets from me, his brother. He wants to make Nino rich against me. And then use him against me. Jesus Christ! How many people has that game of his worked on? Do you know? No one knows what nest of vipers U Curtu managed to build in those years. There's no doubt that he did.

'Listen to what he tried to do to Tano, who he'd also made a man of honour. You don't know? Okay, listen. Tano was in jail and he [Totó] gets it into his head to kill the judge Filippo Neri, the one who was a prosecution lawyer in the trial of the 114. Nino comes to the meeting and tells us. Tano practically goes for his throat. "No, Nino, tell him not to do it," Tano shouts at him. "Tell him we'll talk about it in there first, tell him not to do anything. If he kills the judge, they'll eat the key of the cell and we'll never get out . . ."

'Peppe, listen to me carefully . . . Tano refuses to understand that U Curtu suffers from *sbirritudine* (surveillance mania). U Curtu is a born traitor. But in the end, if you're a man of honour and you have a fugitive on your territory, what do you do? You keep your territory quiet, with no kidnappings and no people being killed . . . so the cops stay away, and the fugitive has nothing to worry about. But if the man of honour fills the suburb with cops, what is he? I'll tell you what he is: he's a cop, and the son of a cop. In fact, he's worse: he's a *carabiniere*, he's a *carabiniere* on horseback. And Riina's like that. I said to Tano: "What do you mean, half of Cosa Nostra's in the Ucciardone, and this *viddano* wants to kill a judge? He wants to keep us in jail for the rest of our lives."'

'Tano refuses to understand . . . Tano thinks he's still his faithful dog.'

'Tano doesn't understand, as if it wasn't Riina who kept Liggio in jail!' said Di Cristina.

'Oh, really?' exclaimed *cannarozzu d'argento*, his voice distorted by the microphone resting on his throat.

'Yes sir . . .'

'What had happened?'

'Liggio had stopped trusting Totò a hundred per cent. Bah, we never discovered why. You know what these shepherds are like. They don't talk much, they do a lot of *tragedia*, and never tell you anything. The fact remains that someone started saying that Lucianeddu no longer trusted Riina. It was when Luciano said not to turn to U Curtu, but to Binnu, to Provenzano. He explained that U Curtu drank and talked too much. Obviously they went and told him straight away. At that time everybody was happy to chatter away to Totò. Liggio was an animal, and you were scared even to go near him. With Totò, with that great bastard Totò, it was a pleasure . . . Pippo, listen, you're complaining that you didn't understand U Curtu. And Luciano, who was closer to him than anyone else, and even he didn't understand a thing? He hadn't understood that he was smarter than he looked . . .'

'And what happened?'

'What do you mean, what happened? Luciano never got out

of jail because Totò Riina didn't want him to. It was 1974. No, it was after 1974. Liggio had been arrested and he was in Lodi. Riina was on Corso dei Mille, at the house of Pietro Vernengo . . . the Palermitan from Ponte Ammiraglio. And then there were Pietro Giaconia, Ciccio Mafara, and that *picciotto* from Pallavicino . . . Asparino, Asparino Mutolo. Vernengo tells Totò that they could sort out a little squadron and go and break Luciano out of Lodi jail. Riina didn't say anything. They insisted: "What's it going to take? Lodi's child's play . . ." At last U Curtu spoke, and they couldn't believe their ears. He said: "Mind your own business and leave the jailbirds as jailbirds. I'll think about these things. If necessary, I'll come to you." You see, my dear Pippo, how it happened?'

'So Luciano never got out of jail.'

'That's right, he was in jail and he's still in jail. Riina never took the trouble of getting him out.'

'He's a snake, Peppe. We've got to think about U Curtu. We've got to crush his head.'

THE GOOD MOTIVES OF PIPPO AND PEPPE

Pippo Calderone from Catania and Peppe Di Cristina di Riesi weren't just two old friends. They were something more. Old Mafia blood flowed in their veins; they knew which rules needed to be respected: the laws of the family which were more important than the laws of God and men. Calderone and Di Cristini had lots of good reasons to confront U Curtu and the Corleonesi straight away. Things in Catania and Riesi weren't the way they had once been.

In Catania there was a young man who was starting to stand in Pippo's light. He came from the notorious district of San Cristoforo, and his name was Benedetto Santapaola. To some he was

Nitto, to others 'the hunter'. He didn't look anyone in the eyes. He was trigger happy. For Santapaola the life of a human being was worth less than the life of a cockroach. Nitto was a thorn in the side of Pippo Calderone, an open wound in the flesh of the Catanesi.

In the province of Caltanissetta, Giuseppe Di Cristina was no longer the only one in charge. On the other side of his territory there was Francesco Madonia, an old Mafioso from Vallelunga Pratameno who was a friend of Luciano Liggio and Nitto Santapaola. U Curtu had managed to find precious allies in two Cosa Nostra fortresses, with his devious style of doing things, without making a sound, without anyone noticing.

Totò Riina lacked the arrogance and violence of Luciano Liggio. He had followed a different path. He seemed never to ask for anything, or to want anything. He spoke for other people, never for himself. And if he wasn't satisfied he told the others, his protégés, that he, poor thing (*mischinu*), had done everything he could. But that the heads of the families, the *capimandamento*, the Commission, everyone who had always issued commands in Cosa Nostra, hadn't wanted to know. The result was that Totò Riina won faithful friends while he was sowing hatred. U Curtu divided families, he plunged them into rancour and resentment. He approached malcontents and won their trust. And then they kept him informed about the affairs of the *cosca*, about the movements of this one or that one, about what was discussed in the meetings.

During those months other things had happened in Sicily. After the 1968 earthquake the Belice Valley was under reconstruction. Giuseppe Di Cristina discovered that the Corleonesi had everything under control. They had claimed a slice of every contract. And the subcontracts, and the supply of materials, and then all the movement of earth, and then the security services. The only people working in the Belice Valley were people with permission from U Curtu. And U Curtu had taken more and more room in Caltanissetta, with the help of old Francesco Madonia, in Catania, with the support of Nitto Santapaola, in Trapani, with the help of Totò Minore, in Agrigento, with the strength and power of the Ferro family. It was a network of complicity cultivated in secret, a cross-party alliance within Cosa Nostra. What power did Pippo Calderone have to guide the regional Commission?

The most stubborn enemy of Totò Riina was Giuseppe Di Cristina. The Riesi boss was furious about this hypocritical *viddano* becoming so powerful behind his back and behind the back of everyone in Cosa Nostra. He decided to come out into the open. He protested with the Palermitans. Nothing to be done. They didn't care what was going on in Riesi, in Caltanissetta, in Catania. The Palermitans tolerated U Curtu. Sooner or later – they thought – they would defeat him. When? When the time came and when it was necessary. No sooner and no later. There was time . . .

In Palermo they had other things to think about. They were all stretched to the limit, all concerned with the idea of abandoning cigarette smuggling to take up drug trafficking. Their problem wasn't Riesi and that fucker Peppe Di Cristina. Their problem was how to organise the trafficking: morphine base, opium, heroin, suppliers, couriers, distributors, ports, airports, funding, the DEA (Drug Enforcement Agency), the FBI . . . And then, how were they to run the business? All together or each on his own? Was the Commission supposed to divide quotas among the families, or were the families supposed to divide them up themselves? Those were the problems facing the Palermitans. Totò Riina didn't count; he had nothing to do with it.

For Giuseppe Di Cristina, on the other hand, he was an idée fixe. He never missed an opportunity to throw oil on the fire. When he went to Palermo the first thing he did was go to Stefano

Bontate's house in Villagrazia. He always talked to him about U Curtu.

'That bastard Totò Riina is going to have to pay for what he did to Corleo, the *esattore*.'

Bontate listened and said, 'Sooner or later he'll pay.'

But he put it off, and put it off again.

Di Cristina insisted, and even got petulant: 'Stefano, what are you thinking? U Curtu doesn't even have to pay for the Ficuzza thing, when he wasted that *carabiniere*!'

The boss of Riesi thought again about what he had just said and got furious. He turned into an animal.

'Stefano, Stefano . . . let's take precautions until the time comes. We can't allow those shepherds to kill a *carabiniere* colonel as if it didn't matter, and as if it's never mentioned again. And then, then . . . you remember when we asked Michele Greco to find out about the death of Russo . . . What did Riina say to him? Do you remember, Stefano? He said that when you kill a cop you don't need to ask questions. As if the Commission didn't exist, as if the rules didn't exist. I said to Michele Greco that he needed to say something too . . . and in fact he's the one who pulls the strings where U Curtu is concerned. In fact he pulls the strings as if he was a puppet. Stefano, Stefano, I'm going back to Riesi, but next time I come to Palermo we have to talk seriously about Totò Riina.'

AFTERNOONS AT LA FAVARELLA

Meetings for the Mafiosi were a ritual and a pleasure. They had lots of meetings during this time, the months of spring and summer 1977. The bosses of the families were seen at the foot of Montagnalonga in Gaetano Badalamenti's little villa and Stefano

Bontate's farm in Fondo Magliocco. For some weeks the meetings had been held at La Favarella.

La Favarella was an estate that stretched from the little ruined church of Maredolce to the last gardens of Ciaculli. It surrounded the country house of Michele Greco, the 'Pope' of Cosa Nostra.

'We're quieter here,' the Pope had insisted to the others. 'Everyone comes his own way, no one can see the cars from outside, it's nice and cool. We have a good meal and a good talk.' The others agreed.

At La Favarella they always said the same things and always asked the same questions. Then they almost always gave the same answers. What had those dirty dogs got into their heads? Sending everything flying: rules, friendships, deals? Always doing what they wanted? Killing when they decided to kill and making money when they decided to make money? Where the Mafiosi of Caltanissetta or Agrigento or Trapani raged about the Corleonesi, for the Palermo Mafia they were just a source of irritation. Irritation because business could have steamed ahead. There was not a real cloud in the sky. The judges 'adjusted' trials. Fugitives were warm in bed with their wives. The politicians did what they were supposed to do: they issued contracts, fiddled accounts, were generally available. As for the cops, they might as well not have existed.

Cosa Nostra hadn't been so much at ease with itself since the days of the dynamite-filled Giuliettas. The Mafia, after the trials of Catanzaro and Bari, after the big fuss that Liggio had caused by escaping, had gained that invisibility that allowed them to live and get fat. The Italian state had its own problems with terrorism. The Red Brigades were killing people every day. Police and magistrates had other things to do besides chasing Cosa Nostra.

'We have all the conditions necessary to live a quiet life,' Giuseppe Settecasi of Agrigento and Filippo Rimi of Alcamo complained one afternoon at a meeting in La Favarella, 'and instead here we are glaring at everybody. Do you or don't you know that even parliament's looking only one way for the time being?'

Salvatore Greco was Michele's brother. He was a few years younger than the Pope, and was called 'the Senator' because of his good relations with many deputies in the Sicilian Regional Assembly. That afternoon the Senator had arrived in Ciaculli waving a piece of paper. Then he had read it out to everyone.

'Mafia crime is showing a tendency to change slowly, but in an emphatically gradual way, into a common form of organised crime, no longer marked by typical elements ... on the other hand the grip that the Mafia has had for so long on the apparatus of formal power is tending to slacken, if not to disappear completely.'

'Who wrote that?' Tano Badalamenti, the most ignorant of them all, asked suddenly.

'Parliament. It's the report from the anti-Mafia commission,' replied the Senator, the corners of his mouth twisted into a half-smile.

'And what does this piece of paper actually mean to me?' Badalamenti, never a genius at the best of times, asked again.

'It means, my dear Tano, that the people in Rome believe that the Mafia, as it once was, no longer exists. They believe that the Mafia of the past is turning into a collection of softies (*scassapaghiari*), petty thieves who will fuck themselves over sooner or later,' Salvatore Greco went on.

'And we're letting them believe that,' said Tano Badalamenti, who had understood at last what was written on that piece of paper.

'Yes, we've just got to get on with our business,' the Senator agreed.

If only the Corleonesi understood . . .' Don Tano concluded bitterly.

'The Corleonesi! The Corleonesi!' Giuseppe Di Cristina started shouting. 'They don't understand and they never will. Let's kill that bastard U Curtu and then we can rest easy . . . all of us . . . I say all of us because there's stuff for you as well . . .'

No one had ever spoken so clearly at a meeting between the bosses of the families of western Sicily. Even those who didn't want to hear had heard. Even those who didn't want to see, now had incontestable proof that the *viddani* were 'at the gates of Palermo', as a slightly worried Totuccio Inzerillo put it. Totuccio Inzerillo's uncle was Saro Di Maggio. He was a very old man, about to pass the reins of the di Passo family of Rigano to his favourite nephew.

His uncle replied: 'Totuccio, U Curtu can't do anything here in Palermo, we all agree about that . . . because as soon as he lifts his head we'll kick him in the teeth and send him back to Corleone to grow wheat . . .'

Everyone laughed. Apart from one man, Giuseppe Di Cristina. They'd done the talking part at La Favarella, and now it was time to eat. And on the embers they started roasting *cacuoccioli* and *carne di crasto* – artichokes marinaded in oil and lamb chops.

THE MEETING WITH THE CAPTAIN

There was a traitor at La Favarella – the master of the house, Michele Greco. 'The Pope' was a *muffutu* – a spy – for the Corleonesi. And the first information he passed to U Curtu concerned the boss of the Riesi.

Michele Greco told Totò Riina: 'A few days ago Peppe Di Cristina was behaving like a lunatic. At one point he shouted,

"Killing Russo was a disaster." The guy he killed with you people from Corleone . . .'

A week later, Giuseppe Di Cristina just managed to save his own life by chance. His loyal bodyguard had the same round face, the same pronounced nose, the same big jaw, and he wore the same blue beret. That day he was in his BMW as well. The hitmen got confused and shot him full of the bullets intended for the Riesi boss.

Giuseppe Di Cristina didn't let even twenty-four hours pass. He phoned the police station and asked to speak to Brigadier Giuseppe Di Salvo. The brigadier alerted his captain. They made an appointment and met up the following night in a cottage in the area of Judeca.

Captain Alfio Pettinato was open-mouthed. Di Cristina spoke and the police officer listened. The meeting took only an hour, but that was enough to reveal a thousand secrets.

'I'll tell you, Captain, who killed Colonel Nini Russo. You don't know this, but I always thought very highly of the colonel for his competence and skill, even though he pursued me doggedly . . .'

'Who killed him?' the captain cut in.

'It was Riina and Provenzano. They'd already suggested his death in a meeting in Palermo between the end of '76 and the start of '77. Tano Badalamenti and Saro Di Maggio said no to the Corleonesi. They said you couldn't make war on the state, that Cosa Nostra rules said to be inside the state, indeed to help the state when necessary, if there was a reciprocal advantage. And instead those wretches killed Colonel Russo anyway. Then we had a meeting in Palermo and I spoke clearly . . . I explained that killing Russo had been a disaster that would only cause us grief. By way of reply those sons of bitches set up a trap for me . . . You've got to stop them now, Captain, because they're not just dangerous for me, more importantly they're dangerous for you . . .'

Captain Pettinato stared at Di Cristina and saw the terror in his eyes. The man was a like a cornered animal.

'Dangerous for us? Why?'

'The plan to kill Judge Cesare Terranova is already under way. They want to kill him and lay his death on me, Captain. Those *tragediatori* want to make people think that I was the one who killed him, to take revenge on him . . . Terranova had investigated me for the Ciuni method. It's an old method of the Corleonesi. They were the ones who killed the prosecutor Pietro Scaglione to cause problems for Vincenzo Rimi. And now they want to try again with me. You have to stop them.'

'But what can we do in your view – where will we find them?' the *carabiniere* cut in.

'I'm not saying it'll be easy, but I'll give you the right information to dig them out, those two beasts, Totò U Curtu and Binnu Provenzano. They're a pair of animals, Captain. At a guess, between them they've already killed about eighty people. To find them you're going to need to get the whole of San Giuseppe Jato under control. Bernardo Brusca is their man and he's helping them. They're also being helped by Peppe Gambino, *u tignusu*, Mariano Agate of Mazara del Vallo, Nené Geraci of Partinico. And the Nuvoletta brothers from Marano di Napoli, who are Liggio and Riina's straw men in the fruit-growing sector . . . You've got to stop them, Captain Pettinato. Next week I'm taking delivery of an armoured vehicle that has cost me about 30 million. I want to make sure my ass is covered. You know, Captain, I have some venial sins on my conscience, and quite a few mortal ones as well . . .'

Giuseppe Di Cristina didn't feel like a cop. And he didn't feel like a traitor that night when he left that cottage in the area of Judeca. He didn't feel like a traitor a week later, either, when along with Pippo Calderone he decided to move against the

Corleonesi using their own weapon, *tragedia*. Only a Palermitan, Tano Badalamenti, was informed of their intentions.

Inside Cosa Nostra a plot can take many forms and many roads; there was no turning back on the road that Di Cristina and Calderone took. They built the *tragedia* around U Curtu by striking his colleague from Nisseno, Francesco Madonia di Vallelunga Pratameno. They wanted to set him against Stefano Bontate. They wanted the Palermitan to humiliate Madonia. They wanted old Madonia to take up the gauntlet. If that happened, there were only two possibilities: either Totò Riina would defend his ally, and the Palermitans would have been dragged into conflict with the Corleonesi, or U Curtu would abandon Francesco Madonia to his sad fate. In both cases the power of the *viddani* would be compromised, both in Catania and in Riesi.

The *tragedia* was staged by Giuseppe Di Cristina. An unlikely transgression was invented, on the part of Piddu Madonia, the son of the boss of Vallelunga. But it didn't work. Stefano Bontate refused to get involved. Giuseppe Di Cristina lost his head. And on 18 April 1978 he had Francesco Madonia killed at the foot of the castle of Falconara.

Sometimes, even in Cosa Nostra, two and two make four. Di Cristina and Calderone had killed a head of the family without permission from the Commission. They had to pay for it – no two ways about it. Totò Riina asked for them both to be killed.

'Those are the rules,' U Curtu reminded Michele Greco. The Pope referred to Stefano Bontate. And he added: 'And then he told me . . .'

'What else does he want?' asked Bontate, losing his temper.

'Well, Tano . . .'

'What about Tano?'

'Totò says that Tano knew and didn't stop Madonia from being killed. He's just as responsible as Calderone and Di Cristina. In fact he thinks he's responsible for the plot . . .'

'Get to the point, Michele. What does he want?'

'He wants Tano to be put "outside the family".'

'*Posato?*' Relocated.

'Yes, *posato* . . . Tano mustn't be killed.'

Stefano Bontate said nothing. Tano Badalamenti was ignorant, *con il palmo e con la giunta*,[1] but his prestige had kept Cosa Nostra united during the difficult years, when men of honour were in rags and in jail. His peasant wisdom had been essential for the reconstruction of the Commission after the trial of the 114. Badalamenti *posato*. He couldn't have known the secrets of the family any longer, he couldn't even have talked to the men of honour. Bontate couldn't imagine Cosa Nostra without Badalamenti. But he knew that if the rules weren't respected, the Corleonesi would turn Cosa Nostra into a lawless jungle. The boss of Santa Maria del Gesù was convinced that he could prove to the Commission that it was the *viddani* who had kidnapped Luigi Corleo. He could ask for the death of Totò Riina and Binnu Provenzano. And once those two were in the ground, Tano would be able to get back to the family.

'That's what Cosa Nostra is like, Don Michele,' Bontate said.

The Pope understood that U Curtu had done it once again. Tano was worthless now. Stefano Bontate had had to bow. Pippo Calderone and Giuseppe Di Cristina stank of corpses.

---

1 Italian expression used to describe someone very ignorant.

THE FUNERAL ORATION OF THE SNAKE

One morning in May Giuseppe Di Cristina was in Palermo preparing for a raid on the Banco di Sicilia. He was walking along a street in Passo di Rigano. He had only taken a few steps when two men came up behind him and started shooting. The boss was injured, but he managed to grab his automatic. He fired twice. The hitmen fled. Di Cristina took aim again, but the third bullet jammed in the barrel. The two hitmen noticed what had happened, turned round and finished him off with six bullets to the head.

Di Cristina's death caused a scandal. On the evening of the crime Stefano Bontate summoned a meeting in the farm in Fondo Magliocco. Many members of the Inzerillo family were there: about ten *picciotti* from Santa Maria del Gesù, and Saro Di Maggio. Michele Greco came too. Gaetano Badalamenti didn't arrive. Totuccio Inzerillo was as angry as the devil.

'I want to know why they've been killing people in my part of town without telling me anything. Now I'll have the cops on me, with the corpse that they've dumped at my house . . .'

Stefano Bontate said nothing. He was furious, and not because of the death of his friend Peppe Di Cristina. If he had to die he had to die, but not in Passo di Rigano. Once again the Corleonesi had played dirty. They had freed themselves of the boss of Riesi, and found a way to cause problems for Totuccio Inzerillo.

Stefano said to Totuccio: 'Listen, what do you want us to do? Do we have to kill Riina? Let's call a meeting of the Commission and I'll kill him with my bare hands, if that's any use.'

'*Picciotti, picciotti*, violence will get you nowhere. As soon as the first gun goes off in Palermo, there'll be a corpse on every street around here,' said the Pope, who, until that moment, had been listening in a corner.

'And now what are we going to do?' asked Bontate.

Sighing, Michele Greco patiently explained his point of view: 'Listen to me, everybody. Are we going to stop these arguments once and for all? Let's dig a big hole and bury all the *tragedie* in it. Trust me, let's try to forget . . .'

They tried to forget.

Three months later, on 8 September, the Corleonesi killed Pippo Calderone.

'It was as if he was hypnotised by his death,' his brother Nino confessed. 'Pippo was still deluding himself that he could change things in the Catania family. He was deluding himself . . . that day he had to go and see Salvatore Ferrera, the new boss of the province, and the meeting was to be organised by Nitto Santapaola . . . He told him it was in Aci Castello, at Ferrera's house, at six or seven in the evening. Pippo went out calm and confident. He wasn't even armed. When he turned off the main road, at the level crossing near Aci Castello, they ambushed him.'

The Corleonesi had managed to eliminate the most powerful allies that the Palermitans had in eastern Sicily and the inland provinces. U Curtu had won his first battle. He had got what he wanted. 'The best forgiveness is revenge,' he said to his family.

At the first meeting of the regional Commission it was Totò who insisted that he and only he could deliver the funeral oration for 'the late-departed Pippo'. The Corleonese was a snake.

'He delivered a short speech,' Nino Calderone remembered years later. 'He talked about my brother's character, his reputation as a magnanimous and generous man of honour. He remembered the work he had done for a more orderly and harmonious Cosa Nostra. He said that all his troubles had come from his friendship with Di Cristina. He said that Pippo had believed in that wretch, it was true, but in good faith. Certainly he couldn't be blamed for that. Now we had to draw a line under the past and love one another. He actually said those words, U Curtu did. It was hard to tell whether Totò Riina was acting or not at that moment . . . if those noble words came from genuine grief even over someone like him . . . or from the abject satisfaction of the winner who has just eliminated a dangerous enemy and is proud of the quality of his victim. There's no point trying to understand. It's always like that in Cosa Nostra: no fact ever has a single meaning.'

With the deaths of Peppe Di Cristina and Pippo Calderone, on the eve of the 1980s, the rise of Totò Riina's Corleonesi within the Sicilian Cosa Nostra began. As in all struggles for Mafia power, the first dramas were played out on the edge of the empire. The first deaths occurred far from Palermo. The war, even if it had not yet been officially declared, was close. Not everyone understood straight away. Many, a great many, too many men of honour pretended not to understand until the end.

THE MAFIOSO WITHOUT HONOUR

THE MADNESS OF LEUCCIO

'Shoot him! Shoot him!' shouted Uncle Titta. Leuccio was horrified at himself. He was standing, legs spread, in front of the horse, his arm outstretched and his rifle dangling. It was a 12-calibre hammer shotgun. Through his cotton trousers he felt the cold steel of the barrel on his thigh.

'Shoot him, Leuccio!' his uncle shouted again.

Leonardo Vitale looked once more into the horse's bulging eyes, staring at him meekly. It was an old nag with low hocks and a bulging belly, good enough for the plough at best. Leuccio turned his back on his uncle. He drew up his arm and rested the mouth of the rifle against the white patch on the animal's forehead. He closed his eyes and tried not to retch. He fired.

That was the start of the story of Leonardo Vitale, Leuccio, a *picciotto* from Altarello di Baida, the suburb that marked the border between the last buildings in Palermo and the first hills in Monreale. If Leuccio could kill a horse, he could kill a man. He shot Vincenzo Mannino. He had been pointed out to him by his uncle Titta, Giovanbattista Vitale, a Mafiosi with no heirs who wanted a nephew like himself, whatever the cost. Leuccio didn't ask why Mannino had to die. The boy – he was only seventeen

– hid in a Cinquecento on Via Tasca Lanza and waited. When he saw Mannino coming he rested the rifle on the bonnet and shot him straight in the chest.

He became a man of honour in a cottage in Fondo Uscibene. It was the first time many people had seen him. But there were also the two old men who had brought him up, his uncle Titta and old Salvatore Inzerillo. They punctured his finger with a bitter orange thorn, and burned a *santina* into his hands . . . They kissed him on the mouth, but 'on the lips, no tongue'.

When the performance was over, Leonardo Vitale wrote: 'I have been mocked by life, misfortune has rained down on me since I was a child. Then the Mafia came with its fake laws, its fake ideals: fighting thieves, helping the weak and, however, killing. Lunatics! You have to be a Mafioso to have any success. That's what they taught me and I obeyed. My mistake was to be born, to have lived in a society in which everyone's a Mafioso, and that's why they're respected, while those who aren't are despised . . .'

Then he was in a criminal asylum. They locked him up in there for six years, after he had 'sung'.

At eight o'clock in the evening on 30 March 1973 he had crossed the gardens in Piazza della Vittoria and turned up at the police station. He told them everything. He told them about the black well that had swallowed him up. He talked about when Giuseppe Bologna had accused his uncle of being an informer. 'Kill him!' his uncle had commanded. He remembered when Ciccio Di Marco had robbed the shop belonging to a man of honour. 'Kill him!' his uncle had commanded. He explained what his work was. Laying bombs, burning cars, destroying orchards, frightening those who had building sites on Viale della Regione Siciliana and had said, 'No, I'm not paying'. Then he, Leuccio, turned up again to demand the money after a chat with his uncle Titta. Forty thousand lire a month, sometimes sixty thousand. Five hundred thousand lire every now and again.

It was the 1960s, and he had seen the tower blocks going up one after the other on Via Perpignano, on Corso Calatafimi, in Mezzomonreale, in Boccadifalco, Cruillas, Borgo Nuovo and Uditore. He told the police everything. Leuccio gave them hundreds and hundreds of names. Including the ones that were frightening even to say. Vito Ciancimino, a puppet in the hands of the Corleonesi. Pino Trapani, the communal planning officer. Pippo Calò, the one who had once had a butcher's shop in Porta Nuova. Prince Alessandro Vanni Calvello from San Vincenzo. And, at the top of them all, one name: Salvatore Riina.

Leuccio Vitale lowered his voice: 'He's one of the bosses. Riina tells you what you can and can't do. When two families find themselves in conflict, they turn to *zu* (uncle) Totò. He listens to the arguments and decides. Once, us lot from Altarello were fighting with the della Noce family. The builder Giovanni Pilo had opened a construction site and he was supposed to pay a *pizzo*[1] to my uncle Titta. Instead Raffaele Spina, the La Noce representative, claimed it for his family. What to do, what not to do; before any guns are fired, a meeting is organised with Riina. *Zu* Totò listens, listens and in the end says: "I have La Noce in my heart," and "I'm giving the *pizzo* to La Noce." Why? Hey, who knows! The Corleonese liked the La Noce family better – maybe because the family there had found him a warm bed and a safe house and smart *picciotti* when uncle Totò went down to Palermo. Perhaps because my uncle Titta wasn't that likeable a guy and always did his own thing. However, U Curtu's word was law.'

---

1 A form of extortion – demanding to receive a percentage of all profits of a commercial activity in exchange for 'protection'.

At police headquarters Leonardo Vitale exposed his soul to one man whose tie was loose and another one who kept lighting cigarettes and stubbing them out. The one with the loose tie was called Bruno Contrada and he was the head of the flying squad. The one smoking like a Turk was Tonino De Luca of Homicide. They nudged each other and yawned. They said: 'This guy's mad.' Leuccio replied, 'No, I'm not mad. I'm a Mafioso, I'm a man of honour of the family of Altarello di Baida. It's a Cosa Nostra family. Cosa Nostra . . . Now let me tell you . . . Cosa Nostra is a lot of families. Each family is formed of *decine*, units of ten, and has a boss elected by the men of honour, as he was the mayor. The boss chooses a deputy and an adviser. And over every *decina* he puts a *capodecina*, a boss of the unit of ten. The men of honour don't discuss, they obey. I just obeyed. The Mafia is evil itself – an evil that won't let go of anyone it's got in its grip.'

That was what Leonardo Vitale said in that March 1973. Leuccio was the first *pentito* in the modern history of Cosa Nostra. Then he ended up the way he ended up . . .

Highly esteemed professors had declared him 'mentally unstable', psychiatrists and psychologists agreed: that boy from Altarello was mad. So mad that they locked him up in the asylum of Barcellona Pozzo di Cotto.

Eleven years later, in 1984, Leuccio was a free man. One day in December he had gone to mass, had signed the book of 'those under special surveillance' and then gone to San Martino Delle Scale. 'The fresh air in the pine forest blows away dark thoughts.' He saw them arriving on a red motorcycle. They couldn't miss. They didn't miss. Leuccio died two hundred metres, more or less, from where Vincenzo Mannino had been killed twenty-six years before.

Everybody thought Leuccio was mad. Everybody except U Curtu. Totò Riina had the scent of a hunting dog: he could smell danger years in the future and a thousand kilometres away. He knew that that *picciotto* from Altarello would cause trouble to him and the whole of Cosa Nostra. He had him killed as an example, as a symbol. It was after Leuccio's confessions that U Curtu talked to Provenzano about an idea that had been running around in his head. And he confided in his loyal friend Binnu: 'Since then we've stopped introducing our men of honour to the Palermitans, the ones from the Corleone family. So if someone wants to turn grass, they'll be singing *cosa loro* – their thing – and not Cosa Nostra.'

In those days the Palermitans had other things on their minds apart from worrying about Leuccio. The *picciotti* were tired. The acquittals of Catanzaro and Bari had stuck in the throats of the police like a fishbone. And police superintendents and inspectors were starting to use a heavy hand: a single drop of blood and everyone with a Mafia record went straight to the Ucciardone. The Commission met and decided to 'subjugate or kill' the judges and policemen who overdid things, who issued arrest warrants like Christmas presents. Stefano Bontate said: 'If a cop starts causing trouble, we try to get him transferred to the mainland . . . it's the best thing; we can't wage a war on the state. But if he stays here and goes on causing trouble, we sort him out.'

A *decina* of *picciotti* were given the task of collecting information about three cops who wouldn't loosen their grip. They were the head of the flying squad, Bruno Contrada, and his deputies, Boris Giuliano and Tonino De Luca. The *picciotti* followed them for a few months. They discovered where they lived, how they moved, whether they had weaknesses and if so which, where they went to the seaside, who they saw, who they knew, who could approach them to give them some good advice. Some needed to be killed. Like Filadelfio Aparo, a brigadier of public safety. He'd been given the task of finding the fugitives and had put his nose to the ground like a dog to find their trail, suburb after suburb. He was shot down. A fortnight later they also killed Mario Francese, a journalist on *Giornale di Sicilia*. Two crimes to get rid of people who – U Curtu was sure – would sooner or later do them damage. They were signals to make people understand the new policy chosen by Cosa Nostra. There was no need for other messages. They managed to have a large number of policemen transferred. Then Bruno Contrada was silenced as well. There was no need to send him away. He was more useful where he was, at police headquarters. He was 'approached', and he understood.

Saro Riccobono told his family: 'Contrada is in our hands. In fact, if they arrest you, call him and, if they take you to the station, demand to talk just to him.' And the boss of Partanna Mondello wasn't the only member of Cosa Nostra with access to Contrada. The policeman passed information to Totò Riina, to Michele Greco, to Totuccio Inzerillo. With Boris Giuliano, on the other hand, it went a very different way. With the judges, it went even better. At the Palermo tribunal they forgot about the crime of criminal association. The police didn't take statements and the magistrate didn't ask for them. Everyone played along. When a real cop like Boris Giuliano wrote pages and pages of reports, there was always a drawer at the Palace of Justice to hide them away. Until 1979 Cosa Nostra rattled along serenely, and God alone knows how much serenity they needed, now that the bosses were getting involved in the business of the century.

THE DISCOVERY OF AMERICA

Tano was old-fashioned: all honour, family and respect. He had fertile lands and byres full of cattle. Gaetano Badalamenti had been involved in drug trafficking for almost thirty years. He travelled back and forth from Sicily to America, from Cinisi to Detroit, where his brother Emanuele had emigrated immediately after the war.

Don Tano met up with some important people. At the time everyone who worked with drugs worked with the big shots in the American Cosa Nostra. Tano fell in with Lucky Luciano, while the Alcamo, Partinico and Castellammare del Golfo befriended the Bonanno family of New York and the Magaddinos of Buffalo. But Sicilian Cosa Nostra had nothing to do with it. The families were organising themselves in their own right. If a family in Sicily had a brother, a cousin, an uncle or a brother-in-law on the other side of the ocean, it was easy to do business. You asked a fellow-Italian to put a few kilos of 'stuff' in the boot . . . Not everyone could do it, and not everybody did do it, because at the time there wasn't much money in it. You earned more and risked less with cigarettes: Chesterfield, Camel, Pall Mall. In 1959 a case cost 28,000 lire in Tangier and was sold in Rome for 210,000. Cigarettes were a gold mine. Cigarettes had kept Cosa Nostra alive for a quarter of a century.

The gold mine in the late 1970s was heroin. Nunzio La Mattina, Pino Savoca and Tommaso Spadaro were three smugglers from the Arab quarter of the Kalsa. One day they threw their sticks of cigarettes into the sea and bought morphine base from the Turks. Chemists from Marseille refined it, and the Cosa Nostra families sold it. Then a man called Nino Vernengo worked out how to make that magic powder and spoke to the other men of honour: 'All you need is a kitchen, a few steel basins, some heat. There's a big stink and you need some air as well, and that's all.' From that day Vernengo was known as *u dutturi*, the doctor.

At first it was all a disaster. What mattered to Vernengo was the weight on the scales. A lot of kilos on the scales, a lot of dollars in his pocket. He had seen that the Marseillais – to balance out the kilos that the 'paste' lost when it was being boiled – added tropine or benzotropine, which they refined separately. One day the brains behind the operation asked him to refine tropine and sell it with a small quantity of heroin to Pino Greco (*Scarpuzzedda*). They also sent it to America. In the States users dropped like flies: about a hundred people died. Nino Vernengo, *u dutturi*, had to return all the money, down to the last dollar.

It was the early 1970s, and the Palermitans hadn't yet learned the ropes. By the end of the decade things looked very different. Nino Vernengo had learned. Above all Francesco Marino Mannoia had learned. The raw materials had never been in short supply. They arrived by fishing boat to Trapani, by plane to Punta Raisi, by ferry across the straits. The only problem was finding the time and the place to refine it without anyone getting in the way. Mannoia refined his first kilo between the end of 1978 and the start of 1980. And he didn't stop until he was arrested for the first time on 2 December 1980.

He allowed himself a bit of rest for a few weeks when he couldn't spend another minute in the acidic atmosphere of a laboratory. He had to detoxify himself. He turned white as a sheet and red as if he'd been horsewhipped. He struggled to breathe. His skin was covered with pustules and he scratched like a mangy dog. During those days he seemed more dead than alive. And yet even then they wouldn't leave him alone. They had the 'paste' hidden somewhere, and nobody knew how to treat it. They kept asking, 'So, Ciccio my friend, when are you going to be able to work?'

All the families in Palermo were involved in drug trafficking. Every *capofamiglia* decided which of his own men of honour could participate, and what their quota would be. The fonder the *capofamiglia* was of them and the more he trusted them, the greater the likelihood that he would make them rich through the drugs trade. There were many ways of taking part in the business. The man of honour could organise the trafficking by himself if he knew someone reliable in Turkey or Thailand. Or else the man of honour could buy just a slice of the cargo. He could invest his money either alone or in a group. He could take his share of heroin and sell it, or else he could stay at home waiting for other people to sell it abroad. The ones who chose that solution earned the most, because there was a greater risk of the 'stuff' ending up in the hands of the cops.

During the early 1980s Palermo was a refinery operating at full steam. DEA experts maintained that the Sicilians covered a third of the North American market, something like four tons of heroin a year. According to FBI figures it was more than that: six tons a year. A Mafioso like Francesco Marino Mannoia moved from one refinery to another. From Gaetano Fiore, leaving fuel behind the bar at Baby Luna, to the stable at Rosario Spatola's property in Baida. From the kitchen of an old house belonging to the Vernengos in Ponte Ammiraglio to Giovanni Bontate's garage at a cottage on via Villagrazia. From Pietro Aglieri's warehouse at La Guadagna to the villa of another Aglieri on Via Messina Marine. And they weren't even the biggest or best-equipped laboratories. In Alcamo there was one with an electric pump that drew water from a river. It processed eighty kilos a week, four and a half tons a year.

Francesco Marino Mannoia did a bit of work for everybody. For Michele Greco, for Giovanni Bontate, for Gerlando Alberti, *u paccaré* (the imperturbable one). But above all for Stefano Bontate, the head of his family in Santa Maria del Gesù. One day Bontate told him that he'd set up a company with Totuccio Inzerillo and John Gambino.

'Why Inzerillo?' Mannoia asked, curious.

'It's a special moment for Cosa Nostra. Totuccio Inzerillo has been made a *capomandamento*[1]. He took the place of Saro Di Maggio, and now he's part of the Commission, and I need new, strong alliances in the Commission if I want to stand up to the Corleonesi. If Totuccio and I agree, and we make *piccioli* together, that bastard Totò Riina will never set foot in Palermo again. You can be sure of that, one hundred per cent!'

In twenty-four months – between 1979 and 1980 – Francesco Marino Mannoia refined six or seven hundred kilos of morphine. He made 5 million lire a kilo and didn't have to worry about finding a laboratory and paying for it. Bontate and Inzerillo sold heroin to Gambino at 50,000 dollars a kilo, and Gambino sold it on to the American families at 130,000 dollars a kilo. During those two years the families of Santa Maria del Gesù and Passo di Rigano made, just with Mannoia's 'paste', something like 30 or 35 million dollars, and the Gambinos between 78 and 91 million dollars. These were gross prices, of course. Totò Riina just dipped his feet in that river of water.

The *viddani* had no important relations on the other side of the ocean. And they didn't have any trusted friends either. They were nothing to the heads of the five big New York families. Less than nothing. And who in Brooklyn had ever heard of Totò Riina? U Curtu settled for investing the ransom money from kidnappings in morphine base. Minimum quotas: 5 million in one cargo, 7 in another. Ten million when you got a good deal. The Palermitans treated him like a beggar-man.

---

1 Head of the local Mafia; the boss in a specific geographic area.

MONEY, MONEY, MONEY . . .

Corleone was bedlam. Everyone wanted in on the big drugs carousel. Some just set up a company to make a few kilos at once, some wanted more and went up to twenty or fifty kilos a month, some dreamt of having all the morphine base it was possible to ship from the Mediterranean. It was a boundless delirium of greed. The men of honour seemed to have taken leave of their senses. *Piccioli, piccioli, piccioli* – money, money, money . . . No one in Palermo was talking about anything else. Some had mother-of-pearl floors, some had gold taps. They would buy a Jaguar one day and a Ferrari the day after, or build villas with silver swimming pools.

It was money madness. At La Noce and Bolognetta, at Acquasanta and Corso dei Mille. The only thing they talked about was money, about cargoes leaving and coming in, about how much *u zu* Peppino had made, or *u zu* Jachino. The rules had been abandoned. Every man of honour did deals with whomever he felt like – even with traffickers who weren't part of Cosa Nostra and hadn't taken the earth. There were Mafiosi who did deals with people they wouldn't even have looked in the eye a few years before, and would have taken offence if they'd so much as said hello. Adventurers of every shade and colour: Chinese, Thai, Turkish, Moroccan, Corsican, crooks and ne'er-do-wells. U Curtu quivered with rage, furious with Cosa Nostra.

Totò Riina had to ask the Palermitans for permission to have a turn on the carousel. He had to flatter and cajole them. 'I'm not asking on behalf of myself,' he said, lowering his eyes. 'I'm doing it for all the little men who are finally glimpsing a little of God's grace after suffering so much for this Cosa Nostra, for the prison terms they've had to serve, for their families . . .'

Who could have turned him away? His reasoning was perfect in its form. In the end, Totò Riina acquired more and more power, a little at a time.

Until then the Corleonese had ensured that every family put one or two men of honour at his disposal. When they were moving from one suburb to another, he had to be sure to avoid checks and road blocks. At any time, and wherever he happened to be, he had to have someone with him, to find him a safe refuge, to guard the door during the night. But protecting him while he remained a fugitive was only the apparent motive for his requests. The real one was different. The intention of U Curtu – who now had loyal, unknown soldiers in the region of Corleone – was to win the trust of the Palermo families. A group formed around him, men known only to him. Men of honour who had been initiated into a Palermo family, but had in effect become made men in Corleone. From the Partanna Mondello family he had Gaspare Mutolo and Salvatore Micalizzi. The group also included Pietro Vernengo and Ignazio Pullarà of the family of Stefano Bontate. The sons of the Palermitan Francesco Madonia, Giuseppe and Nino, of the family of San Lorenzo. Franco Di Carlo from Altofonte, Giuseppe Giacomo Gambino *u tignusu* from Resuttana and Raffaele Ganci from La Noce . . .

They were all at Totò Riina's disposal. They didn't move a muscle without telling him, and U Curtu tried to get them all on his carousel. When it didn't work, Totò Riina said that 'it was their fault, the fault of the *mammasantissimas* (men in senior positions) who want to gorge on dollars and don't give a damn about the *picciotti.*' U Curtu dispensed arsenic in daily drops. Never making a false move, never doing anything to provoke a violent reaction. He administered his poison in doses just big enough to poison Cosa Nostra slowly and gently.

The Sicilian Mafia needed to be in peace. It was a golden age:

drugs meant wealth. No one was insane enough to unleash a storm in the middle of that sea of money. Not even U Curtu. He and the Corleonesi had never had contacts on the other side of the Atlantic. In the heroin trade they were dependent on the Palermitans. Totò Riina just had to shut up and listen when they talked about the United States, about Kennedy Airport, about landing strips in Miami. It was a game played only by the Inzerillo, Di Maggio, Spatola and Gambino families. And Stefano Bontate was in with them. They were rich, extremely rich. Five families and property worth a billion dollars.

The resources of those five families – more money than all the other families in Cosa Nostra put together – had one sole origin: they were on both sides of the ocean, in Passo di Rigano and New Jersey. They were all related. The mother of the Gambino brothers was a Spatola. The father of the Inzerillos had married a Di Maggio, and the brother of that Di Maggio had married another Spatola. Totuccio Inzerillo, who had inherited the *mandamento* from his uncle Saro Di Maggio, had married a Spatola. Totuccio's New Jersey uncle, Antonio, had married a Gambino. His cousin, who had the same name as himself, Salvatore, had married a Gambino. His cousin Tommaso was the brother-in-law of John Gambino, who had married another Gambino. His cousin Maria Concetta was the wife of John Gambino's younger brother, Giuseppe. The Gambinos had only arrived in New York in 1964, and had settled in New Jersey, in Cherry Hill. They were men of honour of the Sicilian Cosa Nostra. Even though they were nephews of Carlo Gambino, the boss of bosses, they answered only to the Sicilian Cosa Nostra.

How could those bonds ever be broken? Who could be so crazy or suicidal as to go against them? U Curtu didn't even think about it. At least he didn't seem to ... Peace brought money, money brought peace. And a cop was causing trouble. There was somebody sticking his nose into their business. It was now that the bosses of Cosa Nostra found a use for the information about policemen and judges that the foot soldiers had collected a few years before.

A COFFEE AT THE BAR LUX

'Clear off, Tommy, go home. The game's got too risky . . . Let's get out of here.'

Tom Tripodi didn't understand. They'd been working on the inquiry for two years, and the high-ups in the Drug Enforcement Agency had decided to send them undercover to Sicily. He had been in Palermo for three months. He and his colleague had finally started to score some points. At Punta Raisi airport they had confiscated two suitcases on the baggage-claim belt, containing half a million in banknotes. At Kennedy Airport they had intercepted a 10-billion-dollar cargo of heroin.

Tom Tripodi lit another menthol cigarette. He took a long drag on it. For a moment he thought his companion was joking. He looked at him: his face was dark as night, and he was sadder than usual. Something was troubling him.

'What's up, Boris?' the American asked.

Boris Giuliano was a special man, and a special policeman. He was brave, honest and intelligent. Boris Giuliano was the first cop in the world to understand the role of the Sicilians in the international drug traffic. Then – this was the 1970s – the cops in Palermo were convinced that the Mafiosi belonged to a species destined for extinction. 'The old bosses, perhaps . . . after the war . . . today they're common criminals. Drugs? The Marseillais do those, and the Chinese; here they're dragging things back to the dark ages, with extortion and cigarette smuggling . . .'

Boris Giuliano saw things differently. The policeman they called 'the sheriff' was the only one who suspected that the refineries were in Palermo, in Trapani, that the heroin was leaving Sicily for the United States, that a flood of dollars, millions of dollars, was coming back to Sicily. The sheriff was the only Sicilian policeman who tried to decipher the hieroglyphic code of the Mafia. He tried to interpret its marks, to put together its signs, its faint traces, to get to know the new men of honour and the modern methods of the criminal paradigm that was enriching Cosa Nostra.

Boris Giuliano had been to FBI academy in Quantico, Virginia. As far as he was concerned there was no difference between the alleys of the Vucciria in Palermo and the streets of Chinatown in New York. If you wanted to see and not be seen, Via dei Caprettai was like Canal Street, an important but not crucial detail. If you had to shoot at someone, that someone was going to give up the ghost: the sheriff was capable of putting a bullet between your eyes from fifty metres away. He could trail somebody for hours along a deserted street, and his quarry wouldn't suspect a thing. He knew how to lure in a rogue and make him an informer. He knew how to use his head. Boris Giuliano had worked out one essential thing: you had to look for the money. A refinery could open and close. A kilo, twenty kilos of heroin could disappear, but the money couldn't. Dollars left a trace. They were the finger-prints that the Mafia couldn't erase. Banknotes were the thread that the cop wanted to follow, and which he was following, to the best of his ability and on his own, with a Colt number 5 strapped below his armpit, and with the information he had managed to extract from the silence of Palermo.

Those 500,000 dollars that he had found in the suitcases in Punta Raisi had brought Boris Giuliano to the savings banks of the Sicilian provinces. Somebody called Giglio had deposited 300,000 dollars in banknotes. Who was Giglio? Giuliano asked Francesco

Lo Coco, the director of the credit institute. 'I don't know,' he replied. Francesco Lo Coco was a first cousin of Stefano Bontate, but Boris Giuliano didn't know that.

'Tom, listen to me,' Boris said. 'Facing the enemy head-on is getting too dangerous. In this city the walls have ears, and the walls of police headquarters have eyes, ears and a mouth.'

'Are you telling me there's a spy in the station?' asked Tom, who was starting to understand Boris's grim sense of humour.

'I'm not sure, but I think they've seen through our game. They know who you are. Someone's talked.'

'Do you know who it is?' asked Tom Tripodi.

Giuliano lowered his voice. 'I don't know, but I don't trust Bruno.'

'Contrada? The head of the flying squad? Your boss?'

'Yes, Contrada, my boss . . .'

'If they know about me, do they know about you too?'

Giuliano smiled bitterly: 'That's for sure, but I'm the cop, they're the thieves in this life.'

'Same with me. I earn my living as a cop, have you forgotten that?' said Tripodi, rounding off the conversation.

It was the end of June 1979. The Palermo police were keeping an eye on two Mafiosi. They saw them going into a tower block on Via Pecori Giraldi, a narrow side-street off the Romagnolo coast road. The next morning, at dawn, they burst into the flat. They found sawn-off shotguns, Magnum 357s that would have brought down a buffalo and kilos of ammunition. There were eight half-kilo bags of heroin in a wardrobe. All around were traces of the owner of that fortune which – a million more, a million less – were worth 3 billion lire. The documents, the personal effects and the wardrobe said that the heroin belonged to Leoluca Bagarella, Luchino, one of Totò Riina's hitmen. It was the first time they'd caught the Corleonesi red-handed.

The call came in the next day.

'Tell Giuliano his days are numbered.'

Boris took the threat seriously and sent Tripodi back to America. He sent his family on holiday to Piazza Armerina.

Three weeks later the sheriff was dead.

It was 21 July. He went out earlier than usual that morning and, breaking with his habits, went into a bar to have a coffee – the Lux, downstairs from his home. Perhaps he had an appointment with someone he knew. The killer was already waiting for him. Leoluca Bagarella, Luchino, Totò Riina's brother-in-law, shot him in the back. The Corleonese's hands were shaking. He had to pull the trigger four times.

There were lots of reasons to kill Boris Giuliano.

'We just waste him, and as to the others we either buy them or they behave themselves or they pretend not to understand. Whack him,' the Commission had decided. They all agreed – Stefano Bontate's Palermitans and Totò Riina's Corleonesi – to ice the cop who had studied at Quantico. Because there wasn't just the business about the drugs, there were other things too. They were expecting visitors in Palermo, important visitors.

DON MICHELE'S LAST ADVENTURE

When Michele Sindona landed in Sicily he was a spent force. A failed banker brought down on an indictment by the American government. He was a man who knew he had to die for burning Cosa Nostra's money.

Don Michele's troubles had begun with the acquisition of the eighteenth bank of the United States. He had bought the Franklin Bank in New York with money taken from his banks in Italy. Sindona had emptied the coffers for all kinds of crack-brained schemes and speculations. And still, to save it, he had managed to borrow 1 billion and 700 million dollars from the Federal Reserve. The bail-out had failed, and within a week the American crash had brought down Don Michele's four other banks in Europe: the Banca Privata Italiana, Finabank, Amincor and the Hamburg Bankhaus.

Michele Sindona stayed in Sicily for fifty days in August and September 1979. Put up by the Spatola family, chauffeured around by John Gambino in a black Mercedes, given red-carpet treatment by Totuccio Inzerillo and his uncle Saro Di Maggio, and listened to with patience and interest by Stefano Bontate in meetings at the farm in Fondo Magliocco, which could go on for seven, eight or ten hours. Highly secret meetings. Delicate discussions, too delicate for the ears of U Curtu, too refined for those *viddani* from Corleone. Totò Riina couldn't have known that Don Michele was hiding in Palermo.

Michele Sindona didn't die, he didn't die then.

There had been a time when Sindona could have been put on a par with King Midas. Forty per cent of the shares that passed through Milan stock exchange every day were under his direct or indirect control. The head of the Italian government, Giulio Andreotti, pampered and defended him. 'Sindona is the saviour of the lira,' he had declared serenely.

Sindona's group was represented in six banks in four countries. It owned the Ciga international hotel chain and five hundred other companies. Don Michele was the banker of the Holy See. He directed the investments of the Vatican Bank, the Institute of Religious Works, and looked after the affairs of the P2 masonic lodge. And he 'laundered' Cosa Nostra's dirty money.

There were days, back then, when the banker felt like an old puppet-master, capable of controlling, with a barely perceptible movement of his finger, the action of dozens and dozens of puppets, making them jump and dance. The puppets were connected to him by a strong thread, so strong as to be invisible. All the threads led to Moneyrex, his international exchange agency. Moneyrex had 850 banks scattered around the world, and did about 200 billion dollars' worth of business every year. Sindona had amassed sums abroad totalling billions and tens of billions. Thanks to Don Michele, the fortunes of many wealthy and important Italians were stateless, and Cosa Nostra's money was as immaculate as freshly washed sheets.

In the sultry summer of 1979, all that Sindona had left were those threads and a secret register listing the names of five hundred big shots. The banker called it 'the list of the five hundred'. It was his insurance against bankruptcy, disasters and scandals. He had hoped never to have to use it, but he had been mistaken.

And now he was in Sicily, to sell in exchange for his life his last remaining treasure. To pass on to his friends in Palermo the bill that the five hundred mysterious Italians had left in his hands. To gain a bit more time and try one last trick. He had two possibilities. He could force the five hundred to ensure that his judicial vicissitudes, in Italy and the United States, found an honourable solution. Or alternatively, the five hundred, caught by the throat by the menace of unpleasant publicity, might come up with a per -capita share to help him out of his fix. Was 50 billion enough to keep Cosa Nostra happy? In either case he needed the support of a powerful organisation like the Sicilian Mafia. That was why Michele Sindona, with a fake passport in the name of Joseph Bonamic, landed in Palermo that summer with John Gambino of Cherry Hill and Giacomo Vitale, the Mafia and freemason brother-in-law of Stefano Bontate.

Michele Sindona had to persuade his 'friends from Palermo' to forget their rancour, to throw themselves into the adventure, to support him, using their methods. He had to persuade them that he was no use to them dead, but he might be useful alive. He had to persuade them not to see the money they were accumulating with the heroin trade as eternal and untouchable. Where would their billions of dollars end up if someone like him was thrown out of the world of international high finance?

Don Michele was convincing. He managed to come back to New York and face his destiny – alive.

MY DEAR STEFANO, YOU'RE A DEAD MAN

That time the tax collectors of Salemi didn't waste much time on pleasantries. A quick hug, a few words of greeting. Tommaso Buscetta, Masino, sat down on a leather sofa. They poured him a glass of whisky. Ignazio Salvo was pacing up and down the room like a wild animal in a cage. His cousin Nino Salvo threw himself down on an armchair and didn't waste time chattering: 'Let's declare war on those four *viddani*.'

Masino looked first at one, then at the other. He said nothing. Ignazio's eyes gleamed with hatred and a stiffness in his neck and shoulders emphasised his aggression. He said: 'We've got to finish them off. They don't respect anybody. They think they can issue orders in Palermo like they did up in their mountains . . . They think they can fuck with us like they can fuck with the shepherds of Corleone.'

The invitation to go back to Palermo had reached Tommaso Buscetta in jail in Turin. He was finishing a sentence for drug trafficking. Masino left prison that same day. It was a bright day in June.

When the plane made its descent he saw the austere profile

of Montepellegrino, the soft outline of the coast, the blue sea. He was gripped by the emotion that filled him every time he came back to Sicily. Masino loved Palermo, he loved it with the passion of a teenager falling in love for the first time. Anywhere in the world, if he closed his eyes, he could smell its scent of orange blossom; he could remember the sweetness of nights fragrant with jasmine and the strong smell of spices rising from the markets.

'Masino, you alone can do it, you have to give us a hand. We've got to make Riina understand that we're not idiots like Don Michele Navarra,' pleaded Nino Salvo, who worshipped Buscetta like a god.

Tommaso Buscetta barely listened to him. He was thinking about his old Palermo that no longer exited, about *his* Cosa Nostra that had changed so completely. He was thinking that, when he was a *combinato*, to make a man of honour you had to send letters to all the families in the whole of Sicily, to see if anyone had anything to say or pass on about the foot soldier. They could also raise objections: this one's a distant relative of an army officer, this other one's the nephew of a magistrate . . . Cosa Nostra didn't want anything to do with uniforms or people who got their salaries from the state.

'But today,' Masino thought, 'to be a man of honour you just have to know how to shoot. Not in the old days – back then you didn't need to know how to shoot. Some people did, sure. Some people did, but it wasn't something you asked or demanded of a man of honour. Lawyers, princes, engineers were made men of honour and they weren't sent to shoot; they were made Mafiosi because they were useful as what they were. Some people had estates, some could cure injuries, some could get you out of jail, and they were all united in friendship. How lovely it was to feel you were friends with someone you'd never met. You could go to a city, anywhere at all, and you'd be welcomed like a brother. They went with you; you could feel their affection and a deep sense of respect.'

Nino Salvo paused. 'So, what do you say, Masino?'

Buscetta gave a start. Sadness and nostalgia stuck to him like his shirt to his skin. He swallowed down a mouthful of whisky.

'I say it's not worth it . . .'

'Not worth it!' Nino said, almost shouting, his cheeks red with rage. 'It isn't worth making the *viddani* pay for kidnapping my son-in-law? They didn't even let me find the bones, those bastards. It isn't worth presenting them with a bill for what they did to Peppe Di Cristina, to Pippo Calderone, to so many of our mates who are no longer alive, and it's their fault? Fine, it's not worth it for the past. And what about the future? Tell me, is it not worth getting rid of them for the future, now that they've got it into their heads to start getting cocky here in Palermo? Tell me, Masino . . .'

'No, it's not worth it even for the future. Our lovely Cosa Nostra has no future, Nino! Get that into your head!'

Buscetta had been in Palermo for a few days. He had seen how rich the rank-and-file Mafiosi had become, and how the money had gone to their heads. They couldn't think of anything but buying, consuming, spending that mountain of money that each of them wanted to make even higher – all the way from the sea to the sanctuary of Santa Rosalia at the top of Montepellegrino. He went on: 'It isn't Cosa Nostra any more, Nino, it's not ours. It belongs to petty thieves like Pippo Calò and Michele Greco – people U Curtu has connected to strings so that they'll raise their heads or lower them at his command. Stefano Bontate told me that Michele never opens his mouth at Commission meetings. He just bobs his head up and down. He's a coward, a chicken, and a total slave to the Corleonesi . . .'

'Have you seen him?' Ignazio asked.

'Who?'

'Calò.'

'Yes, he called me in.'

'And what did he say?'

'Nothing clear. I worked out that he wanted to make me a vice-head of the family. He doesn't like the idea of me leaving Palermo. Perhaps he wants to put me in his place on the Commission because he's had enough of the Corleonesi ... Perhaps he wants to whack me when it suits him, and it's easier if I'm here. He told me he's going to be refurbishing the historical centre of Palermo along with Vito Ciancimino and Totò U Curtu. He offered me a slice of the cake.'

'And what did you say?'

'I thanked him and told him I don't like sweet things.'

Nino didn't laugh. Buscetta didn't laugh.

Masino had done what he could to make peace between the Palermitans. If they were united, the Corleonesi would be as irritating as a mosquito. But they weren't united. And they never would be again. The heroin money had killed any chance of that. Buscetta was sure of it, and yet the attempt had been made. He had organised a meeting between Pippo Calò, Stefano Bontate and Totuccio Inzerillo. They had seen each other at a Pavesi grill on the motorway between Naples and Rome. A lot of lovely words, a lot of smiles and a lot of promises. They had sworn to consult one another before any meetings of the Commission, to mess up the plans of the Corleonesi and the Grecos. 'I haven't even got time to turn round and that bastard Calò had already betrayed me, putting my son in jail after giving him 10 million from the proceeds of a kidnapping ...' Masino told his cousins from Salemi.

Then Buscetta got to his feet.

'I'm off, Nino. I'm off, Ignazio. Cosa Nostra is cursed. The *viddani* will never know the meaning of respect or honour. On the contrary, they will teach the Palermitans the meaning of betrayal and *tragedia*. Everyone will get lost behind the drugs trade, behind the money coming in from America, until greed and rancour will lead to fathers and sons being killed together like bastards, and the right eye will hate the left. I'm off. I hope to hear from you in Brazil.'

A few days later Tommaso Buscetta met Stefano Bontate and Salvatore Inzerillo at Fondo Magliocco. He looked at his friends, and they seemed to have gone mad. They hated Totò Riina the way you hate the man who raped your mother. It was a kind of monomaniacal delirium that blinded any intelligence or lucidity. They thought about it day and night. In fact U Curtu possessed their souls.

Stefano had said with a crazed gleam in his eye: 'I'm going to kill U Curtu. It's the only way to get things working again. I'm going to kill him during a meeting of the Commission, in front of everybody. I can already imagine the scene. He's sitting there in front of me. I get up slowly, he doesn't notice, I clutch my pistol. Bam. Bam. I shoot him in the face, and that's the end of him. We'll leave him behind us for ever . . .'

Buscetta looked at him as you might look at a man who says he knows how to fly as he dangles from the window of a skyscraper. He said, 'Pull yourself together, my dear Stefano. You're a dead man. I see you already, Stefano; I see you dead.'

THE BUTCHER OF PALERMO

IT WASN'T JUST HATRED

After Boris Giuliano, Cesare Terranova died. At the end of the summer, sixty-six days later.

Salvatore Riina didn't need to close his eyes to see the judge's wide face, hear his voice and the brusque questions he had asked thirteen years before at Ucciardone prison. U Curtu hated him, but that wasn't why he had him killed.

Cesare Terranova died because he was dangerous. He was the only Italian magistrate who knew the Corleonesi, their families, their ferocity, the countryside where they had lived and where they were hidden. Cesare Terranova was perhaps the only servant of the state to have followed, from start to finish, the rise of Totò Riina and Luciano Liggio. From the estate of Strasatto to the murder of Michele Navarra; from the victorious war fought in Corleone to the power that those rough peasants had acquired in the shadow of the Palermitan aristocracy of the Bontate, Inzerillo and Di Maggio families. The judge had taken charge of their story, their secrets and their psychology.

During those years U Curtu had never lost sight of Cesare Terranova, and knew perfectly well what he was going around Italy saying. Terranova was telling the four winds that there was no difference between the 'old' and the 'new' Mafia. It was Mafia, just Mafia. And as such, it was to be defeated with more accurate investigations, more efficient police, harsher laws and more severe trials. Totò Riina had no doubts: Cesare Terranova would strike again. If they gave him time to sit on his chair as a judge in the law courts in Palermo, he would start his inquiries at the precise point where he had interrupted them to become an MP. And he had interrupted them in Corleone, around those five years of Mafia wars, around those sixty-four names, the accused that he had brought before the courts, and all of whom had then been acquitted in the Court of Assizes.

U Curtu was sure that Terranova would resume committal proceedings with the dozens of reports, hundreds of pages and thousands of names that had already drawn blood from Cosa Nostra in Catanzaro and Bari.

'Binnu, *chistu fa dannu assai*, this guy's done enough damage, he's got it in for us,' U Curtu confided in his inseparable friend Provenzano. The judge Terranova had to die. He died.

It was the third time that September that he left home to go to the Palace of Justice. He had given up being an MP for the independent left. After his second period in office he wanted to return to his job as a judge. At the higher council of the magistracy they told him there was a post available as an instructing magistrate in Palermo. It was an important post. In that office anyone who wanted investigations could take them to their conclusion. Cesare Terranova was happy on the morning of 25 September. He still had the pure air of the Madonie Mountains in his lungs, after three months in Petralia Sottana. He had rested, he had relaxed, and doubled his desire to live, to act, to work.

Marshal Lenin Mancuso, his driver, right-hand man and bodyguard since the early 1960s, was waiting for him on the corner of the street, in Via Rutelli. The marshal was in his car. He saw the judge and patiently pulled the car around; he knew that Cesare Terranova wanted to drive as usual. The judge went and stood in front of the car, while the marshal opened the passenger door. Neither of them noticed the man with the floral shirt walking up behind them. He was the first to fire, with a Winchester carbine. The other two started immediately afterwards, with a 38 and a 357 magnum. Within a few seconds the car was as bloody as a slaughterhouse. The man with the floral shirt didn't want to take any risks, and before he left he fired the last shot at close range, into Cesare Terranova's neck.

Totò Riina's face looked as if it was made of stone, and it stayed stony when he heard one word in a faint voice down the phone: '*Murìu*', he's dead. And others would die too. He had confessed as much to Binnu: 'We have to act on our own. If we start talking to the Palermitans, blood will turn to acid and the cops will eat us alive. *Futtimuninni*, we don't care about them, Binnu; let's go it alone . . . The Commission only makes decisions when it suits the Palermitans. When you waste a cop and you haven't talked to the people in Palermo, what are the people in Palermo going to do? Resuscitate the cop? *Futtimuninni*, we don't care about Stefano and Totuccio. For now . . .'

The next one to die was Piersanti Mattarella, the president of the Regional Assembly, and after Mattarella it was Captain Emanuele Basile. It was the feast of the Crucifixion in Monreale. The captain was in dress uniform, walking across the square holding his five-month-old baby girl to his chest. There were three hitmen, three 'sons of the family': Vincenzo Puccio, Giuseppe Madonia and Armando Bonanno. They killed the captain in the middle of the crowd. The officer had made the same mistake as Boris Giuliano: he had come too close to the Corleonesi. He had started following the traces of the dirty money from heroin, and started an investigation where the sheriff had left off.

From Monreale he had headed towards Corleone, towards San Giuseppe Jato, towards Roccamena. He had found clues that started from the lair of Via Pecori Giraldi and reached all the way to Luchino Bagarella and the bank accounts of U Curtu. That was Captain Basile's mistake. But the Corleonesi had made one too.

The three hitmen were caught two kilometres from Monreale, on the road that went down to the military airport in Boccadifalco. Vincenzo Puccio was a man of honour of the family of Michele Greco, Giuseppe Madonia was the son of *zu Ciccio*, the historical ally of Totò Riina in Palermo, and Armando Bonanno was a member of the family of Piana dei Colli.

'There's the proof,' shouted Totuccio Inzerillo to his uncle Saro Si Maggio. 'You wanted the proof that it was them, that they had their feet in Palermo? Now that you've written it in the paper. Michele Greco, Ciccio Madonia and Totò Riina are the same thing; they walk arm in arm, they run together . . . they don't give a damn about the provincial Commission. Uncle, we're still wasting time with rules, negotiations, discussions . . . they aren't listening to us. Lead is what they need, lead.'

Totuccio Inzerillo wanted to demonstrate his strength to the whole of Palermo. He wanted to make the *viddani* understand that the family of Passo di Rigano, his family, was also capable of confronting the state, of carrying out a 'big' murder. Totuccio chose his victim. It was Gaetano Costa, the chief state prosecutor. A month before, the magistrate had signed twenty-two arrest warrants against men of honour of his *cosca*.

Gaetano Costa – it was late afternoon on 6 August – was walking along Via Cavour. He stopped to look at the posters for a cinema, then turned towards the big newsagent's and bookshop that occupied the whole of the pavement. The assassin fired a pistol in his face.

Stefano Bontate had a particular relationship with Totuccio Inzerillo. They were associates, they were also friends, but he also treated him with caution. Totuccio talked too much, he was a hothead: he certainly wasn't like his uncle Saro. But that day Bontate couldn't control himself, he couldn't keep a tone of reproach out of his voice.

'Fuck, Totuccio, did you really have to do that?'

'Yes, I had to do it.'

'But I ask you: what's the point of shooting judges and cops? We're supposed to reach an agreement with the state, otherwise they'll all be down on us . . .'

'And who thinks about the state, Stefano? Wake up, I'm thinking about the Corleonesi. They're not the only ones capable of killing . . .'

'You shouldn't have done it.'

'Why? U Curtu can do whatever he likes and I can't? The Corleonesi can and us lot from Passo di Rigano can't? And who are the bosses, them or us?'

'Totuccio, you have to tell me the truth, did you have prosecutor Costa killed because of the arrest warrants he'd signed against your family?'

'No, Stefano, that wasn't why I had him killed . . . You know, jail is jail and sooner or other we end up there . . . No, I had him killed to make the Corleonesi understand . . .'

That was how Cosa Nostra was. In killing a magistrate, one faction was measuring itself against another. Within ten months the two 'sides' lined up within the Sicilian Mafia had assassinated the investigating magistrate Cesare Terranova and the chief prosecutor Gaetano Costa. For different reasons, for different interests. Alive, together, in those days in the early 1980s, Terranova and Costa could have made a revolution in Palermo.

THE WRONGS OF THE FALCON

The night's frost had scorched the mandarin trees of Ciaculli. It was a cold January, the coldest of the last twenty years. It was snowing in Palermo; the red domes of the church of San Giovanni degli Eremiti were covered with snow; a gleaming white mantle covered the crests of Monte Grifone and the hills of Bellolampo. That day Stefano Bontate was at La Favarella. With him was Totuccio Contorno, his right-hand man, his shadow, his faithful dog.

'The time has come,' Stefano Bontate repeated to himself, out loud, as if making a solemn promise to himself. To fix it in his mind for ever, to free himself from a nightmare.

'I'll kill him with my own bare hands. You, Michele, just have to tell me where I can find U Curtu.'

Michele Greco didn't dare to open his mouth. The Pope had thrown water on the fire at meeting after meeting. This time he didn't even try. He had never seen Bontate so calmly determined to settle his scores with the Corleonese; he had understood that there was no turning back. Stefano gazed blank-eyed and uninterested at a non-existent point among the trees. Totuccio Contorno moved away and left him alone with his thoughts.

'U Curtu must die,' Stefano Bontate said in a faint voice.

The phrase had been festering in his throat for years. It was an obsession that was devouring his life. Since the kidnapping of Luigi Corleo, Salvo's brother-in-law, he should have freed himself from Totò Riina. But he had bowed to the rules he had been taught. A man of honour always tells the truth to another man of honour. He had asked U Curtu if the Corleonesi were behind Corleo's disappearance. Totò Riina had told him he didn't know anything about it. The *viddano* was lying and Bontate knew it. But he had to prove it, he had to show the boss of the Commission to request – and be granted – permission to kill him. It was another sacred rule. The lie about Corleo had only been the first of many that U Curtu had told. Then Bontate had a moment of vexation. He had been told that the Corleonesi called him 'the Falcon'. He of all people, known in all corners of Sicily as the 'Prince of Villagrazia' for his style, for his elegant manners, his old-style way of being a Mafioso. He, the son of Don Paolino . . .

From that day in 1981 Stefano Bontate looked for Totò Riina, to kill him. He talked to Totuccio Inzerillo about it, and the rumour spread among the men of honour of their families.

There was just one order: find U Curtu. But U Curtu was a ghost. Bontate and Inzerillo sent ambassadors to all the suburbs of Palermo. They went to Francesco Madonia in San Lorenzo, they went to Giuseppe Giacomo Gambino in Resuttana, to Raffaele Ganci at La Noce. They were U Curtu's puppets.

'Where is *u zu* Totò?' asked Bontate.

'He's left,' they replied.

And they smiled, they always smiled. Totò Riina had chosen his men well, and taught them that you had to smile, you always had to smile whatever happened, even if the walls of Jericho were falling down. Then Bontate and Inzerillo had U Curtu's foot soldiers followed. They tailed Gambino for weeks. Nothing. They followed the sons of Francesco Madonia. Nothing. They kept an eye on the Ganci family. Nothing at all.

They changed tactics, and organised units that scoured the city from Piana dei Colli to Croceverde, from Falsomiele to Pagliarelli. They called trusted foot soldiers from Catania to Palermo. They loaded them into cars that drove up and down, up and down the suburbs. The *picciotti* didn't even know who was supposed to die. The bosses told him it was 'an important person'.

Turi Pillera from Catania was quick with his hands; he knew

how to fire a gun. When Totuccio Inzerillo invited him to get into his car to 'go for a spin' Turi Pillera thought his time had come. The world of Cosa Nostra was one of fear and betrayal. The Catanese tried to remember where he might have made a mistake, what he might have done that was so serious that it meant he had to die. His hands were sweaty and cold when Totuccio said to him, 'We have to waste a big shot. If we find him, we ice him, okay?' Turi Pillera remained impassive, but his heart was thumping in his chest.

'Totuccio, that's why I'm here. I'm at your disposal,' the Catanese replied, feeling as if he'd come back from the dead.

The car darted along the streets of Palermo and Turi Pillera noticed that Inzerillo was glowering. He was tense. He was smoking one cigarette after another. He was looking around like a wild beast in search of prey. Totuccio was at the wheel of a flame-red BMW. Pillera was in the back seat. In the front, next to Inzerillo, there was a man of honour from Passo di Rigano, Salvatore Montalto. The *picciotto* was relaxed, as calm as someone who's going to the beach at San Vito Lo Capo for a swim, not to 'ice important people'. In the dusk of late afternoon, the Catanese even thought he saw the hint of a smile on Salvatore Montalto's lips.

Turi Pillera wasn't mistaken: Montalto was a traitor, one of U Curtu's spies. He told Totò Riina, he told him everything. And he also told him they would be searching a few Palermo suburbs that evening. Salvatore Montalto was deriving malicious enjoyment from Totuccio Inzerillo's agitation.

For four weeks all attempts to surprise the Corleonese in one of his refuges or in the street came to nothing. Stefano Bontate decided to set a trap for him. He talked for a long time to Michele Greco and persuaded him to make U Curtu agree to a meeting at Fondo Magliocco. Stefano Bontate was by now incapable of reasoning. He still thought the Pope of Ciaculli was above all factions; he hadn't noticed that he had taken the side of the Corleonesi. Totò Riina sent a message to say that he would go to the meeting.

The next evening the most valorous men of honour of the family of Santa Maria del Gesù, the ones who were best at killing, arrived at Fondo Magliocco. Totuccio Contorno was there, and the Pullarà brothers. And Totuccio Inzerillo and his men from Passo di Rigano came too. There were fourteen of them waiting for U Curtu. Half of them – six or seven – were Judases. They waited for a long time. Then they heard a car horn and opened the gate. It was dark already, at eight in the evening. Stefano Bontate ran towards the white Mercedes that was coming into his estate. He opened the door. He almost threw himself into the Mercedes. He was already prepared to go for U Curtu's throat. He wanted to kill him with his bare hands, in front of everyone.

Totò Riina wasn't in the car. The only people who had gone to Fondo Magliocco were his butchers. And there they were, sitting in the Mercedes staring with a smile at Stefano Bontate, whose face was purple with rage. It was the first time his people had seen Bontate at Fondo Magliocco.

The Falcon had organised a plot against Riina. Riina had known about the plot and hadn't reported it to the Commission. Instead U Curtu had given the boss of Santa Maria del Gesù enough rope to hang himself. He had played with him as a cat plays with a mouse. Everyone could testify that Stefano Bontate wanted to kill the Corleonese. Everyone could say that Stefano had violated the rules of Cosa Nostra. That was the most serious crime as far as the Mafia was concerned, and the sentence was death. Stefano Bontate and all the men of honour who had taken part in the plot were marked men.

Wearing his priestly expression, Michele Greco said to the

other bosses in the Commission: 'Stefano put himself on the wrong side.'

THE TOMATOES WEREN'T YET RIPE

There was a stone arch, and on the arch there was a tabernacle. The white avenue started there, at a bend in the road which climbed towards Altofonte Park. The villa was two hundred metres on from there. It was a rustic construction protected by a high wall. After the electric gate, a gravel drive passed through well-tended orchards planted with apple, medlar and pear trees. Then the drive turned around the house, to the garage.

Leoluca Bagarella parked his car.

Totò Riina was working in the vegetable garden. He was bent over between two rows of tomatoes that were still too sharp to eat. They could just see his back. U Curtu was clean shaven, and wearing an aquamarine tartan polo shirt that revealed his paunch. U Curtu's oldest children, Maria Concetta and Giovanni Francesco were going up and down the slide beside the vegetable garden. Totò's first daughter was already seven, and his first son five. Ninetta Bagarella appeared at the French windows of the kitchen on the ground floor. She was holding Giuseppe Salvatore by the hand and little Lucia in her arms. Ninetta greeted her brother. Luchino said to his brother-in-law: 'It's all ready.'

'I'm ready too, we can go now,' U Curtu replied.

Totò Riina was leaving Palermo, to take refuge in a country house belonging to Bernardo Brusca, trusty Brusca. It was in San Giuseppe Jato, thirty kilometres from the villa with the high wall and only twelve kilometres from his own Corleone.

The previous evening they had had their last operational

meeting at the restaurant La Nave. Raffaele Ganci was wolfing down caponata – aubergine, tomato and capers – with bread, while repeating for the fifteenth time the details of the operation, reminding everyone of the part they had to play. Totò Riina listened in silence and lowered his head in a sign of approval. U Curtu had only one problem: he had to go into hiding. Palermo was about to turn into a city at war.

The men of honour had already been on a war footing for several days. They had taken possession of a flat in Via Messina Marine. They ate, slept and lived there. They were Pino Greco Scarpuzzedda, Mario Prestifilippo, Nino Madonia, Giuseppe Lucchese (*u Lucchiseddu*), Nino Rotolo and Giuseppe Giacomo Gambino. They spent their time playing cards, chatting and lubricating their guns. They had an arsenal: 12-calibre rifles loaded with shot, 357 Magnums, 38-calibre pistols, thousands of rounds of ammunition. In a case they also had two Kalashnikovs acquired by Nitto Santapaola's Catanesi. It was the first time that the Palermo Mafiosi had used the lethally powerful AK47.

Everything was ready. The stolen cars had been hidden in a warehouse on Corso dei Mille. They had already been stuffed with newspaper so that they would burn more easily immediately after the crime. The *picciotti* were just waiting for the *battuta*, the last bit of information, the news that would reveal where the designated victim would be, and with whom. And above all at what time. It was supposed to be delivered by Giovanbattista Pullarà and Giovanni Teresi *u pacchiuni*, 'the fat guy'. They were the two taitors of Santa Maria del Gesù, the 'Judases'. The christ they were going to betray was Stefano Bontate, the most powerful Mafioso in Palermo.

They betrayed him on 22 April. Raffaele Ganci announced it to the *Picciotti* on Via Messina Marine. He said only: 'It's set for tomorrow.'

Nino Madonia replied excitedly: 'What do you think, is Stefano going to like the *pocket coffee*?'

His *pocket coffee* sweets (a popular kind of coffee-flavoured chocolate) were the bullets of his AK47.

On 23 April 1981 Stefano Bontate turned forty-two. Glasses were still being clinked in the cottage on the old farm of Aloi when the *picciotti* got moving. A little cortège of cars and motorbikes sped along the Palermo coast road. The Honda with Pino Greco and Giuseppe Lucchese was at their head, followed by a Fiat 131, a Fiat 128 and an A112, all laden with U Curtu's butchers. The cars reached Via Oreto and slowly arranged themselves around the four sides of Piazza di Falsomiele. The Honda drove up and down the streets of the suburb waiting for the Falcon to arrive.

Stefano Bontate left the farm at half-past eight in the evening to go home and change. After the family reunion he wanted to allow himself a more intimate celebration. He got into his brand new Giulietta Super with its test plate, one of fifteen hundred models made. He set off at full speed along the narrow streets of the suburb. The Honda intercepted him just before the ring road. The motorbike slipped along the right-hand side of the Giulietta. Out of the corner of his eye Bontate saw that the passenger sitting behind the driver was getting up, with his feet on the footboards and his hands holding something. He just had time to turn round and reach for the pistol under his armpit. The first rifle blast hit him in the face, as did the second and then the third. Stefano Bontate fell against the wheel. The Giulietta continued on its way and crashed against a low stone wall.

The Honda turned into Piazza di Falsomiele and Pino Greco Scarpuzzedda raised an arm. All the others, inside the car, knew what he meant. They turned on their engines and set off again. There were no longer only three cars. A little way off there was also a rust-coloured 126. The man sitting in the driver's seat was Luchino Bagarella, and U Curtu was next to him.

That evening Totò Riina ate cheese under the pergola of the country house of San Giuseppe Jato. The only person with him was Bernardo Brusca. U Curtu wanted to talk. He said: 'The Palermitans still haven't understood who the Corleonesi are. And when they do work it out, it will be too late for them. By then Palermo will already be ours. All of Sicily will be ours.'

Then Totò Riina got to his feet. He was tired, he was yawning. He set off towards home. Suddenly he turned towards Brusca. And before he disappeared behind the door a hiss issued from his mouth: 'The Falcon is dead, now it's the other guy's turn . . .'

FOUR BILLION REASONS

Totuccio Inzerillo didn't weep for Stefano Bontate. Cosa Nostra didn't weep. They didn't even weep for friends. If necessary they avenged them. And that was what Totuccio Inzerillo, the head of the family of Passo di Rigano and heir to a Magia dynasty of Sicilians, Americans and Sicilian-Americans, decided to do. With time Totuccio Inzerillo would even have sorted out the Corleonesi. There was no longer any reason to get bogged down in diplomacy and hypocrisy, to pursue the duplicities of Michele Greco or the prudence of Uncle Saro Di Maggio.

'If only they'd listened to me three years ago . . .' he thought.

But there was no point having regrets. The only thing to do was maintain one's sangfroid. The only precaution he took was an armoured car. He didn't change his habits, he didn't hide, he didn't surround himself with an armed escort.

'U Curtu won't kill me, he can't kill me,' he admitted with a laugh to his family from Passo di Rigano.

The month before, Totuccio had sent a cargo to America. It consisted of two hundred and more kilos of 'white stuff' destined for his cousins in New Jersey. Fifty kilograms of that heroin belonged to U Curtu. Totuccio still owed 4 billion lire 'to that bastard from Corleone'.

'Four billion reasons to keep me alive and well – he'll see to it that my health is guaranteed,' Totuccio said on the phone to his brother Pietro, who had called him from Brooklyn. 'U Curtu sent me a *picciotto* . . . I told him the money hadn't yet arrived from America. Before it gets here, U Curtu will be under the ground, being eaten by the worms.'

In that spring of 1981 Totuccio Inzerillo went on trafficking with his relatives on the other side of the ocean.

His American cousin, John Gambino, had told him: 'Our grandfathers invented Las Vegas; they built something big. And as for us, what can we do with all this money that we're earning with heroin?'

Totuccio Inzerillo listened to him. John explained: 'Another Las Vegas, that's what we can do! We take Atlantic City in New Jersey, we fill it with casinos, discos, brothels and hotels and we build the east coast Las Vegas.' The project took form in Philadelphia; the Inzerillos had guaranteed themselves twenty per cent of an operation worth 130 billion. Totuccio already felt his share was in his pocket. It was an impressive investment, a river of money that would flood Via Castellana, the street that bisected Passo di Rigano.

Totuccio Inzerillo was so euphoric about his American investment that he couldn't sleep at night. He looked numb. And he couldn't see what was happening right in front of his nose, in his suburb, among his own men. He would stake everything on the loyalty of his *picciotti*. And he would make a terrible mistake. His three *capidecino* had been servants to U Curtu for years. Totò Montalto had also betrayed his brother to become a *capomandamento* in Villabate, as Riina had promised him. Salvatore Buscemi wanted to take Inzerillo's place in Passo di Rigano. And then there was Francesco Bonura, who had got it into his head to be *capofamiglia* in Uditore. Totò Riina had cultivated their ambitions in silence and in secret discussions. The hatred felt by those men was as ripe as a grape at harvest time. U Curtu just had to patiently collect the bunches.

The Corleonesi also saw each other again at the restaurant La Nave. Totò Riina wanted Totuccio dead straight away. And the 4 billion? 'Bullshit . . . with all that's gonna come later,' he confided to Raffaele Ganci.

It was Giuseppe Montalto, Totò Montalto's son, who delivered the crucial information on the night of 10 to 11 May: 'Tomorrow morning Totuccio Inzerillo will go to his woman . . .'

The attack group was ready to go. The *picciotti* knew who Totuccio's woman was, they knew she lived in a tower block on Via Brunelleschi. Would the Kalashnikov be able to pierce the armoured windows of Totuccio's Alfetta? The *piccotti* proved that one during the night by firing them at the reinforced window of a jeweller's shop on Via Libertà.

'The *pocket coffee* works, it works . . .' Nino Madonia reported later.

It was ten minutes to midday in Via Brunelleschi. Giuseppe Marchese parked his van beside Totuccio Inzerillo's armoured Alfetta and went on the lookout. When he saw him coming out of a door of the block at number 50 he alerted the others: 'He's here.'

Pino Greco Scarpuzzedda let Totuccio Inzerillo take the last few steps of his life. Then all of a sudden he burst open the sliding door of the van and started firing. Giuseppe Marchese had stayed at the wheel and saw the flashes and bullets passing just in front of his face. Totoccio Inzerillo fell three metres away from the useless armoured Alfetta.

The death of the boss of Passo di Rigano was celebrated a few days later in a villa in Monreale. It was a balmy evening. The little crowd that had gathered in the countryside were fired up by the warm wind heralding the summer and the bottles of *Monsciandò* (Moët & Chandon). Nino Madonia was raving about the precision of the *pocket coffee*, and Giuseppe Giacomo Gambino was mocking Giuseppe Marchese, the youngest of Totò Riina's hitmen, a wild young man that U Curtu had been keeping an eye on for several months. Gambino said to Marchese, laughing at him: '*Piuzzu*, what's up? Still got a whistling in your ears?'

The bosses were a little way off, far from all the others. They were talking, sitting around a table. Their voice was a murmur. When they fell silent, they looked at the foot soldiers of the new army they'd just formed. U Curtu was at the head of the table. On his right was Bernardo Brusca from San Giuseppe Jato, on his left, Nené Geraci from Partinico. Totò Riina was counting on two old villagers like himself. And above all he was counting on his butchers. He knew they would hand him the heads of his enemies and give him power within Cosa Nostra.

The *viddano* of Corleone wanted to reorganise the Sicilian Mafia. He had a plan. He didn't even talk to Binnu Provenzano about it. But it was still a bit too early to show his cards. First of all he had to get rid of all the Palermitans.

TOO MUCH ENVY, TOO MANY DODGY THINGS . . .

All the snakes that U Curtu had bred left their lairs and went around the world killing people. You just had to be called Bontate or Inzerillo, Buscetta or Badalamenti, or have shown respect to those bosses. Those who refused to mix with the Corleonesi died. Those who refused to salute U Curtu's attack-dogs died. Sons, cousins, nephews, fathers died. They were 'interrogated', tortured, strangled, reduced to ashes on a gridiron. Or dissolved in acid or thrown into the sea with their feet in concrete.

It was called a Mafia war, but it wasn't a war. In wars the grief is divided in two: people die on both sides, in both armies. In the slaughter that was starting inside Cosa Nostra, the dead – like tunas in the annual *slaughter* – were all of a single species: the Palermitans.

Twenty-one Inzerillos died. Pino Greco Scarpuzzedda repeated a litany: 'Not so much as a seed must be left of them.' One day he kidnapped Giuseppe Inzerillo. He was only fifteen. He was Totuccio's son, who had promised to avenge his father. Pino Greco cut off his right arm with a sea-urchin fisherman's knife. And before he finished, he said, '*Mischinu*, you wretch, now how are you going to shoot Totò Riina, eh?'

The pain and fear had already killed Giuseppe. But Pino Greco went on talking to him as if he was alive. He insulted and taunted him, and shot a corpse in the back of the neck. The body of the youngest Inzerillo was dissolved in a tub of hydrochloric acid. His uncle Santino – Totuccio's brother – was lured into a trap by the same men of honour from Passo di Rigano. When they saw him going into a fuel store with his uncle Calogero, U Curtu's foot soldiers got ready and grabbed him. Santino yelled at the top of his voice. He threatened his killers. He had gone mad. His rage stopped him from feeling fear, his madness made death sweeter. He and his uncle were strangled with cords. Then Santino ended up on a grill, two metres square, at the country house of Salvatore Liga, nicknamed *Tatuneddu*.

A few days later, in the boot of a Cadillac on the other side of the Atlantic, they found the corpse of Pietro Inzerillo wrapped in a plastic bag. He was *incaprettato*, killed the way lambs are slaughtered in the days leading up to Easter: hands and feet tied with a rope running around their necks. When the muscles of the legs go, the rope stretches and grips the throat. Death comes slowly, by self-strangulation. In Pietro Inzerillo's mouth they found twenty dollars. Another ten were found between his balls. Pietro, who was 'half a man', had had 'eyes bigger than his stomach'.

The Corleonesi killed eleven members of the Badalamenti family. Even the ones who had nothing to do with trafficking and uncle Tano's business, like his nephew Nino. They pursued him halfway across Europe and found him in Germany. They tortured him, killed him, cut him into pieces. But the family of Santa Maria del Gesù disappeared. Out of a hundred and twenty men of honour, sixty died. Some betrayed their family, a very few managed to flee. They were known as *i scappati*, the ones that got away.

In that year, 1981, almost five hundred people died. And the Corleonesi killed another five hundred in the twelve months of 1982 and the first four months of 1983. There had never been such blood, never such ferocity. The rule was different: killing only when it was necessary, when it was useful.

Not a day went by when Masino Buscetta didn't receive news of death from Sicily. Masino had predicted it. He had known the *viddani* would end up like that. But he still couldn't explain such cruelty; he couldn't understand that pointless massacre. The Falcon had been killed now. And Totuccio Inzerillo had suffered the same fate. Why, why were they so unrelenting?

Tommaso Buscetta phoned Palermo, looking for Nino Salvo, the 'tax collector'. Pointless. Nino was in hiding in Greece. Then Masino called Salvo's brother-in-law, the engineer Ignazio Lo Presti.

'Hello, I'm . . . how are you?'

'What do you think . . . life's amazing.'

'I know.'

'We're going crazy here.'

'I heard, I heard . . .'

'There's too much dodgy stuff, too nasty, my dear brother . . . you no longer know who to turn to . . . Too much envy, too many betrayals, too much dodgy stuff.'

'But I'll keep on calling . . . it should be something confidential . . .'

'If you think of coming . . . we can organise it for you . . .'

'First I want to talk to Nino. Find him for me . . . I'll keep on calling . . . then we'll see what happens on the way back.'

Tommaso Buscetta was the only one who could do anything to stop Totò Riina. That was what the powerful *esattori* of Salemi, Nino and Ignazio Salvo, thought. It was what U Curtu thought as well. Masino could feel the Corleonesi breathing down his neck. One day he found out that Michele Greco had called New York and spoken to the Sicilian-Americans. 'Don't worry about what's happening here, we'll send you regular tasks but you'll tell me where to find Masino . . .'

Months passed, and the Salvos bowed to the new bosses of Cosa Nostra. So did Salvo Lima, the Christian Democrat who was linked to Bontate. So did the Caruanas and the Cutreras, the biggest drugs traffickers in South America. And so did John Gambino, who hurried to Italy, to Palermo, to meet U Curtu. When he went back to America he advised the 'villagers' to think not of the dead, but of the living.

And he said, 'Corleone's in charge now.'

Tommaso Buscetta witnessed the beginning of the end of the Cosa Nostra that he had known. The Corleonesi began the massacre to bring him out into the open. First they kidnapped his Brazilian brother-in-law, Homero Guimares Junior, the brother of his wife, Almejda. Then U Curtu made Antonino and Benedetto, Masino's sons, disappear. They were also 'interrogated' about their father's hiding place. They didn't talk, so they were burned alive. On one of those bloody Christmas Eves, they killed Buscetta's father-in-law in a pizzeria, as well as his brother and nephew in the family glassworks.

'Why, why?' Masino asked in desperation.

THE SHADOW OF THE ENTITY

Life had taught Tommaso Buscetta that rancour is a useless emotion. It took away your clarity of mind and wiped out your rationality. Masino struggled not to be overwhelmed by fear, pain and hatred.

He said to himself: 'I have other children to protect, I have a wife to defend and I have no weapons or friends who could help me. Only my brain can save me.'

He remained level-headed. He thought: 'The slaughter in Palermo can't be explained only by the ferocity of the Corleonesi . . . The Corleonesi have always been hyenas who devour others as they have devoured themselves . . . But this ferocity wasn't there before . . . absolutely . . . not even on their part. There are things happening in Palermo that go beyond Mafia problems . . . beyond Cosa Nostra . . . beyond Totò Riina. I see another hand involved, I see the shadow of an Entity . . . Behind or beside or above or below, somewhere there is that same Entity that moved to keep Aldo Moro from being saved . . .

'I was in jail at the time . . . Bontate told me to approach the Red Brigades to see if anything could be done . . . Stefano insisted and Pippo Calò resisted. Stefano's political friends wanted Moro free, Calò's political friends wanted him dead . . . Eventually Calò also said to him, "Stefano, don't you understand that the top men in your party don't want to save that guy's skin?"

'That's when strange things start happening, that year . . . and they continue the year after. The year after, I was still in jail in Cuneo. Stefano sent me a message, telling me to talk to the terrorists. If General Dalla Chiesa was killed somewhere in Italy, would the terrorists take the blame? And send out one of their fliers? That was what I had to ask. I chatted up a Brigade member who was in a cell with me, and who was important because he'd taken part in the Moro kidnapping. And I said to him . . . obviously making no direct assertions, in the Mafia style: "It would be good to kill General Dalla Chiesa because he's bothering you. But if someone killed General Dalla Chiesa, would you claim the killing?' He said, "We'll only claim it if one of us is involved."

'I sent the message back and General Dalla Chiesa remained alive . . . Yes, but what interest would Cosa Nostra have in killing General Dalla Chiesa, who had only imprisoned terrorists and hadn't bothered the Mafia? Well, Cosa Nostra would have no interest in doing that. The interest belonged to the Entity . . . that same entity which, still in 1970, asked Nino Salvo if he could kill a journalist in Rome, one Mino Pecorelli, who was causing trouble. Mino was then disappeared, and no one could stop me thinking that the death of Pecorelli and the killing of Dalla Chiesa are the same thing . . .

'Tano Badalamenti also said to me, "Pecorelli and Dalla Chiesa walk arm in arm." All those years there was a strange mixture of things . . . Pecorelli had just been killed, that lawyer in Milan had been killed, what was his name? The one who was on Sindona's back . . . Ambrosoli . . . Someone had asked for Dalla Chiesa to be killed, and Sindona appears in Sicily.

'I think: they're going to kill him, because of the money that he's been making Cosa Nostra lose. But that's not it . . . When I ask Stefano Bontate what he's come to do, he tells me, "He came to tell us that he supported Sicilian separatism, and was asking us for a hand with the coup . . ."

'I ask him, I ask Bontate, "What did you reply?"

'And he tells me, "That guy's crazy, we kicked him in the arse . . ."

'I didn't say it to him, but I thought, "*Minchia*, it took you fifty days to kick him in the arse?"

'Stefano didn't always tell me everything . . . he only told me what he wanted to . . . the rule about always telling the truth when you're talking about Cosa Nostra is one thing, chattering about family dealings is quite another one . . . Obviously Sindona was a family affair. I can imagine what happened at Rosario Spatola's in-laws' country house, with a fine September light, in the shade, in the garden . . . They were all of them, the Inzerillos, the Spatolas, the Gambinos, Stefano, all sitting around the banker . . . and the banker talks and talks . . . He knows that if he doesn't persuade them, he's a dead man. He knows that if he's to go back to America, either he gives him money or he gives him something else. And given that he'd lost his money, he has to give him something else . . . And what do you give someone like that in exchange? Your secrets, that's what you can give him.

'That's why they kept him in Palermo for fifty days . . . Nothing to do with a coup, nothing to do with people getting their arses kicked . . . Those guys, Stefano, Totuccio, Don Saro, squeezed him like a lemon and when he had nothing more to tell them they sent him back to America. And what they were left with was plenty of ammunition for blackmail . . .

'Poor Stefano, eventually Sindona's secrets were as nothing compared to his own.

'Okay, Sindona knew a lot about political entities in Rome, and if one of those included the Entity that had asked for the disappearance of Pecorelli and Dalla Chiesa, that Entity was in Stefano's hands ... Who knows what Stefano had done? I wouldn't be surprised if, at some point, after doing loads of favours, he had started asking for some in return ... asking favours without asking, in the Mafia style ... And that Entity understood that it was completely in his hands, that it couldn't say no because Stefano knew about so many things; if he felt that way he could take it and crush it like a bug.

'Stefano must have thought he had everything sorted out, and in fact here we are ... The Entity had to be organised and, why not start with that stool pigeon Calò ... Like switching parishes ... The Entity made Calò, and his friends in Corleone – Ciancimino, Salvino Lima, the Salvo family – understand that, yes, it was a friend of Stefano's, but it could also be friends with other people ... and that if Stefano came to a bad end ... it could be an even better friend; it could only be one thing. And the people who gave satisfaction in the Corleonese style, killing first Stefano and then all the Bontates and, after Totuccio, all the Inzerillos and the Di Maggios ... The Corleonesi never leave witnesses. The Entity can be certain of that.'

THE DICTATOR

THE LUNCH INVITATION

It was the patron saint's day in Roccamena. The village band played a military march that mingled with the music of the carousel. The 'great bastard' ('*gran cornuto*') had appeared in the piazza between the stalls of roasted pumpkin seeds and chickpeas. Giuseppe ('Pino') Marchese and Balduccio Di Maggio weren't waiting. They knew only that he was known as 'Cain'. They didn't know what his name was or why they had to kill him. They'd been following him for a few stops of the underground. Then they'd fired two bullets into his head. Some women had screamed. No one had moved a muscle.

The appointment was in Dammusi, in San Giuseppe Jato, on the lands of Bernardo Brusca.

'How did it go?' U Curtu asked without apprehension when the butchers got out of the car.

'It went the way it was supposed to go,' Balduccio replied.

'Any complications?' repeated *u zu* Totò.

'At one point I got hungry,' Pino Marchese said seriously.

U Curtu smiled at the coldness of the boy killer. He called a *picciotto* and said to him, 'Go and get some *sfincioni* (Sicilian pizza), roast chicken, pizzas and arancini ... Get them hot, make sure they fry them in front of you.'

When they sat down at the table, U Curtu was surrounded by his general staff. Totò Riina looked around complacently. This was the Cosa Nostra that he liked. He said so, speaking in an unusually loud voice: 'Cosa Nostra should be like this. Five united families grabbing the whole of Sicily.'

The others listened smugly, but in silence.

'Let's raise a toast,' the Corleonese went on. 'And remember to pour a glass for our Luchino . . .' Leoluca Bagarella was in jail.

'We'll always have a glass ready for him . . .'

Totò Riina was in a good mood that evening. At last he was the boss. For once he didn't hide his feelings behind a motionless, stony face. That dream of wealth and power that he had cultivated in secret since 1964, in his cell in the 'young adults' department of the Ucciardone, was now a tangible reality. He could have paved the road from Palermo to Corleone with hundred-thousand-lire notes, gone back to the village with more money than anyone in those mountains had ever had. But it wasn't money that could satisfy U Curtu. He had become rich, extremely rich, but eventually he had noticed that he wasn't interested in money, that money didn't fulfil his needs. He wanted to command, to have prestige, he wanted to be more 'important' than the men who had come before him. U Curtu wanted absolute power over Cosa Nostra.

He almost succeeded. Like a sadistic and vindictive god, he could decide whether men lived or died. Like a head of government, he could appoint ministers and dismiss them the next day. Like a magician, he could push a man towards the stars and drop him in a filthy pigsty immediately afterwards. By now Totò Riina had everything he had ever wished for. U Curtu had changed the shape of Cosa Nostra. Another few months, another few deaths, and Cosa Nostra would be his.

When the Corleonese had first known it, the Sicilian Mafia had been a state. It had its territory, its people, a set of laws with a system composed of institutions, norms and sanctions. There was even an infallible system of taxation: everyone paid taxes, everyone paid bribes to the organisation. Escape was impossible. The sovereign territory of Cosa Nostra was Sicily, and Sicily was divided into provinces, the provinces into *mandamenti*, the *mandamenti* into families of men of honour. The men of honour were the people of Cosa Nostra. They had to respect rules of behaviour, and anyone infringing them was punished, whether with death, expulsion or suspension, whether they were a foot soldier, the head of a family or a bigwig on the Commission. The *capofamiglia* was elected by the men of honour and became the godfather of the suburb. But if an important decision needed to be made, he had to turn to the *capomandamento*, elected by all the other heads of families. And the *capomandamento* couldn't govern autonomously if, for example, he had decided to *ammuccarsi* (kill) a cop or a man of honour from another family guilty of a slight. That was how things were in Cosa Nostra when Riina decided to make it his.

'In this Cosa Nostra,' the Corleonese had complained to Michele Greco, 'any fucking *capomandamento* who wakes up in the morning calls a meeting of the Commission . . . They spend whole days deciding whether or not they're going to waste a seller of ricotta . . . And what do you expect? This Cosa Nostra is fucked – it's a democracy! Trapani wants cooked, Mazara wants raw. In San Cataldo they say white, in Caltanissetta they say black. And the Palermitans, while we're on the subject? Twenty-four families in Palermo is too many, I've been saying that for years. Four would be enough, or five at the most. The *mandamenti* need to be bigger, and consist of five families too. The *capomandamento* should be chosen not by the families but by the Commission, which, with fewer *mandamenti*, will be more concentrated . . . This is, I think, what Cosa Nostra needs to be. Today, in fact, the

Palermitans *sciusciano* (chatter and chatter), they fill their mouths with rules, tradition and values . . . everyone's thinking about his wallet . . . the bosses make bucketloads of money and the *picciotti* starve . . .

'And what's this *pupiata* (puppet show) about elections? Are you trying to tell me anyone elected that great bastard Michele Navarra? And what did Lucianeddu do? We were strong and we took everything. As natural as the wind and the rain. This Cosa Nostra needs to be changed the way you change an old house. It has to be a Cosa of a few families who keep control of everything, who decide who's to be the head of the family in Altarello and who's the *capomandamento* in Resuttana.'

Cosa Nostra, which was, in its own way of course, a democratic state, became a dictatorship in only two years. The Corleonesi weren't just a family, they'd become a current, an alignment, a party. The affairs of Cosa Nostra effectively changed from one day to the next. The Sicilian Mafia had altered its structure, its DNA.

If a man of honour wasn't Corleonese, allowing that he was still alive, couldn't hold any responsibility, he couldn't lay claim to any decent business deal, contract, trafficking or building permit. He didn't even have the right to live a tranquil life. Because one day he might get the message: 'U Curtu wants to see you.'

The Mafioso had to go to the meeting. There was no alternative. If he didn't go, his fate was sealed. He became someone who wasn't respected, who couldn't be trusted, a traitor. If he went, he didn't know if he would ever see his wife and children again. And he couldn't put his mind at rest even if, once he had paid his visit to *u zu* Totò, the man who looked like an old uncle offered him a delicious meal. You knew it was all part of his system . . .

He didn't shout in his face: 'You've done such and such a thing, you bastard!'

No, he found a table laid specially for him. *Caponata, pasta con le sarde, custicieddi di maiali chini, cannoli di ricotta* (aubergine and tomatoes, pasta with sardines, stuffed pork chops and ricotta pastries) . . . Over lunch they laughed, they joked, they enjoyed themselves. Afterwards U Curtu strangled him. The whole population of men of honour lived in terror of receiving a message from U Curtu and finding a table spread with every luxury.

From lunch to lunch, only Totò Riina's hand-chosen men, the ones he had kept by his side when conquering Cosa Nostra, had found a place on the Commission. The ones who had, on behalf of the Corleonese, betrayed bosses, friends and relations. They were Michele Greco and Pino Greco Scarpuzzedda, Giuseppe Giacomo Gambino, Francesco Madonia, Bernardo Brusca, Totò Montalto, Pippo Calò, old Nené Geraci and Antonino (Nino) Rotolo. There was also Giuseppe Bono from Bolognetta, who was addicted to gambling and women but 'had contacts' in America.

A CUPOLA OF PARANOIA

Cosa Nostra was ruled by terror. You could die over nothing. Over a word, a look. All you needed to do was dither over an order to kill a crony, give one question too many or one answer too few, to be squashed like a fly on a window-pane.

The men of honour were frightened. Frightened to think and talk. Totò Riina's paranoia had taken hold of Cosa Nostra. Friends were wary of friends. Brothers were suspicious of brothers, sons of fathers. People spied on each other to catch the sign of betrayal in an insignificant gesture. Inside Cosa Nostra it was said during those years: 'He's not there, but he hears everything.'

U Curtu didn't just hear what was murmured in Cosa Nostra. The Corleonesi had ears everywhere: in police headquarters, in parliament, in the political parties, in jails, in banks, in newspapers, in local and regional government. They had 'approached' lawyers and doctors, judges and policemen, politicians and civil servants. U Curtu controlled the state as he controlled the suburbs of Palermo. And he reacted as he did in the suburbs of Palermo to anyone – in the state – who refused to play the game. His butchers could be unleashed on a whim.

It was the early 1980s and the terror that was engulfing Cosa Nostra was like the nightmare that oppressed Palermo and Sicily. Anyone who refused to bow their head was killed like a dog.

Pio La Torre was killed like a dog, at 9.30 in the morning on 30 April 1982. A motorcycle blocked the way of the Fiat 132 belonging to the regional secretary of the Christian Democrats. The driver, Rosario Di Salvo, braked. The first burst of bullets was meant for La Torre. Di Salvo managed to draw his pistol. He was injured and fired a few shots. They killed him too, with a shot to the back of the neck. Ten minutes later, in Corleone, a young man entered the Good Friends' Club and called out contentedly: '. . . *piupiupiu . . . e moriu u Piu* . . . peep peep peep . . . Pio's died.'

Cosa Nostra breathed a sigh of relief. Woe betide those who touched Mafia money. 'A man of honour would rather be in jail with money than at liberty without,' Asparino Mutolo said.

Pio La Torre wanted to do both: put the Mafiosi in jail and strip them of their wealth as well. He had seen cart-drivers becoming billionaires, councillors displaying gold and villas. He had seen the Salvos of Salemi becoming more and more powerful, and the Limas and Cianciminos still in the front rows, in spite of the anti-Mafia investigations. He knew he had to get his hands on Cosa Nostra's dirty money, in the banks, in the current accounts, in the mysterious companies who made the decisions about building contracts. La Torre had presented a law in thirty-six articles legitimising property checks, introduced the crime of

Mafia association, reformed public calls for tenders and forbade subcontracting.

One day the Commission met in La Favarella. If Michele Greco was worried, the Madonia and Resuttan families were extremely worried.

Nino Madonia said: 'We don't want to take risks. If this law is passed, all our money's going to go up in smoke. We've already started taking money to Germany. We're buying land and buildings. Then we'll see . . .'

Michele Greco was watching U Curtu and waiting to see what he would say. He said nothing.

Salvatore Greco, the Senator, was irritated by the Madonia family's feverish apprehension. As usual in difficult moments, the Senator had been to Rome to collect information. He returned reassured. And now he wanted to reassure his cronies: 'It's just a proposal for legislation. By the time it's approved, if it is approved, we old folk will be dead. And you too, Nino, will have time to die before they take away your *piccioli*.'

'My father doesn't believe it, Don Salvatore . . .'

'You've got to tell your father to have patience and trust. Our friends in Rome say the law won't be passed . . .'

Totò Riina didn't speak during the meeting. That was nothing new. He spoke only to say goodbye when he left in his white Mercedes. No one asked him what he thought. 'Perhaps he wants to talk to someone before he decides what to do,' the Grecos said to each other. U Curtu, on the other hand, had very clear ideas. The next day he called Scarpuzzedda and Mario Prestifilippo. He complained about Pio La Torre and the *tragedia* he was playing out.

'If someone has a sore finger, it's better to cut his arm off; it makes things safer,' Totò Riina concluded. The butchers knew the line. Two weeks later, Pio La Torre was dead.

In September Carlo Albero Dalla Chiese was assassinated too.

'Two years late, when he hadn't yet caused the Mafia any trouble, even though he was the prefect of Palermo,' Buscetta thought.

Masino hadn't forgotten that Carlo Alberto Dalla Chiesa had to die in 1979 on the orders of the Entity that had requested some blood-red favours of Cosa Nostra. Like the death of the general. Like eternal silence for Mino Pecorelli, a journalist who played with secrets bigger than he could deal with.

'Now', Masino thought, 'there was no longer any need to cover the general's murder. He was sent to Sicily to bother the Mafia. It was a physiological fact that he had to die. No one would have asked too many questions.'

U Curtu really thought he had 'grabbed' the whole island. And now he was reorganising *mandamenti* and families; now he was issuing command batons to the soldiers in his army, and he didn't want anyone stirring up trouble.

For months the investigating magistrate Rocco Chinnici had been looking into Cosa Nostra's affairs. He was saying that 'seventy per cent of the funds provided by the Sicilian Regional Assembly to agricultural operations goes directly or indirectly to Mafia families'. He explained that 'there is no public work in Sicily that doesn't cost, as happened in the Belice Valley, four or five times as much as anticipated, not because prices have risen but because that's how the Mafia enterprise wants it.'

Councillor Rocco Chinnici had another responsibility: he gave free rein to his judge, Giovanni Falcone, who had already done a great deal of damage with his investigation into the Spatola construction company. The state prosecutor Pizzillo had advised Chinnici 'to bury him with a trial about theft and kidnapping, because Falcone is ruining the Sicilian economy.' Rocco Chinnici pretended not to hear, and he let his judge go on chasing the Mafia. On 9 July 1983 Giovanni had signed fourteen arrest warrants against U Curtu and Binnu Provenzano, against the Greco brothers of Ciaculli and Nitto Santapaola 'the hunter' for the Dalla Chiesa murder.

This time it wasn't just the finger that was hurting, it was the whole arm. Rocco Chinnici was blown up in a car bomb at 8.05 on 20 July when he was leaving home. That morning U Curtu ordered another bottle of champagne.

'*Monsciandò*, I insist . . .'

In three years Cosa Nostra killed three senior magistrates, the president of the Sicilian Regional Assembly, the provincial secretary of the governing party and the regional secretary of the opposition party. The Corleonese butchers 'wasted' three *carabinieri*, six police officers, eight businessmen, the prefect Carlo Alberto Dalla Chiesa, a journalist and several dozen inconvenient witnesses. U Curtu had eliminated all the men who represented the state in Sicily, and who refused to bow. He had ordered the killing of a thousand Mafiosi from the old Cosa Nostra. He was a snake. He was the most dangerous man ever born in Sicily.

MASINO'S DARK NOVEL

Tommaso Buscetta's eyes were closed, and his face the same colour as the fluorescent light. He was lying across the second row of seats in business class on the Boeing 747 flying from Rio de Janeiro to Rome. He had tried to kill himself with strychnine. And now he had water in his lungs, and his heart refused to start beating regularly again. The doctor was leaning over him, shaking his head with concern. Masino was panting. For seconds at a time, when his breath caught in his throat, it looked as if he was definitely going to die. The doctor gave him an injection. Buscetta seemed to come back to life. He asked to talk to the cop who was bringing him back to Italy.

The cop's name was Gianni De Gennaro. The doctor called him over: 'He wants to talk to you.'

De Gennaro abandoned the half-drunk glass of whisky with which he was beginning his lunch, and went over to the Porta Nuova Mafioso. He had to put his ear to Buscetta's lips to grasp the meaning of his vague whispered words.

'I didn't understand, say it again,' he said as he got up.

He had understood, in fact, but he couldn't believe it. The cop knew that the Brazilians had tortured Masino: they had pulled his fingernails out, they had 'stroked' him with an electric current and dangled him out of an aeroplane in the sky over São Paulo, only to hear him repeat over and over again, 'My name is Buscetta Tommaso . . .'

Buscetta whispered again into the policeman's ear: 'I'll tell you everything I know, officer.'

The policeman forgot his whisky, he forgot his lunch, he forgot that he hadn't prayed for twenty-five years. He found himself murmuring: 'Mother of God, please don't let him die. Please, Jesus Christ, don't let this son of a bitch die now, of all times.'

The heavens heard the policeman's prayers. Buscetta didn't die. As soon as they landed at Fiumicino, De Gennaro called Palermo. He asked to speak to Giovanni Falcone. He told him: 'I have Buscetta here. He wants to talk.'

Falcone listened imperturbably. Calmly, he replied: 'I'll be in Rome tomorrow.'

He hung up again and thought, with an ironic smile: 'De Gennaro's drunk'.

On 16 July 1984, at 12.30, Giovanni Falcone sat facing Tommaso

Buscetta in a room in the criminal investigations department in the EUR district of Rome. The light struggled through the high, dusty windows.

'I'm not an informer, I'm not a *pentito*; I haven't betrayed Cosa Nostra. Cosa Nostra has betrayed itself,' Buscetta began. For three months, sitting opposite Falcone, the Mafioso told the judge what the Sicilian Cosa Nostra was, who it had been betrayed by and why.

'Before Tommaso Buscetta', Giovanni Falcone explained, 'we had only a superficial idea of the Mafia phenomenon. With Buscetta, we started to take a look inside. He supplied us with plenty of evidence about Cosa Nostra's structure, recruitment techniques and operation, but above all he gave us a wide, over-all, sweeping vision of the phenomenon. He gave us an essential key to it, a language, a code. For us he was like a language teacher who lets you go and speak to the Turks without using gestures. He taught us a method. Without a method you don't understand anything. With Buscetta we reached the edge of the precipice, where no one had dared to go because there were plenty of good excuses for refusing to see, for playing things down, for splitting hairs and over-analysing investigations, for denying the unified character of Cosa Nostra.'

What the Mafia had for four decades managed to keep more secret than the mystery of Fatima – the top-down structure of the organisation – was finally out in the open. The names, the history and the power of the Corleonesi were all out in the open, and at the mercy of the judge's intelligence and tenacity. Buscetta revealed that at the top of the pyramid, at the top of that organisation, as powerful as a god and treacherous as a snake, as power-obsessed as a dictator, there was Salvatore Riina, U Curtu.

Buscetta said, 'He looks like a peasant, your honour, but he's

intelligent, he's sly, he's obsessed with surveillance ('*sbirritudine*').
He's always behaved like a cop, turning to the police to eliminate his enemies, if he couldn't have them killed. No, he wasn't
an informer. He had the weakness, if I might put it that way, of
sending anonymous letters. He wrote plenty of those, *u viddanu*!
I think, your honour, that he was the one who had Liggio ar-
rested. Yes, Lucianeddu ... in 1974 ... in Milan. The arrest of
Luciano is a fact that can't be explained, or rather one that can
only be explained that way. Liggio had put U Curtu, next to
Badalamenti and Bontate, in the triumvirate that governed Cosa
Nostra. Tano ended up in jail and Riina, outside, started kidnapping people. He kidnapped the son of Count Arturo Cassina.
When Tano got out, he asked U Curtu, "Why did you do it? Didn't
I tell you there weren't going to be any kidnappings in Sicily?"
Liggio, who was also involved in the kidnappings, takes him off
the Commission and puts himself on it. Riina had fought hard to
end up in command, and his nose was out of joint. So incredibly,
a short time later, with no clues or evidence, the *carabinieri* pick
up Liggio in Milan. They knock at the door and arrest a quiet,
respectable gentleman in a middle-class flat, with a woman and
a child.

'Riina, the cop, had done his spying. He goes back to the top
and starts his demolition job on Badalamenti. In three years he
gets him out, sends him into exile, and the body-count begins
... They called it the Mafia war. It wasn't a war, your honour, it
was a massacre, a manhunt launched by the Corleonesi against
everybody who, regardless of which family they belonged
to, was or had been friends of Stefano Bontate and Totuccio
Inzerillo.

'I myself belong to the family of Pippo Calò. I should be a
victor, as they say, shouldn't I? And in fact I've been persecuted
and I've had so much mourning in my family, just because of my

friendship with Bontate and Inzerillo. That manhunt, it was that hyena Riina who wanted it, and he killed my children and lots of members of my family. It was animals like Bernardo Provenzano who wanted it; *viddani* like Bernardo Brusca, a guy who would stink even if you poured a litre of cologne all over him. They're the most wretched people in the history of the world since Nero, your honour.

'Salvatore is the brains behind it, your honour, forget about Liggio, who's just a clown. U Curtu is the brains and Pino Greco Scarpuzzedda is the arm. They were the ones who killed Colonel Russo. They were the ones who wanted Terranova dead. It was Riina U Curtu who forced the murder of Piersanti Mattarella on the Commission. It was Riina who had Captain Basile killed, and the secretary of the Christian Democrats, Michele Reina. He killed State Prosecutor Scaglione in person, with Liggio, and he organised the death of Dalla Chiesa to do a favour to a few politicians by getting rid of the troublesome presence of the general.'

Giovanni Falcone recorded Buscetta's statement in tiny, round handwriting, ending up with hundreds of pages and mysteries. And he ordered Gianni De Gennaro to organise 3,600 meetings.

The policeman said to Buscetta: 'Perhaps I've made the mistake of my life in asking Jesus Christ to leave you alive.'

Seventy-four days later Giovanni Falcone signed 366 arrest warrants, brought 300 charges and shed light on 121 murders.

Under the guidance of the judge Antonino Capornetto and thanks to the work of Paolo Borsellino, Leonardo Guarnotta and Giuseppe Di Lello Finuoli, the Investigating Office of the Palermo Court became a steamroller. The pool of judges constructed a monumental indictment totalling forty-two volumes and 8,067 pages, the first trial 'against the Mafia organisation called Cosa Nostra, a very dangerous criminal association which, through violence and intimidation, has sown and continues to sow death and terror . . .'

The document was described as 'a black novel that grips the bones and freezes the blood . . . a strato-cumulus of monstrous realities that concern the whole county. A frightening tangle of terror, iniquity, ferocity and death. A blend of coarseness and subtlety, of feudal archaism and technological, criminal modernity in which murder is the rule.'

For the first time Cosa Nostra was naked in the eyes of the world.

ONLY THE PAINTER WAS ACQUITTED

It was raining and windy. It was cold, that morning on 10 February 1986. Luciano Liggio went alone into the courtroom bunker. And he remained alone – alone, among the 474 defendants in the first Cosa Nostra maxi-trial – in cell number 23. He looked distractedly at the lawyers' bench, and sat down heavily. From the inside pocket of his jacket he took a Havana cigar half as long as a man's forearm and as thick as two fingers. Pippo Calò stared blankly at him from cell 22. Bernardo Brusca, in 19, gave him a derisory look of contempt.

Lucianeddu was no longer a Mafia boss. He was an actor. The youngest soldiers of Cosa Nostra, in cells 8, 12 and 18, nudged each other and smiled. Everyone in the Ucciardone knew that Lucianeddu brought in those cigars that he never smoked, and stored them jealously in big wooden boxes that no one ever opened. He only took a Havana when he went down to the courtroom. And he waved it around in front of the television cameras and the journalists' notebooks – a marshal's baton, as evidence that his power was still intact.

Lucianeddu was just a shadow of what he had been fifteen or twenty years before. The youngest soldiers knew it, and whispered, 'Look how well he plays the part of the boss.'

Lucianeddu could do anything. He just had to keep his mouth shut about Corleone and the old affairs of the family. Luciano Liggio had made it known that he had a hobby, painting. It ended up in the newspaper. He painted fields, Sicilian landscapes, sunsets. The director of the Ucciardone, Orazio Faramo, said he was proud of their model inmate. Luciano's lawyer expressed his admiration: 'It's a style halfway between realism and divisionism: we could call him Liggio the painter.'

An exhibition was organised in a gallery on Via Dante, and his paintings sold like hot cakes at the opening. The men of honour in the Ucciardone laughed. 'Didn't everybody know that many of the boss's paintings were done by Asparino Mutolo?'

Lucianeddu could do anything . . . That caricature of a Mafia boss was useful to him. The journalists looked at him and said, 'Is this Cosa Nostra? Is this Liggio, who's been in jail for ten years, the godfather of Cosa Nostra? Is this the boss of bosses, who's behaving as if time had stopped, who thinks he's still frightening?'

'Leave him alone and let him get on with it,' U Curtu had ordered his men, locked up in jail. Luciano Liggio had to go into the bunker courtroom, roll his eyes, roll his cigar between his index and middle fingers, to behave as if he was the number one among the Corleonesi. 'The important thing,' U Curtu said, 'is that he doesn't talk . . . because if he does talk, to prove that he's not entirely worthless, he's capable of speaking out of turn . . .'

When Lucianeddu asked to speak, during Tommaso Buscetta's questioning, there was surprise in the cells. And, immediately afterwards, there was also a shiver of apprehension.

Liggio admitted that he knew Buscetta. Then they invited him to tell him about when, in 1970, they were both given the task of negotiating Cosa Nostra's involvement in a coup with Prince Junio Valerio Borghese.[1]

'Didn't I tell you about those things with Signor Buscetta, your honour? Signor Buscetta is a fraud; he's an informer who doesn't tell the whole truth . . . he only talks about other people and never about himself . . . and his own problems . . .'

Buscetta didn't even reply. But the president of the court, Alfonso Giordano, did reply: 'These circumstances, Signor Liggio, are in the record of your interrogation.'

This time the men of honour in the cages didn't laugh. U Curtu didn't laugh either, and the next day he sent a message to the Ucciardone. Two *picciotti* approached Luciano Liggio and reminded him to keep his mouth shut. In the bunker courtroom of Palermo Lucianeddu didn't say another word.

That trial would pass as well, as the trial in Bari and the big trial in Catanzaro had passed. There would be a bit of a commotion, the foot soldiers would do a bit of jail and with time everything would be back in the right place. The same as before, the same as always. U Curtu went to a lot of trouble to reassure his men. He was extravagant with money. And the families of the *picciotti* were never short of cash. He had understood that it was a delicate moment. He couldn't get rid of all his hatred by killing people. Instinct led him to kill one of those 'bastards from the Investigating Office', the judges in the maxi-trial. Or some lawyers who were working reluctantly, and couldn't find the specious argument required to blow everything sky-high. But too much attention was being devoted to the bunker court and Cosa Nostra; there were

---

1   The Golpe Borghese was an attempted neo-fascist Italian coup d'état allegedly planned for the night of 7 or 8 December 1970.

too many journalists and too many television cameras around the place.

'Keep calm, keep calm,' the Corleonese said over and over again to the men of honour. This would pass as well. They would still have to think about what happened next. And the Corleonese was thinking about what happened next. He sent messages to the Cosa Nostra politicians, to the judges who had been 'approached', to the cops who were on the payroll. He also called his friends in Rome, asking for some of them to come to Sicily, to Palermo. Totò Riina explained Cosa Nostra's position. If the *pentiti* were believed, if the sentences were definitive, there would be a mass-slaughter in Sicily that the whole world would remember. The magistrates promised. The cops promised. The politicians in Rome promised.

'In the Court of Cassation . . . everything will change in the Court of Cassation,' they swore.

On 16 December 1987, at 7.30 in the evening, after thirty-five days in the council chamber, 349 hearings, 1,314 cross-questionings, 645 defence summations, 4,676 years in jail and 28 life sentences requested by the counsel for the prosecution, the court resumed.

For almost two years the presiding judge, Alfonso Giordano, had just been a little black dot for the men of honour lined up in their cages. That day the president of the Court of Assizes looked like a giant. He spent hours reading the terms of the sentence. And word after word he rained down, like water from a cloud-burst, life sentences and jail terms on the defendants, 2,665 years of prison and 19 life sentences.

Giordano read: 'Salvatore Riina, life sentence. Bernardo Provenzano, life sentence. Francesco Madonia, life sentence. Michele Greco, life sentence. Totò Montalto, life sentence. Antonino, Giuseppe and Filippo Marchese, life sentence. Giovanbattista

THE BOSS OF BOSSES

Pullarà, life sentence. Benedetto Santapaola, life sentence. Giuseppe Lucchese, life sentence. Giuseppe Calò, twenty-three years. Giuseppe Bono, twenty-three years. Bernardo Brusca, twenty-three years. Mariano Agate, twenty-two years. Salvatore Greco, eighteen years. Antonino Rotolo, eighteen years. Gaspare Mutolo, ten years. Vincenzo Puccio, ten years. Giuseppe Giacomo Gambino, eight years. Giacomo Riina, seven years and six months. Giuseppe Leggio, seven years. Leoluca Bagarella, six years . . . Luciano Liggio, acquitted.'

'The Mafia has been defeated at last,' the ministers in Rome declared triumphantly. A dangerous euphoria spread around Italy, and the city of Palermo become a symbol of revolt, of frontier, trench, bulwark against the Mafia. For months and months words and rivers of ink were spread about how the state had won. But there was fear in Palermo. No one dug any further into the secrets of Cosa Nostra now that it had been put on trial and found guilty. No one knew the balances and alliances of the new Mafia. U Curtu was still in hiding.

THE GREASY POLE

The bank account had a code and the key word was Vito. Every month he paid in almost 300 million lire. Some of the money had made its way to Canada through the American Cosa Nostra. Some more had ended up in safes in Lugano and Geneva, but the most consistent part of the fortune accumulated over thirty years was never found. Vito Ciancimino was an extremely rich man. Vito Ciancimino was in the hands of Totò Riina's Corleonesi.

On behalf of U Curtu he had managed the reconstruction of the districts of Palermo. He had distributed contracts and work and regulated the traffic in bribes and favours. The former errand-boy at the barber shop in Corleone was Totò Riina's most loyal right-hand man in the world of politics. He was a mayor, a councillor, and also the provincial director of the Christian Democrats. He reached agreements with ministers and under-secretaries, he talked to presidents of the council and made decisions concerning party conferences and elections. Vito Ciancimino was a powerful man, extremely powerful. All of a sudden, one day, he looked as if he was finished. He was arrested, sent into internal exile and arrested again. Following Don Vito's money, judge Falcone's investigations revealed the business affairs of the 'peasants'.

During those months, a new wind was blowing in Palermo. The old bosses were dropping one by one. Excluded from award-ing council contracts, after fifty-one years, was Count Arturo Cassina. Excluded from Palermo's municipal council was the republican Aristide Gunnella, the subject of so many rumours. Excluded from the Christian Democrats were a handful of sena-tors and deputies who all had a whiff of the Mafia about them. It was a time of renewal. The mayor Leoluca Orlando was dream-ing of a European Palermo.

The council building opened up its rooms; these were the days of the Palermo spring. Days of clashes with the Romanian no-menklatura, of feuds between the parties in Sicily, of wars fought in broad daylight and underground conflicts. There was a mayor who wanted a revolution, but the bureaucratic machine of the city council was still in the hands of Vito Ciancimino and his friends. One autumn day thousands of construction workers took to the streets. They sang the praises of Don Vito, who was locked up in a maximum security prison. They all clutched the same plac-ards: 'Long live Ciancimino', 'Long live the Mafia, which provides work . . .'

The former barber-shop assistant from Corleone was now

under police surveillance in a small village in the Apennines in Abruzzo. He had been living in Rotello for a few months. No one would ever have suspected that, a thousand kilometres away from his internal exile, he might still be managing all the big building contracts in Palermo. And yet the Corleonese former mayor still controlled the billions involved in public works. With a few clean companies, and blue-chipped straw men, behind the screen of Roman firms that had mysteriously slipped into the jungle of Palermo.

'He's always involved in the distribution of the big contracts – Vito Ciancimino is always there,' Judge Falcone guaranteed in 1989. Then the magistrate discovered another name that led him to Totò Riina's contracts. It was the name of Giuseppe Modesto of Camporeale, a small businessman who had been a protagonist in the Belice Valley Garcia dam-building project. His companies went on getting work throughout the province. Falcone remembered an old report from the *carabinieri*. 'Various leads suggest that Modesto is linked to Salvatore Riina's Mafia group and to the *cosca* of Roccamena', it said in a 1977 file. Giuseppe Modesto's company was still fully active.

But something had changed, something was changing. There was no longer just one man in charge of the contracts like Vito Ciancimino or builders like Giuseppe Modesto thrashing the competition at auction. The local control of business, suburb by suburb, province by province, had become a sophisticated system of distribution of work and wealth. Just as Cosa Nostra had transformed from a 'democracy' into a dictatorship, U Curtu reorganised the management of the greasy pole, and created a central office for building contracts. U Curtu had appointed his own ministers of public works, who answered only to him. Like Angelo Siino, a small builder from San Giuseppe Jato. Siino frequented regional councillors and examined building plans on behalf of U Curtu. Month after month, the companies belonging to the Corleonesi had been involved in the big carve-up of the contracts. Hundreds, thousands of billions on aqueducts, roads, ports, airports, desalination plants. There were rumours that U Curtu ran large concerns in central and northern Italy, giants of the construction industry. His men controlled the whole of the Sicilian concrete sector. An empire.

A big mystery continued to surround Totò Riina and his affairs, his relations with politics, his links with freemasonry. The Corleonese emissaries cultivated undercover contacts with the powerful; they discussed strategies and exchanged favours. Many men of honour donned the masonic apron: in Trapani, in Caltanissetta, in Palermo. During those years a 'secret government' was born, encompassing areas of the state and professions, strong economic areas and respectable men.

Totò Riina's Cosa Nostra became even more invisible and protected, like a snake among the foliage, using mimicry as a chameleon does. For years in Palermo everyone had said that Salvo Lima and Vita Ciancimino were like water and fire. Bitter enemies since the end of the 1970s; representatives of diverse interests: Lima with the old Mafia, Ciancimino with the aggressive provincial Mafia. Stories were told about their hatred, about nights of the long knives that concluded regional conferences and town-council meetings. It was all for show. Salvo Lima and Vito Ciancimino were and had always been *the same thing*. They both took orders from U Curtu.

HYPOCHONDRIACS

He was the boss of bosses. From Castellammare del Golfo to Trapani, from Mazara to Riesi, from the districts of Catania to the suburbs of Palermo there was not a single family or *mandamento* that the Corleonese didn't control with one of his puppets. He was at the top of the pyramid. His faithful dogs praised him shamelessly: '*Zu* Totò, no one inside this beautiful Cosa Nostra has ever issued commands as you do. What were Calò Vizzini, Genco Russo, Don Paolino Bontà compared to you . . . Nothing, nothing . . .'

Totò Riina was aware of his power. Sometimes he yielded to the temptation to see it as something eternal. He felt at peace, and apart from that 'weight on his stomach' that was Giovanni Falcone he saw no external threats. And yet the state wasn't Falcone. In fact the state had always found that particular judge a source of irritation.

'The maxi-trial went the way it went,' U Curtu reflected, 'but with time things would have sorted themselves out. Salvo Lima got busy, and so did our friend in Rome.' He'd informed the foot soldiers.

'There are so many technicalities we can still use . . . The first sentence should be accepted, as Lima said, as "a political act", and then this trial too will get lost somewhere along the way . . . We won't bother about the cost – money isn't a problem. If things need to be paid for, we'll pay . . . we have plenty of friends at the Palace of Justice . . .'

There was only one shadow that gave U Curtu cause for concern. Pino Greco. Sarpuzzedda had got too big for his boots; his power had gone to his head. He was an unforeseen obstacle. The *picciotti* worshipped him. They had turned him into a legend. He had killed Stefano Bontate and Totuccio Inzerillo, General Dalla Chiesa and a hundred others. Now that the ability to kill was all that counted within Cosa Nostra, Pino Greco was the most loved and the most feared. For his 'battles' he had been given the Ciaculli *mandamento*, but '*il crasto*' (the sheep), Riina said contemptuously to Raffaele Ganci, 'won't stop there. He's reorganising the fighting unit . . . he's initiating new *picciotti*, and not telling me who they are . . . He's up to something . . .'

That was enough for a death sentence. U Curtu dug up the lethal, delicate weapon that was *tragedia*. 'Pino Greco,' he said when there were enough men of honour to listen, 'has adopted the same vices as the bastards he killed. All he thinks about is money and himself. He doesn't care about the family, and he doesn't know how to keep the suburb in order.'

That was the signal. The loyal attack-dogs launched themselves at their prey. A few days later, a stable on Piazza Scaffa, within the *mandamento* of Ciaculli, was stained with the blood of eight men. Pino Greco found the corpses in his territory without even guessing at what had happened. He knew that the bell was tolling for him, and took refuge in a secret house in Bagheria. He died, like all of Riina's enemies, after being betrayed. He was betrayed by Giuseppe Lucchese, whom Scarpa saw as a brother. Pino Greco had only just woken up and was making coffee. He was in his pyjama bottoms. Luccineddu crept up behind him.

There was another shadow threatening the Corleonese's power. Riina couldn't even see it coming. It was a shadow that was growing in jail. The *picciotti* in the Ucciardone knew that they needed to be patient. But there were many ways of being in jail, and the men of honour were used to being comfortable there. The most comfortable of all were the men of the five families closest to Totò Riina's heart. U Curtu took a lot of trouble, he spent money, he talked, he sorted things out just for them. For Bernardo Brusca of San Giuseppe Jato, for the Madonia family of San Lorenzo, for the Gancis of La Noce, for the Gambinos of Resuttana and the Montaltos of Uditore.

Bernardo Brusca lived like a lord. Riina had found a room for him in Palermo's city hospital, in a room where the only other people were men from his family. They made his bed with fresh linen sheets, stretched as tight as they would have been in a five-star hotel. When he woke up in the morning, the *picciotti* were already standing there with breakfast ready for him. They helped him get out of bed. They walked with him to the table. They waited until he had sat down before sitting down themselves. They waited for him to eat before they ate. A fine life for the Corleonesi.

The creature comforts that U Curtu provided for his 'close' friends created bad feeling among the *picciotti*, and made it possible for Vincenzo Puccio – who had taken the place of Scarpa in the *mandamento* of Ciaculli – to come into the open with a plan he had had in mind for some time. Vincenzo Puccio wasn't afraid to go and wage war on U Curtu. He had the best 'fighting unit' in Cosa Nostra. But he lacked authority. He sought it among the senior figures of the older generation. He found it in eighty-year-old Antonino Mineo, who had been the Mafia boss in Bagheria.

'*U zu Ninu è cristianu basatu* (Uncle Nino is a sound character),' Puccio said in the courtyard of the Ucciardone, 'he follows the rules of the old Mafia. Zio Nino has reasons not to agree with the Corleonesi.' Vincenzo Puccio thought he was moving with due caution in his attempt to overthrow U Curtu's dictatorship. It was the first coup that threatened Totò Riina's power. The Mafioso from Ciaculli also wanted to have the agreement of a Corleonesi. And Giuseppe Leggio, who respected Giacomo Riina, U Curtu's uncle, granted it to him.

Vincenzo Puccio felt that he was well enough protected to move on to the final part of his plan. He wanted to escape from the Ucciardone with a handful of trusted men – the *Picciotti* were already preparing to dig a tunnel under the prison walls – and hunt down the dictator.

'As soon as I get out, I'm going to cut that bastard Riina's head off,' he promised. He told Giuseppe and Antonio Marchese, and during visiting hours they gave their sisters a note for Totò Riina. Then days later the coup failed. Antonino Mineo was killed, and so was Giuseppe Leggio. On 11 January 1989, Vincenzo Puccio was murdered in the Ucciardone; two hours later, at the cemetery Dei Rotoli, his brother Pietro was murdered as well.

The Corleonese seemed invincible, and that was how Riina felt. Inside and outside Cosa Nostra. Inside and outside Sicily.

THE TERRORIST

THE SETTLING OF SCORES

The cars left the SS117 and filed along the path through the pine forest. After the village of Valguarnera Caropepe there were fruit trees and vines, big olive groves and almond trees in blossom. When the cars passed over the top of the hill, the landscape changed. There were only abandoned shacks scattered in a brown, treeless plain. Bend after bend, they reached a crossroads and headed north. The farm appeared half a kilometre later. It looked like a fortress. It was the shape of a horseshoe, built in yellow tufa stone. The cars stopped, and five men went into the farm. One was U Curtu.

The summit had been prepared 'to discuss something very important'. It was March, in 1992. In the deserted, unfamiliar fields of the province of Enna, Totò Riina brought together the four most loyal Mafia bosses to declare total war on the Italian state. It was the last challenge of the Corleonesi. It was the settling of scores.

U Curtu was sitting behind a wooden table. Standing around it were the representatives of the Sicilian Cosa Nostra. Binnu Provenzano had come from Corleone, Benedetto Santapaola from Catania and Piddu Madonia from Caltanissetta. And from

Palermo, a man that none of those present – apart from Totò Riina – had ever seen before. He was hastily introduced by U Curtu, and no one asked any questions. Later a *pentito* said he was probably a man from Catania called Angelo. In fact he was a Palermitan, and his real name was Michelangelo La Barbera, a Mafioso from Passo di Rigano, the new *capomandamento* of Cosa Nostra in the suburb below the ghostly mountains of Bellolampo. La Barbera was also there that evening in the horseshoe-shaped farm half a kilometre north of the pine forest.

The boss of bosses was as tense as a violin string, with penetrating, flashing eyes. For the first time his feelings were clearly visible on his face: hatred, rage and death.

Totò Riina whispered: 'And now we've got to get moving . . .'

A month before – it was the last day of January – the Court of Cassation had confirmed the life sentences of the maxi-trial and hundreds and hundreds of years in prison. The ruling had recognised the validity of the 'Buscetta theorem' and Judge Falcone had won the battle of his life. There was now a fixed point in Italian jurisprudence that it would be difficult to erase. 'Cosa Nostra was a criminal, top-down structure . . .'

The killing of prosecuting barrister Antonino Scopelliti had led nowhere. The pressure on Salvo Lima and the money thrown into corruption, threats, kidnapping and 'sorting out' the maxi-trial had led nowhere. 'Falcone got away with it,' hissed one of the five Mafiosi closed away in the farmhouse.

U Curtu raised his hand and told him to be quiet. He was going to do all the talking tonight.

'It's been the most disastrous year . . . the guys in Rome don't hear us, they don't want to hear us . . . and that *crasto* (sheep) Lima has ousted us . . .' U Curtu was foaming with rage. And he started to remember everything that had happened over the previous twelve months.

'First he fucked with the Martelli decree. Many of us were already out and they put us back in again by extending bail time . . . then he fucked with 41-bis,[1] the Mafia, and anyone arrested under 41-bis, couldn't be put under house arrest . . . and it's not over yet. Falcone is still doing his *sbirritudini*, his surveillance stuff, he's come up with the Anti-Mafia Investigations Directorate, which De Gennaro is going to run. And now he wants the main anti-Mafia investigation authority job for himself . . . Do you know what that means? That these two are trying to crush us.'

Totò Riina got to his feet and started nervously pacing up and down.

'Falcone's investigation should have been cancelled on formal grounds. My brother-in-law Luchino told us the procedure would be referred to the investigating magistrate . . . we, poor idiots, were convinced that we would kill two birds with one stone . . . all acquitted and Falcone knocked from his perch . . . Instead *we* were the ones who were taken down; we've all got life sentences to deal with . . .'

Piddu Madonia lit a cigarette and said, without much conviction: 'But it will pass, it will pass, *zu* Totò . . .'

U Curtu gave him a look of contempt and didn't reply. He continued with his monologue: 'In the Court of Cassation we should have had guarantees, and they went to all that trouble to get rid of Corrado Carnevale . . . we told Lima that if he didn't stick to the agreement we'd kill him and his whole family . . . Not a bit

---

1   Introduced in 1975, Article 41-bis of the Prison Administration Act (also known as Italy's 'hard prison regime') is a provision that allows the minister of justice or the minister of the interior to suspend certain prison regulations. It is used against people imprisoned for particular crimes, including those of Mafia involvement. It is only suspended when a prisoner co-operates with the authorities, when a court annuls it or when a prisoner dies.

of it . . . even our friend in Rome stopped listening to us . . . but what do they think, what the hell have they got into their heads, those *fitusi*? Don't they know who we are, don't they know who the Corleonesi are?'

Totò Riina paused for a moment and glared at the four other men. Then the tone of his voice changed. His rage had subsided, engulfed by his crazed lucidity. He pursed his lips: 'In a few days . . . let's say two or three . . . tell the *picciotti* things are going to heat up . . . tell them to sort themselves out as they see fit . . .'

The cars drove back up the SS117 at nightfall. They took the sliproad leading to the Catania–Palermo motorway. At the junction they disappeared into the darkness, in opposite directions.

A few days later, in Palermo, some Mafiosi who had three, four or five years still to serve turned up at police headquarters, or at the Ucciardone, or at police posts in hospitals. Someone from the prosecutors' office informed Giovanni Falcone. The director of Penal Affairs in the ministry pulled a face. He understood that something was moving in Sicily.

THE LAST DAY OF THE UNTOUCHABLE MAN

There was only one untouchable man who could walk around Palermo without an escort and without fear. That man was Salvo Lima.

For thirty-five years he had controlled the government of the city. He had twice been mayor and twice under-secretary. For three terms he had been in Strasbourg, in the European Parliament. Salvo Lima was the guardian of 'Sicilian interests'. He guaranteed the balance between legal and criminal power that the Italian state had accepted for the island. Salvo Lima was a man of honour. He was in the prime of life, and convinced that he would live to be a hundred.

The history of Palermo – and not only Palermo – changed the day U Curtu had him killed.

There are many ways of living or dying in Palermo. The one that the Corleonesi chose to kill Salvino Lima was the simplest and clearest. They shot him in the back. Running along the avenues of Mondello, among the banana and ficus trees that hid the art nouveau villas of the Palermitan bourgeoisie, along the streets that bore the names of young noblewomen of the early twentieth century. Via Principessa Adelasia, Via Principessa Iolanda, Via Principessa Giovanna. In the green maze of Mondello, Salvo Lima was shot down at nine o'clock in the morning on 12 March 1992 near a rubbish bin. They covered the corpse with a sheet. The fire service arrived and washed away the blood that still covered the pavement.

'The list doesn't stop with Lima,' an anonymous voice told Palermo police headquarters at 15.42 that day.

On the last day of his life Salvo Lima had woken at dawn. He had had two coffees as he waited for his friends to turn up, the loyal men of the Andreotti tendency. A meeting at seven in the morning to decide the last moves in the electoral campaign, the vote in April for the renewal of parliament. 'We have to do things properly – Giulio's on his way,' Salvino recommended to Alfredo Li Vecchi, the university professor who acted as his chauffeur when he was in Palermo. The Sicilian trip of the president of the council of ministers, Giulio Andreotti, had been fixed for 23 March, when a convention was due to open at the Palace Hotel in Mondello.

'*Minchia, si l'ammuccaru* (Fuck, they've killed him) . . .' was the only response to Salvo Lima's death in the suburbs of Palermo. No words could express the violence of a crime as overwhelming as an earthquake. Salvo Lima was the incarnation of Sicilian power. One other comment was that of the boss Totò Montalto in Spoleto prison: 'They've killed him at last . . .'

Totò Riina and his Corleonesi had killed Salvo Lima a few months after the life sentences had been passed by the Court of Cassation. For the first time Cosa Nostra had been defeated in the Italian courts, with the ruling that was the beginning of the end of the end for the Corleonesi. Cosa Nostra's system of protection no longer worked as it once had.

The road between Palermo and Rome had become more tortuous over the years, more difficult for the Mafiosi and their allies to travel. The party that Cosa Nostra had supported since the end of the war – Christian Democracy – was divided and torn by feuds. The man on whom Cosa Nostra had depended to such an extent – Salvo Lima – no longer guaranteed anything. Neither impunity nor the political backing of Rome. With another Cosa Nostra, with different bosses at the top of the organisation, Palermo and Rome might have gone on talking to each other; they would have gone on communicating, swapping words and rules. But Cosa Nostra was in the hands of U Curtu. And Totò Riina only knew how to kill people who didn't obey his orders.

The president of the council, Giulio Andreotti, landed in Palermo a few days after the crime 'to defend the memory of Salvo and the good name of the Sicilians'. The national secretary of the Christian Democrats, Arnaldo Forlani, warned him that 'they wanted to break up the state and divide the national community'. They both said that Salvo Lima was a victim of the Mafia.

The elections came twenty-five days after the killing in the avenues of Mondello. Four weeks that seemed like a century. The strongest faction in the Sicilian Christian Democrats was wiped out between Saturday and Monday, 5 and 7 April. After that vote

Salvo Lima's pro-Andreotti faction had ceased to exist. Vanished in Caltanissetta, decimated in Agrigento, wiped out in Trapani. It had broken up in its Palermo fortress. After the killing, which had shaken the whole of Italy, only one of Salvo Lima's men, the former president of the Regional Assembly, Mario D'Acquisto, took his seat. U Curtu had hit the bullseye, with four pistol-shots: on the morning of 12 March 1992, Totò Riina's Corleonesi had wiped the empire of one of the godfathers of the island from the face of the earth. His armies had disappeared in the Sicilian mists, his 300,000 votes scattered to the four winds.

What happened next opened up a phase of struggles and deceit. The Mafia doesn't only strike with shotguns and Kalashnikovs. The Mafia covers the whole field. It announces its moves, it shows its cards in order to 'give advice'; it also warns and threatens with favours, 'acts of kindness', gifts that it's impossible to refuse. Like votes. Some politicians in Palermo and Agrigento took plenty of votes after the killing of Salvo Lima. They took too many votes that they didn't want.

'They're the true victors in Sicily . . . What an overwhelming advance, what an impetuous success!' Salvo Lima's retreating troops hurried to observe, giving the full names of the new Christian Democrat bosses in Sicily – bosses who didn't want to be bosses. They would have to negotiate with U Curtu. They would have to strike deals with that beast Totò Riina.

In Sicily, reality goes far beyond fantasy. At a certain point in their lives Sicilians often foretell their own futures. Out of the deepest darkness, everything in Sicily becomes predictable: everything is foretold, everything is taken as read. And there's an expression that prepares for the omen: 'It's all written . . .' Salvo Lima hadn't managed to see his own future. But those who survived him saw their own futures, and started to tremble.

AND HE WALKED TOWARDS DEATH

Smoke had risen slowly, the black smoke was driven by the wind that blew from the mountains towards the Mare di Capaci. The air was foul with the smell of naphthalene and cordite. Prosecutor Paolo Borsellino rubbed his stinging eyes and covered his face with a handkerchief. He climbed over the remains of an engine, blackened and incandescent bits of iron.

'Your honour, over here . . .'

The policeman guided him through the carcasses of the armoured cars and pointed to what remained of the white Croma that had been at the head of the convoy. Paolo Borsellino turned round quickly and walked a few metres along the shattered thoroughfare, looking at the inferno. At that moment he realised that he too was a dead man.

On the evening of 23 May 1992 the deputy state prosecutor Paolo Emanuele Borsellino no longer had any tears to weep for his friend Giovanni, for Francesca, for the young men in the escort. His heart was filled with grief, his mind full of thoughts of death. Cosa Nostra had just finished the most atrocious military action in its history, and the Corleonese had left his signature on the motorway. Paolo Borsellino knew it wasn't over. 'This is just the start,' he thought as he headed back towards Palermo on the day of the death of Giovanni Falcone.

The corridors of the court were in darkness, but the eighteen rooms of the prosecutors' office were harshly lit. Paolo Borsellino called three young judges into his office. He looked at them without speaking for a few moments, then said, 'We have to ask ourselves three questions: why did they kill Giovanni; why did they kill him now; why did they kill him in Palermo?'

The three young magistrates stared at him with tears in their eyes. He smoked one cigarette after another, took off his jacket and threw it on the sofa, and rolled up his shirt-sleeves. Then he hid his face in his hands and, remembering his friend Giovanni, tried to think.

'In my view there's a coincidence between the massacre and some information I was given a few days ago: Giovanni, contrary to what most people believed, had a majority in the Higher Council of the Magistracy, and was about to be appointed national anti-Mafia prosecutor,' Borsellino told them. His colleagues listened in silence. He went on: 'In spite of very strong opposition to his candidacy he had succeeded – and that sensational piece of news had spread quickly around the Palace of Justice. I want to tell you one precise thing: I don't know if the news that Falcone was about to become the new anti-Mafia prosecutor was known outside . . . I don't believe it was.'

The magistrates held their breath. They were frozen to the spot. Paolo Borsellino got to his feet and went and sat on the sofa. He thought out loud: 'But this is only the first point, the first question . . . Giovanni died today because today was the last time he was going to be coming here to Palermo with any regularity. And they knew that – someone had alerted them . . . His habit of coming down to Sicily almost every week, and always during the weekend, would have been interrupted because his wife Francesca had finally been given the opportunity to stay in Rome for a long time . . . I don't think that fact has ever been in the public domain or published in a newspaper . . . but everyone in here knew.'

Paolo Borsellino went on smoking and remembering, remembering and smoking. Remembering was the only way to try and understand; it was the only way not to be overwhelmed by grief. He had run out of Dunhill Lights and threw the empty pack in a wastepaper basket, opened the drawer of his desk and took out another pack.

His voice was low, a whisper: 'The news was circulating that Giovanni might be the new minister of the interior . . . Do you realise what that would have meant for them, for the Mafiosi?'

Paolo Borsellino didn't say everything that was going through his mind. He didn't say anything about the shadow he sensed beside Cosa Nostra. He didn't say that he saw something more than the bestiality of the Corleonesi in this new terrorist tendency. Cosa Nostra had settled its score with Judge Falcone, but someone else had been involved as well. That evening Paolo Borsellino didn't reveal his presentiments to his young colleagues: that they were going to kill him too. At three in the morning he left the Palace of Justice and went back to the civic hospital. At dawn he was back in court.

For fifty-seven days and fifty-seven nights, Paolo Borsellino lived with the weight of death on his shoulders. There was only one possible means of escape: time, to use speed to grab the Corleonesi by the throat before Totò Riina killed him.

For fifty-seven days and fifty-seven nights, Paolo Borsellino didn't live. He died slowly, week after week, hour after hour, in full view of the city of Palermo, which knew and foretold . . .

The deputy prosecutor asked for an investigation and opened another, another and yet another. He flew to Germany to pursue the trail of the assassins of Marshal Giuliano Guazzelli, assassinated in Agrigento three months before. He left for Rome to listen to the secrets of a *pentito* from San Cataldo. He spent hours in the general prosecutors' office explaining to the magistrates of Caltanissetta the best way to get to Capaci.

'I've got to hurry up, I've got to hurry up,' Paolo Borsellino confessed to his best friend. It was a race against time. He had to close the circle around the Corleonesi.

The man who could close that circle had arrived. He was Asparino Mutolo, the most recent Cosa Nostra *pentito*. He was capable of opening up a gap in the criminal organisation. But he had to be listened to now. His declarations needed to be recorded; they had to understand first and then strike.

'I want to talk to Judge Borsellino . . . The things I have to say are quite alarming . . . I'll only talk to him,' Mutolo told the police and the magistrates.

The chief state prosecutor in Palermo was called Pietro Giammanco. He said to his deputies: 'We choose who needs to be questioner, he doesn't choose for us.' And Deputy Prosecutor Vittorio Aliquò was sent from Palermo.

When Asparino Mutolo saw not Borsellino but another magistrate, he closed his eyes and closed his mouth. Days were wasted. Time passed inexorably.

On Sunday afternoon, Paolo Borsellino allowed himself two hours off. He was exhausted. To distract himself he stayed glued to the television, watching the cyclists in the Tour de France climbing the Galibier under the roasting son. Then he called his mother: 'I'm on my way.'

Cosa Nostra were listening in. The car bomb was already parked below his mother's building. At about five o'clock on 19 July the armoured cars arrived in Via Mariano D'Amelio. One of U Curtu's thugs pressed the button.

THE CIRCLES OF HELL IN PIANOSA

The Mafiosi weren't used to harsh imprisonment. Hundreds of them had spent their whole lives in a cell, but they would never have imagined ending their days on the islands of Pianosa and Asinara. After the summer massacres, the bosses experienced real prison for the first time. They were deported like prisoners of war. The Italian government had taken up the challenge. All the imprisoned men of honour were locked up and isolated in two maximum security prisons.

'The killing of Falcone and Borsellino was the biggest mistake that Cosa Nostra could have made,' two or three ministers proclaimed, and some *capofamiglia* secretly thought the same.

The Ucciardone was besieged one moonlit night. A battalion of paratroopers guarded the three districts of Palermo that surrounded the prison, and the police and *carabinieri* went into the wings and slipped inside the cells of the seventh and eighth section, where forty-seven Mafia bosses and eighty-one *picciotti* were being kept. They woke them up and loaded them onto army trucks. At dawn the following day they took them to the islands of Pianosa and Asinara. They were still weary from the journey and the surprise when they were informed of the rules of the new jail: they wouldn't be able to see wives or children more than once a month, they wouldn't be able to cook their meals in the cells or receive any from outside, they wouldn't see their lawyers every week . . .

The *capimafia* didn't even have time to miss the 'family' atmosphere in the Ucciardone: banquets with fresh lobsters from the fish farms of San Vito Lo Capo, flowing champagne, prison guards always at their disposal, doctors providing fake certificates and opening the doors of the civic hospital. They didn't have time because they knew they were in a circle of Hell.

The prison guards had neither faces nor voices. Their faces were covered by balaclavas, and they had orders not to speak. The prison regime was extremely harsh: total isolation.

Weeks passed, and the Mafia population locked up in Pianosa and Asinara cursed the inventors of the super-jails. Whole families had ended up in Pianosa, *cosche* decimated by police raids, *capidecina* and *capimandamento* with their armies in prison camps. Like the Madonia family of San Lorenzo, like the Greco family of

Ciaculli, the Milanos of Porta Nuova or the Vernengos of Ponte Ammiraglio. All the men were in jail, and only women and children were free.

The days in jail were extremely long, the nights interminable. And the men of honour, sleepless on their beds, started working out what had happened over the past year, the past few years of Cosa Nostra. The shock of the maxi-trial, the anti-crime decrees, the hunt for fugitives, and the cops who had stopped pursuing them solely with words. What on earth had happened? Why had the world suddenly changed direction? Some Mafiosi were scared even to think about it: 'These are the gifts of U Curtu, of his ferocity, of his politics. He's the one who took us to this point.' Some others thought about older rules: We weren't supposed to be fighting against the state, we were supposed to be part of it, to live in peace with the state, that's always been our strength.'

Tommaso Buscetta explained those old laws to the anti-Mafia representatives. He said, 'What really troubles the Mafia is not being able to fulfil the promises made to the prisoners. The man of honour goes to jail sure that his family will be all right, that they won't go hungry. And that as much as possible will be done to get them out. There will never be a man of honour, there has never – excuse me – been a man of honour with any worries on that score. Now he's worried that those commitments won't be fulfilled. That's serious. Very serious. When I say that Totò Riina is in his death throes, it's because the state has really called his bluff. What matters to him is not the life sentences, but his moral undertakings to the people who have followed him. Like the Madonia family. He led them to ruin. They're all in jail, with life sentences. And U Curtu is going to be very, very bitter right now.'

The torments of the men of honour coincided with a very long summer. They knew that outside things were going badly, that the authorities had been looking into their finances, that U Curtu hadn't managed to have the trials 'put right'. They were in prison, Totò Riina had let them rot in prison.

In the cells of Pianosa and Asinara they saw the state funerals of Giovanni Falcone and his wife Francesca on television. They saw a slender, sweet-eyed girl who had moved the whole of Italy: Rosaria Schifani, the young window of a policeman blown up in Capaci. Rosaria spoke to his murderers: 'I forgive you, but fall on your knees.'

Images of the funerals of the victims of the Capaci massacre victims were broadcast and re-broadcast on television for days, weeks, months. Once, in Pianosa, one of U Curtu's butchers looked at Rosaria and started crying. He locked himself in the toilet so that the other men wouldn't see. Pino Marchese had decided to abandon U Curtu to his fate.

There was a big helicopter in the large courtyard of Pianosa prison. The director of the Anti-Mafia Investigations Directorate, Gianni De Gennaro, flew it there day and night. De Gennaro had issued the instruction: 'The tanks must always be full of fuel, and the pilot ready to take off at any time.'

No one had really understood the thoughts going through the policeman's mind. They understood a short time later, when one, two, three, ten Mafia prisoners asked forgiveness for their sins and repented. They were immediately transferred to 'safe houses', far from Pianosa and far from Palermo.

THEY CALLED HIM UNCLE GIULIO

Drama and shame entered Totò Riina's life. U Curtu had a *pentito* in the family: Giuseppe (Pinuzzu) Marchese was his brother-in-law's brother-in-law. It was an indirect link, but in the logic of

Cosa Nostra he was still a relative. To tell the truth, Pinuzzu was something more as well. He was the seventeen-year-old boy that the Corleonese had raised like a thoroughbred horse. U Curtu liked to repeat to his killers:

'Pinuzzu is going to be the smartest of them all.'

In September 1992 Giuseppe Marchese became *pentito* number 224 on the witness protection programme of the Ministry of Grace and Justice.

Pinuzzu was the brother of Luchino Bagarella's wife. U Curtu was deeply hurt, he was bleeding; it was a wound that would never heal.

In the spring of 1991 Luchino married Vincenzina Marchese. The Corleonese had been sentenced to six years in prison, but he had been freed on a technicality. He had taken advantage of the fact to organise his wedding after a long engagement. On the morning of 24 April, a cream-coloured Rolls-Royce drove away from the little church of Casa Professa. It first drove along the alleys of La Magione and then carried on along the coast road. The Rolls-Royce stopped in front of Villa Igiea, the splendid hotel that belonged to the Florio family. Vincenzina was dressed in white, Luchino in blue. There were seventy guests at the wedding feast, all from Corleone and the surrounding area. It was the last time Luchino was seen in public. After that he went on the run.

No one talked about that wedding again until Pinuzzu repented. Then people in several houses in Corleone suffered in silence. And hidden away in those four walls they said to each other the only thing they could say: 'We shouldn't have let Luchino do it . . . he shouldn't have married her . . . he isn't *like us*, he isn't from our village, he's different, he's Palermitan . . .'

Giuseppe Marchese began his revelations by confessing his crimes. He talked about U Curtu's refuges, he revealed how he killed people and had people killed. And he told Inspector

De Gennaro how the massacres of 1992 had come about. The Lima murder, the Capaci dynamite, the Via D'Amelio car bomb. Pinuzzu listed the men closest to Totò Riina and the list of dead that the Corleonese had left behind him. His memories also included a list of police officers 'approached' by the Mafia: the first was Bruno Contrada, a secret service officer who had been head of the Palermo flying squad for many years.

Pinuzzu described the Corleonese as a traitor. In fact, the traitor of Cosa Nostra. He said, 'There's no more room for me in this Cosa Nostra.'

Then he started talking about the maxi-trial, about the pressure exerted on Salvo Lima 'and on other people who had taken a pile of money', about 'characters in Rome' whose identity he didn't know.

'Giuseppe Madonia talked to me about them in Pianosa, but he was very reserved – no names . . .'

Pinuzzu didn't go any further; he didn't stray into unfamiliar territory. Pinuzzu was only Totò Riina's 'favourite hitman'.

Those names were given and those stories told before and after September 1992: years of slaughter and years of repentance.

In June, Asparino Mutolo, the *picciotto* from Pallavicino who had been Riina's cellmate in the Ucciardone a quarter of a century before, and who had taught him to play draughts, had jumped the barricade. In October Leonardo Messina, *capodecina* of San Cataldo, a village just outside Caltanissetta, had spilled the beans. Leonardo was the first Mafioso to give the name of a man who had been president of the council seven times: 'Salvo Lima had been very close to the men of Cosa Nostra, and had acted as Giulio Andreotti's intermediary in the interests of the Sicilian Mafia . . . Lima was in contact with Andreotti, particularly with reference to the "interests" concerning trials against members of the organisation . . . in our circles we called him *lo Zio*, Uncle . . .'

Asparino Mutolo expatiated for weeks about the fixing (*aggiustamento*) of trials, and the unconditional trust that men of honour had in the judge who was to rule on their cases, the president of the first penal section of the Court of Cassation, Corrado Carnevale. Then Asparino came out with the same name: 'Andreotti is the person Lima turned to constantly for the decisions to be made in Rome.'

Gaspare Mutolo and Leonardo Messina drew up a list of men of honour. It included lawyers, notaries, doctors and businessmen. And many 'neighbours' – magistrates, policemen, engineers, architects, civil servants in the Regional Assembly. It was the army of supporters, it was the strength of Cosa Nostra.

An earthquake had devastated and undermined the most powerful criminal organisation in the world. The numbers of *pentiti* were growing from one day to the next. By the end of 1992 there were almost three hundred of them. They revealed the unknown planet in which they had lived. They had seen U Curtu and his Contadini from close up. The last *pentiti* all belonged to the Corleonesi faction. They had no deaths to avenge by making their confessions. They rewrote the history of Cosa Nostra after the crimes reported by Tommaso Buscetta and Salvatore Contorno, Antonino Calderone and Francesco Marino Mannoia.

Masino, Totuccio, *zu* Nino and Ciccio came back on the scene to put on record what they had hushed up at the start of the 1980s. They talked about the relationship between Cosa Nostra and the politicians.

The first one to do so was Tommaso Buscetta. He started again where he had stopped eight years before with Judge Falcone: with the 'tax collectors', Nino and Ignazio Salvo. 'The Salvos were the bridge between Rome and Palermo, with and without Salvino Lima.' Masina remembered a visit of 'thanks' from Tano Badalamenti to Giulio Andreotti for a trial that had gone well:

'Badalamenti confided in me on his return that Andreotti had personally congratulated him, telling him they needed men like him in every street in every city in Italy.'

At last he revealed the name of the mysterious Entity: 'It's Giulio Andreotti'.

Francesco Marino Mannoia followed his example: 'Totò Riina was extremely close to Lima and Ciancimino.'

He remembered an encounter that had happened shortly after the assassination of the president of the Regional Assembly, Piersanti Mattarella, in the first months of 1980. It was a summit in a villa deep in the leafy suburb of Altarello. Mannoia went there with his boss, Stefano Bontate. He saw Giulio Andreotti.

'He was in a dark-coloured Alfa Romeo. He was with the "tax collectors" Nino and Ignazio Salvo.'

The Mafioso didn't go into the villa. He waited outside. He heard shouting. Marino Mannoia said, 'When we left, Stefano Bontate told me Andreotti had come to clear up the Mattarella murder. Stefano was furious. He had told him to his face that we're in charge in Sicily.'

Was that when the Falcon reminded the Entity of the death of Aldo Moro, the mysteries of Michele Sindona, the crime of Mino Pecorelli?

The last *pentito* arrived at the end of the year. Very special, he was the chauffeur who had driven Totò Riina the length and breadth of Sicily for years. His name was Baldassare Di Maggio, Balduccio, the son of a shepherd from San Giuseppe Jato. Balduccio too revealed deeds, misdeeds and murders. Balduccio too reported a meeting 'at a very high level' that he had seen with his own eyes. Salvo Lima was there, and Ignazio Salvo, and Giulio Andreotti and U Curtu were there as well. Balduccio didn't hear what they said, but then he reported: 'The Corleonese kissed Andreotti'.

Secrets of old and new *pentiti*, mysteries of Sicily. The *pentiti* confessed, and meanwhile U Curtu's butchers went on killing. Ignazio Salvo died at the end of the summer, killed in his villa in the rocks of Santa Flavia, past the patrician houses of Bagheria. Ignazio Salvo wasn't just a man of honour who could no longer guarantee his services to U Curtu. Ignazio Salvo was a witness to the history of the Corleonesi.

Christmas hadn't yet come when a violent campaign was launched against the *pentiti*. And U Curtu wasn't the only one pulling the strings. Tommaso Buscetta warned him: First they'll try to discredit the collaborators with justice and the judges, then they'll plant bombs and blow up whole districts . . . the Corleonese is in league with the Colombians, and he's going to kill innocent people . . .'

Tommaso Buscetta said one other thing before he left Italy for ever. It was his prophecy: 'U Curtu will die. Either he'll be killed or he'll kill himself. That's my judgement.'

THE STORY OF BIAGIO M.

It was four o'clock in the afternoon, and Biagio M. was still in the fields. The grey clouds parted from time to time and a tepid sun warmed the valleys and lit up the Rocca di Marineo. Winter was nearly over, and the first two weeks of January had brought neither cold nor rain. Suddenly Biagio saw four, six, perhaps ten police cars driving along the twisting road from Marabino. They were driving in single file, brushing the low stone walls on the bends, and setting off again at full speed on the brief straight segments. They were coming from Palermo.

Biagio M. was a peasant who had spent his whole life in the fields around the Forest of La Ficuzza. He had no children or nephews.

He was a widower, and his wife Maria had died of a heart attack in 1968, at the time of the earthquake. Biagio was a man on his own. He had always worked the earth, for sixty-three years. He felt tired and old, weighed down by thoughts and memories.

The sun was beginning to sink behind the mountains. At four o'clock in the afternoon he went back up the path. An hour later he arrived in Corleone. He was in Piazza Garibaldi, and he went into his usual club to play his usual game of cards. He mentioned the convoy of *carabinieri* he had seen making for the village. Behind he heard just one voice. Two words.

'*U pigghiaru.*' 'They got them.'

No one said anything else and no one mentioned any names.

At eight in the morning they had arrested Totò Riina: in Palermo, near Viale Lazio. After a quarter of a century Totò had landed on the ground, with his face in the dust and a pistol pointed at his temple.

Biagio shivered. The peasant came out of the club without paying any attention to the 'sensational news from Sicily' they were already announcing on the evening bulletins.

His legs and memories carried him to Piazza Soprana, the part of the village where he was born, and where the house no longer stood. Totò's house was still behind the church of Santa Rosalia, on the corner of Via Rua del Piano and Via Ravenna. It was like going back in time; in those deserted streets, days and feelings, joys and disappointments re-emerged like ghosts. And so did the life of Salvatore Riina, the orphaned son of a father whom he had known among the alleyways and found again as a refugee twenty years later. A Mafioso, the boss of all the Mafiosi. Biagio still couldn't understand – and God alone knew how any times he had tried – how that little peasant from Via Rua del Piano had become the godfather of Sicily, the dictator of Cosa Nostra.

Biagio took the steep little streets leading off Piazza Soprana and climbed and climbed until he reached the Saracen Tower. A cold wind was blowing, which stung cheeks and hands, the sky was black and starless. 'Totò was the worst of us . . . and he became the most famous and the richest and the most powerful. Everyone knows him,' thought Biagio. He remembered hundreds of names, hundreds and hundreds of faces, hundreds and hundreds of dead people. Poor Menicu Di Matteo, killed in San Giovanni. And Placido, generous Placido who dreamed of another future. And Michele Navarra, who felt like God the father in Corleone. And poor wretches like Paolo Riina, *u trunzu*, who died without ever knowing why. And old Mafiosi like Carmelo Lo Bue and the Maiuri brothers who died for a war that they didn't want to fight . . . All killed like beasts to the slaughter, by Totò U Curtu. By the guys from Strasatto.

There were lights and there were men shouting orders in the street that ran along below the Saracen Tower. They were *carabinieri*, other *carabinieri* searching the houses on Piazza Soprana, on Vicolo Scorsone, on Via Rua del Piano.

'It isn't over yet,' Biagio whispered as he came down from the hill and walked homewards at midnight.

The next day Biagio didn't go to the fields. It was an uneasy Saturday. Piazza Garibaldi was swathed in silence, as if something was about to happen. Something happened that evening, at around seven o'clock.

Biagio recognised her straight away, by her eyes. They were just as they had been thirty years before: black as pitch, sly, alert, slightly veiled with sadness and weariness of living. It was her, it was Ninetta.

Antonina Bagarella had gone back to Corleone. Thirty-six hours after the capture of Totò Riina. With her two sons and her two daughters. Tano was there too, Tanuzzu, Totò's brother.

Corleone's ghosts were made of flesh and blood. Biagio

thought again of Ninetta and her wretched life. Hidden out of love, forced into hiding. He felt neither sympathy nor sorrow. He didn't feel anything. Ninetta had chosen Totò's life, the life of a murderer. Biagio M. looked at the two men and the two women. Giuseppe Salvatore and Giovanni Francesco, Maria Concetta and little Lucia. He hated Salvatore Riina.

Forty-five days after the capture of the boss of bosses of Cosa Nostra, the peasant from Corleone boarded the coach for Palermo. It was the first one, which reached the city at around nine. Biagio M. hadn't been down to Palermo for seven years, when he had gone to social services to stop his wife Maria's pension.

Biagio wanted to see Totò again; he wanted to recognise the little boy he had left in the fields of Frattina and La Venere del Poggio. It was the first of March and 'after a month and a half of isolation' in the bunker court in Palermo Salvatore came in. Biagio walked along the grim walls of the Ucciardone and started sweating. He was uneasy. He wasn't sure he really wanted to meet this man who had brought only blood and grief to Sicily. The sacrifice of many men, the names of murdered policeman and judges, the last terrible massacres of the summer were still vivid in Biagio's memory. Those memories tormented him. It was a furious disquiet because he couldn't give any meaning to all that violence. Why had they left a murderer like Totò Riina at liberty? Why had that rough peasant been able to win money, impunity and power? Why?

On the steps of the bunker court Biagio found a big crowd that wanted to see the face of the boss of bosses. It appeared in the distance, sunk between the slightly stooping shoulders of a thickset man with unusually long arms. Biagio saw him and couldn't help smiling. He was as he had known him. He was the little boy from Piazza Soprana. With that face halfway between devil and clown, those slits that were his eyes, those thin lips.

When Totò Riina started speaking, his whimpering voice reached all the way to the steps of the bunker. It was that voice that Biagio still had ringing in his ears when one day, forty or perhaps fifty years before, Totò, staring at him with those snake-like eyes, had said to him: 'Biagio, I despise people like you. I can crush them whenever I feel like it. I'm the kind of person who always goes the whole way . . .'

They never met again. Biagio didn't forget.

And now he was listening to the boss of bosses talking about the lies of the *pentiti*, the *tragedie* they created, how those stool pigeons walked arm in arm with each other.

Biagio M. had lived in a Mafia village. He could tell a man of honour from the movement of his eyes, the gesture of a hand, the tone of the voice. He came out of the bunker courthouse of the Ucciardone looking for a thread, the trace of a reason. How had Totò managed to become the boss of bosses? Who had granted him permission? He was a man who had lived by killing and trying not to be killed. He had taken Ninetta and her sons by the hand and walked with them into the nightmare. And the nightmare had also walked with Sicily, with the Sicilians. And with Cosa Nostra.

Biagio M. went back to Corleone. He felt less tired and less old. Everything had a beginning and an end. Even the Mafia. He thought that the beginning of the end of the Mafia was Totò Riina's mask. He liked to think that the Corleone would go down in history as the man who had led Cosa Nostra to ruin.

PART THREE

FROM FATHER TO SON

FROM FATHER TO SON

THE PURE BLOOD OF THE SONS OF CORLEONE

The Ucciardone prison, one winter morning in the year 2000. A woman walks slowly along the corridor that runs along the prison walls and then disappears into the special section, the one where the inmates might as well be buried in the ground. She is wrapped in a black coat, hair gathered under a scarf, dark glasses. As she does on the first Tuesday of every month, Ninetta has come to Palermo to visit Giovanni, her son, already on a life sentence at the age of twenty-four. Behind her is little Lucia, then her older daughter, Maria Concetta. Last of all, a few metres behind, comes Giuseppe Salvatore, *u picciriddu*, the youngest son in the family, Salvo.

The door opens. There's another boy waiting in the room. He is alone, sitting motionless on a chair. They look for one another. Ninetta's hands slide along the armoured glass as if to stroke him. They send each other kisses through the transparent slab that denies any physical contact to the prisoners held under Article 41-bis, the severe prison regime for Mafia detainees. Their eyes meet for several minutes. In the silence, stifled emotions. Then at last mother and son greet one another, and start telling each other about the last four very long weeks: Giovanni in the Ucciardone and all of them in the village. The brothers too yield to reminiscence. The CCTV cameras come on, the bugs record their every whisper.

They talk about their father and his teachings. Their father is Totò Riina, the boss of bosses of Sicilian Cosa Nostra, imprisoned in 1993.

'You remember, Salvo? Papa always used to tell us we were *catu e corda*, bucket and rope; we're like the bucket that ends up at the bottom of the well and the rope you need to pull it back up. We were born always to be together, one tied to the other. Salvo, never forget: the two of us are like twins,' Giovanni whispered to him.

The younger brother replies: 'You see, there are things that Papa said to me too, and which I can't forget.' Their mother nods approvingly at her boys: 'Well done, Gianni, well done, Salvo, well done both of you. I like to hear you talking like that.' Salvo pretends to be disappointed, and gives a start. Then he smiles and raises his voice: 'Who do you think you're talking to? My father's from Corleone, my mother's from Corleone, what sort of blood do you expect me to have?' Ninetta looks at them both. Then, turning serious, she says reassuringly, in a solemn voice: 'Pure blood.'

The sons of Corleone never betray anyone. The name they bear marks their lives for ever. With a furrow. Like a brand. Those sons of Corleone are born and bred to be like their fathers. To do them honour. To preserve their breed, generation after generation.

The sons of *u zu* Totò: they had to become what they became.

During that winter in 2000 Totò Riina, his son Giovanni and his brother-in-law Leoluca Bagarella – the brother of Antonina, known as Ninetta – were held in three maximum-security prisons. One in the north of Italy, another in the middle and a third in the south. Less than two years later *u picciriddu*, Salvo, the youngest male descendant of the clan, would be arrested as well. Pure blood of Corleone.

They all went back to the village on 16 January 1993, less than twenty years after the capture of the *capomafia,* who, just a few months previously, had ordered the death of Giovanni Falcone and Paolo Borsellino.

Mother and sons left the villa in Palermo behind them, beyond the ring road. Via Bernini, a little road with two gates and two exits: one towards the suburb and the other towards the airport. It was their last known refuge. At nightfall they came to Corleone in a taxi. They reappeared like ghosts.

Ninetta holds the hand of Lucia, who is twelve years old. Maria Concetta is barely eighteen. Giovanni and Salvo are two adolescents of sixteen and fifteen.

They all go and live in Via Scorsone, really more of an alley, in the upper part of the village. The old houses of volcanic stone rebuilt after the Belice earthquake in 1968, the wooden shutters replaced by aluminium fixtures, frosted glass on the windows, marble stairs, coloured tiles. The sun never shines on Via Scorsone; the air is stale, the walls sweat with damp and absorb everyone's moods.

Giovanni, Maria Concetta, Salvo and Lucia, who have always lived in hiding with their father and mother, now – for the first time since they were born in that clinic on Via Dante in Palermo – can say their own names without worrying. They have identity cards, an official address. 24 Via Scorsone. It's the house of the Bagarellas, where fifty years earlier Ninetta had met the man who would always be her husband, and for at least two decades the godfather of Sicily.

Those boys have been to Corleone before. They know all the *trazzere,* the paths that cut across the fields of wheat and climb hills covered with olive trees and vines. Giovanni and Salvo move among the cottages scattered around the old estate of Piano della Scala or on the edge of the sanctuary of Tagliavia, in the ravines of the Rocche di Rao, in the gorges that appear like wrinkles on the Montagna dei Cavalli. They doubtless spent several years of their childhood there. The most wanted Mafioso in Sicily also hid in his village, the most protected place for a hunted man, the most sheltered lair. Totò lived in hiding in his own village of Corleone, with his whole family.

They're back. And they're the sons of the most feared man in the Sicilian Mafia. They've made him a prisoner, but in Cosa Nostra that doesn't mean anything: he's still the boss. A boss so different from all the others who came before: paranoid, obsessed with betrayals and conspiracies. Astute, highly skilled at deriving strength from other people's weaknesses. Violent in his behaviour too, never accommodating even in his manners: a tyrant. His sons grow up like him. And in Corleone they soon let people know.

They want to have everyone at their feet. Every gesture has to carry weight. They pose as little bosses, giving orders and demanding devotion. They're angry, just like their father. They don't behave like the sons of the other godfather, Bernardo Provenzano, the old friend of Totò Riina. Angelo and Francesco Paolo came back into town too, all of a sudden. It was in the spring, before the massacres of 1992. But the other two, the Provenzanos, did everything they could to go unnoticed. They went to school in Bisacquino, helped their mother, Saveria, in the laundry that had just opened in the centre of Corleone. They were often seen in the bars or walking along Corso Bentivegna. Angelo and Francesco Paolo had good manners, they were polite. They seemed to have stayed far from the life of their father, a fugitive for forty years. He has been a wanted man since one particular evening in September 1963.

Giovanni and Salvo Riina make a show of themselves in the streets of the village, riding around on motocross bikes. They go up and down from the piazza to the street behind the police station. They slip into the town hall and disappear among the roads in the surrounding countryside, for hours at a time, sometimes for days.

Then they appear in the village. In their own way. In the month of the long truck-drivers' strike in Sicily. There are road blocks, revolts, supermarkets attacked in Palermo and Catania, queues several kilometres long for the ferries across the Strait – the prefects of the nine provinces order petrol rationing across the whole of the island. Every fuel distributor has some set aside for the emergency services: ambulances, firemen, the police. But Salvo doesn't care about the truck-drivers' strike or anything else. He wants his petrol. And on the phone he tells his brother Giovanni about one of his escapades. He doesn't know that the Anti-Mafia Investigation Directorate is listening in.

It's an evening in the third week of the strike when Salvo goes to see Vito, who runs the filling station behind the old Ospedale dei Bianchi. 'Vito, come here,' he says. Vito greets him and approaches him, stammering: 'What's up, Salvo? I'm out of petrol – try tomorrow or the day after.' Salvo grins. 'But I need it now.' Vito starts shaking: 'I've got 200 litres, but they're all for the forces of law and order.' And Salvo tells his brother the words he shouted in Vito's face: 'I told him, "Come here, come here. I'm your force of law and order . . ." And I nicked a forty-litre barrel off him . . .'

They never eat pizza with the other boys from Corleone. They reserve a room for the select few. They can't be with other people at any old table. They always need to dominate everybody. And day after day, they become more and more tough and arrogant. They feel the weight of their father on them. They have to show their Mafia spirit. He's brought them up to be the bosses of Corleone.

Until both of them found themselves in the middle of a legal scandal. They are charged with insulting behaviour.

A captain in the *carabinieri* suspected them from the start. He suspected Giovanni and Salvo and some of their contemporaries; they told him that one night someone had disfigured the stone commemorating the judges Falcone and Borsellino. It had been unveiled a few weeks previously in the piazza in front of the town hall. They defaced it by hitting it with rocks. An insult. How can you commemorate those two magistrates so solemnly with a monument, in Totò Riina's Corleone of all places?

Giovanni and Salvo are interrogated at the barracks, and charged. A few days later the *carabinieri* identify another six boys who were in the square. They confess. They assumed all the guilt and take a plea bargain. And even though it says in the files of the deputy prosecutor who followed the investigations that those six young men 'acted in the interests and on behalf of the young Riinas', Giovanni and Salvo are never brought to trial. There isn't a single piece of evidence against them. And those six boys never give their names away.

The *carabinieri* captain thinks of them again and immediately starts making inquiries when the mayor of Corleone finds a calf's head on his doorstep. A warning.

The mayor talks too much about legality and rules, and every spring he invites Don Ciotti and his boys to lands he has confiscated from the bosses. Ever since his election Cipriani has wanted to erase the bad name that Corleone had acquired in the world thanks to his Mafia. The mayor was given an armoured car and a police escort. Giovanni is reported again, this time for threatening behaviour. But once again there is no evidence, and once again there is no trial.

THE BOSS OF BOSSES

The day before the macabre discovery in front of the mayor's house, Totò Riina's older son has been noticed by a brigadier who is patrolling the countryside. Giovanni is under a tree, bent over the carcass of a recently slaughtered animal. The calf's head is missing.

Ninetta never goes out. She spends days at a time locked up in the little building on Via Scorsone, with its door shut and its windows barred. Only occasionally she was seen kneeling before the altar of Santa Rosalia, the little church that clings to the ridge of the rock that climbs towards the Aldisio tunnel. Always at sunset, and always alone.

Ninetta never goes shopping down in the town square. She never socialises with the women who live on her alley. She never confides in anyone. The few times she walks along the street, other people lower their eyes. And her telephone never rings. No one ever calls her, and she never calls anyone. Ninetta Bagarella buries herself away in her house like a prisoner, like her husband Totò in the Asinara.

Alone in a cell, filmed by a CCTV camera day and night, under surveillance like an animal in a cave. Prevented from meeting other prisoners, receiving letters, reading newspapers, cooking. His food was brought in each morning from a school or hospital canteen chosen at random by the superintendent of the prison register office, then it was tasted by the warders in turn. They act as guinea pigs for the fear of poison, on the orders of the prison authorities.

Totò is a man who keeps too many secrets – about the money made from drug trafficking, about his relations with ministers in Rome and whole gangs of MPs from the Sicilian Regional Assembly, about machinations within the state, and about those 'highly elegant minds' that he was surrounded by when he planned the massacres in Capaci and Via D'Amelio.

His name has already been associated with over fifteen years' worth of trials held in Sicily. Extraordinary crimes, morphine-base trafficking, extortion, public building contracts. And over the next ten years he will remain the most mysterious point of intersection in relations between the Mafia, politicians and big business in Italy. At the epicentre of pacts and encounters – some that actually happened and others that were never proven – between former president Giulio Andreotti and senior members of the 'families'. He is behind economic alliances that have trapped Marcello Dell'Utri, Silvio Berlusconi's Sicilian friend. A puppeteer in negotiations and blackmail involving civil servants within the minister of the interior such as Bruno Contrada, the Palermo policeman who's become a big shot in the secret services. Many of those events are about to come to light. They assume the form of investigations and then of other trials. The accused are all high-ranking men.

There are sentences that cause outrage, and acquittals that cause equal amounts of outrage. The Corleonesi is keeping nerves on edge in the corridors of power in Rome and Palermo.

Totò Riina doesn't say a word from the day of his capture.

Only once do the chief prosecutors of Palermo, Gian Carlo Caselli and Pierluigi Vigna of Florence, try to go and see him. They want to test his availability for a 'more in-depth investigation'. They are to be very disappointed.

It's 22 April 1996, three years and three months after his arrest. The two magistrates have him transported secretly to a bunker courtroom in Tuscany. Their questioning lasts only a few minutes.

Vigna starts to break the silence when he finds himself face to face with the godfather: 'A considerable number of people say that you are the head of Cosa Nostra, so I found myself wondering whether you might be willing to talk . . .' Totò Riina replied: 'Please don't even say the word.' Vigna goes on: 'No, let me finish . . .' And Riina replies, 'Stop there and go no further. You and Judge Caselli have the wrong person. I was expecting you both. Prosecutor Vigna, please spare your breath.' Caselli tries to approach him on another occasion: 'Why do you refuse to listen even to the suggestion of a discussion?' The boss of bosses: 'I have nothing to listen to and I'm hungry, I have pains in my kidneys. please leave me alone and let's pretend nothing happened.' Caselli asks again: 'Could you please explain that phrase: I was expecting you both . . .' Riina: 'I know what you're trying to do and what you're trying to get at.' Caselli: 'Doing our job, our duty'. Riina: 'Go on, go on, just keep on doing your work . . .' Vigna interrupts him: 'Sure, I wanted to see.' Riina: 'For the love of God, who's stopping you . . .' Vigna: 'Certainly not you.'

The two prosecutors get up and leave.

Totò Riina has been sentenced by the state, and then he has sentenced himself to the life of a man who is buried alive, for ever. He already had heirs: his sons.

But his greatest torment – as he will confide some years later to Ninetta in one of the two-hour visits a month in the maximum-security prison – is not having walked his oldest daughter, Maria Concetta, up the aisle.

Maria Concetta has just finished secondary school, and has fallen in love with Antonino 'Tony' Ciaravello. Her engagement has her father's blessing. Tony is from the village. Fat and exuberant, he has studied at the Conservatory and plays the trombone. He is also a DJ on a local radio station and wants to become a businessman, in Corleone.

Since he's been seen in the village with Maria Concetta, no one has dared to call him by the nickname *'Salsiccia & Baccalà'*

– 'Sausage and Codfish' – given to him because of his stout girth. From now on he's Tony and that's that. In fact he's 'the fiancé from Corleone'. The future husband. And above all the future son-in-law.

From Maria Concetta he gets the dowry of respect and a few problems. The officers at the station begin an investigation. The police superintendent of Palermo, Antonio Manganelli, the current chief of police, suggests him to the court for 'special surveillance'.

Tony defends himself. 'My only crime is to love.' He tells everybody: 'They're doing this to me as a snub to him.' 'He' was Totò Riina.

Maria Concetta and Tonino also set up a company selling agricultural machinery, Agrimar, a tractor dealership, a big warehouse and five showroom windows on the outskirts of the village on the road to Palermo. They launch a website – www.corleone.it (now abandoned) – which explains 'who we are', and publicises tractors and threshers. They are joined in the business by Salvo, who is barely an adult.

After a three-year engagement, Maria Concetta and Tony finally get married.

On 6 September 2001 he waits on the steps on the main church in the village, wearing a blue suit and his hair thick with gel. She, in an ivory-coloured dress, gets out of a black Mercedes. The Riinas have invited three hundred guests, all from Corleone, not a single one from the neighbouring villages, let alone Palermo. That's also how it was at Villa Igiea, at the wedding feast of uncle 'Luchino', Leoluca Bargella, when he married Vincenzina Marchese ten years before. The priest who celebrates the wedding in Corleone wishes them well, and remembers 'the suffering of relatives in jail'. They all bow their heads and make the sign of the cross.

In the first pew on the right-hand side of the church there is another Maria Concetta, ninety-three years old. She is the paternal grandmother, Totò Riina's mother. And then there is Francesco Grizzafi, the favourite nephew of the boss of bosses. There's also a third Maria Concetta at the wedding in Corleone: a pretty girl, the daughter of the bride's mother's cousin, another Bagarella. She was engaged to Salvo Riina for a few months. Another union between close relatives. Blood of the same blood.

It's the first time that the Riina and Bagarella families have come together in a public celebration.

The banquet at the La Schiera restaurant is a lavish one. And then there's a honeymoon, very secret. Tony and Maria Concetta would never say where they spent their first night as a married couple. It was a family tradition: Totò Riina had done exactly the same.

That Saturday towards the end of the summer, Maria Concetta was walked down the aisle of the Chiesa Matrice in Corleone by the last male in the Riina family, the youngest, Salvo. In terms of honour and obligation, it should have been his older brother. But Giovanni is in jail. He has strangled a Mafioso with his bare hands – his first homicide. And he has also ordered the death of three villagers. Now the only free man in the family is Salvo, *u picciriddu*.

THE FIRST TIME OF THE FIRST MALE

Someone is following them. Tailing them. In Corleone – *their* Corleone. It's already two years since they came back.

Giovanni Riina and his brother Salvo notice it on the night between 24 and 25 January 1995. A blue car, a station wagon is driving along behind them with its headlights turned out. It accelerates down Corso Bentivegna, falls behind, speeds up and falls behind again. Then it disappears around a corner, into the darkness that climbs up the road towards Bisacquino.

There was someone checking the movements of the two sons of the boss of bosses of Cosa Nostra. He was taking a note of their movements and their habits – he never let them out of his sight. Who could have been brave or stupid enough to keep under surveillance the heirs of the most powerful Mafioso the Sicilian Cosa Nostra had ever known? Did they want to frighten the two boys? Kidnap them? Or actually kill them?

A few days before that night Salvo recognised a car parked a few metres from his house, in the street that cuts across Via Scorsone before heading further downhill. He also saw it the Saturday before, and also on the afternoon of Epiphany.

Salvo scents danger. He talked about it to his uncle Luchino, currently in hiding.

His uncle sometimes came up to Corleone to see him. Or else he and his brother Giovanni would go down to a shack in Giambascio, a rural district on the edge of San Giuseppe Jato. He was almost always in the company of Giovanni Brusca, the man who held the remote control on the hill in Capaci on 23 May 1992. And Vito Vitale, a rough, fierce Mafioso, a new star of the Corleonesi. Brusca and Vitale are also in hiding.

Salvo Riina says to his uncle Leoluca: 'There's a suspicious car driving around Via Scorsone too often, with some guys in it I don't like the look of. I feel I'm being watched.' Giovanni tried to describe the occupants of the car: 'I've seen a dark guy and perhaps a thin one in the car. It isn't just a fantasy of mine: they aren't just shadows, we've also been followed . . .'

His uncle maintains his composure. But he knows that someone in Corleone is preparing to launch an attack. He advises first Salvo and then his brother Giovanni to stay on their guard, to write down the registration numbers of the cars of the outsiders who are driving around the village in those days. He advises his nephews not to tell anyone or ask any of their friends for help. Totò Riina's sons do as they are told. On the morning of 27 January they tell their uncle the registration numbers of the two cars, a Mercedes and an Alfa 33.

Leoluca Bagarella immediately launches an 'investigation'. He orders one of his men to contact someone who can tell him the identity of the owners of the two cars. The task is given to Antonio Calvaruso, a Mafioso who, a year later – in January 1996 – will decide to collaborate with the Anti-Mafia Investigation Directorate and the state prosecutor's office in Palermo.

Calvaruso, reconstructing those events, will later report: 'Giovanni Brusca knew a surveyor in the Department of Motor Vehicles. He gave me his name and I set about finding him. Thanks to him and another contact we had in the Automobile Club, we managed to find out who the owners were.'

They compare notes and Bagarella puts two and two together. The owner of the Mercedes is a delicatessen owner from Palermo. He seems to be 'sound'. He has no previous convictions, and doesn't even seem to have any contacts among the cops. Leoluca Bagarella has him 'watched' for a whole morning. He discovers that the delicatessen owner isn't as much of a stranger as he seemed at first sight: he visits the house of Marcello Grado's mother.

The Grados are a family from the suburb of Santa Maria del Gesù with links to the Bontates and the Inzerillos, the enemies of the Corleonesi who were wiped out in the big Mafia war of the 1980s. And they are also related to Salvatore 'Totuccio' Contorno, a hitman for the old *cosche* who – even after 'repenting' – returns to Palermo to avenge himself on his enemies. Bagarella starts to get frightened, fearing for his nephews' lives, and his own.

Then he asks a Mafioso from the suburb of San Lorenzo about

one Gian Matteo Sole, the owner of the Alfa 33. They tell him the man is related to Marcello Grado. He is his brother-in-law, they assure him. At that point Leoluca Bagarello decides to get rid of them.

The *pentito* Calvaruso later goes on to reveal: 'Bagarella reached the concusion that the Grados and Totuccio Contorno were trying to give Totò Riina a sign by killing his sons. And he gave vent to his rage.'

Calvaruso remembers something else, too: 'One day when someone whispered to him the news that Contorno had also been seen moving about around Via Malaspina, the street in Palermo where Bagarella was hiding, he had a panic attack, and from then on he only ever went out armed.'

Totò Riina's brother-in-law is tormented by the idea that the survivors of the 'old guard' might come back to Sicily to settle their scores with the boss of bosses and all his people. He is convinced that their hatred has never abated.

He repeats: 'They'll do something, you'll see. And not only Totuccio Contorno and his relatives, but also some members of the Inzerillo family. Killing them isn't just in my interst, killing them is in everybody's interest . . .'

It isn't just a matter of the Corleone family. It's the whole Cosa Nostra, re-established by Totò Riina, who is afraid of what the Mafiosi who survived the slaughter of 1981 might do.

Before 'sorting out' those two – Grado and his brother-in-law – Bagarella wants to discover which villagers are spying on the movements of Giovanni and Salvo Riina. Who provides the *battuta*, the final order; who can move around in Corleone without the help of someone in the place? And then: who owns the station wagon that followed Giovanni and Salvo's car during the night of 24 and 25 January? They aren't from Palermo. They're from Corleone.

THE BOSS OF BOSSES

It is Giovanni Riina who recognises the man in the station wagon three days later. He runs to his uncle: 'It's Francesco Saporito.' Then he brings Bagarella's friends to the square in front of the town hall, and points out another of the men who had been tailing him: 'That's the other one, it's Giuseppe Giammona.'

Giovanni Riina mutters: '*Rumpitici i corna.*' Cut their horns off. Kill them both.

Francesco Saporito works as a labourer on a building site in the Ficuzza forest. He's thirty years old. Giuseppe Giammona is twenty-two and a shopkeeper, with a drapery business in the middle of the village. They are brothers-in-law. Giovanna, Giuseppe's sister, is married to Francesco.

Leoluca Bagarella launched the usual 'investigation' into all their friends and relations. He is convinced that Saporito is in some way connected to Pino Leggio, an old boss who in turn is closely connected with old *capimafia* from Bagheria who are lined up against the Corleonesi. And then he imagines – his brother-in-law, uncle Totò, has been infected by the same insane conspiracy theory – that they must also be friends of Grado's.

Saporito and Giammona are always together. What one one of them thinks, Bagarella suspects, the other thinks too. Bagarella puts two and two together once more. He calls a meeting of his men in the rural district of Giambascio.

Giovanni Brusca is there, and so is his brother Enzo, and Vito Vitale from Partinico, and Vincenzo Chiodo and Giuseppe Monticiciolo of San Giuseppe Jato. Together they organise the murder.

They get hold of disc signals and flashing lights, planning to disguise themselves as police officers and stop Giuseppe Giammona at a road block, before loading him onto a van and taking him into the countryside to 'question' him. But then Bagarella thinks the kidnapping sounded too complicated. He brings guns to Giambascio. Three calibre-38 revolvers, a 357 Magnum, a rifle loaded with gunshot, a Thompson submachine gun and a Kalashnikov. They give another three pistols to Giovanni Riina. One automatic and two revolvers. He and his brother have to defend themselves. They always have to go around armed.

They start with Giuseppe Giammona. It's Saturday 28 January, three days after Totò Riina's sons got frightened in their car on Corso Bentivegna.

They divide up into three groups. The ones doing the shooting get into a red Peugeot. They are Enzo Brusca and Vito Vitale. They reach Corleone at sunset. On Corso Bentivegna there are hundreds of people walking by. They park the car a few metres from the clothes shop, put on surgical latex gloves, grab their pistols and go inside.

'How can I help you?' asks Tania, Giuseppe's fiancée who is standing behind the window. 'Like this,' Vitale replies. He takes out his 357 Magnum, aims it at the young man and fires. Four shots to the head. Then they walk slowly away through the crowd. The red Peugeot is burned at night, in an alley leading up to Montelepre.

There hadn't been a murder in Corleone for eighteen years. After the killing of Ciccio Coniglio on the boss's orders for poking his nose into the secret of the burial of Calogero Bagarella, only one other person had been shot. His name was Giovanni Palazzolo, a livestock breeder.

The last 'maschiata', the last firework display, was in July 1977. That was the rule they had imposed on the Corleonesi. No crimes in the village. Don't shit on your own doorstep.

But this time they are threatening the lives of Giovanni and Salvo; this time they have to demonstrate what will happen to anyone who risked challenging the boss of bosses.

Bernardo Provenzano, the other grand old man in the Sicilian Mafia, lets it be known from his safe house that it would be better to wait before taking up arms and killing someone in the village. He wants to reflect on the consequences. For him one homicide was already too much, let alone two or even three.

Bagarella replies: 'You do the thinking, Binnu, and in the meantime what shall I do? Wait for them to kill my nephews?'

At the funeral of Giuseppe Giammona, Giovanni Riina's friends make their houses available to hide the hitmen. They film all the men in church on their video cameras. They want to capture their faces; they want Giovanni to recognise someone else among the people they've been tailing.

Less than a month later, on 22 February, it is Francesco Saporito's turn. And that of his wife Giovanna. They are slaughtered in front of their baby son.

They prepare the same weapons. Pistols and rifles and submachine guns. They set off in three cars again, in single file from Giambascio towards Corleone. Leoluca Bagarella and Vito Vitale put on wigs, and then the usual latex gloves. They drive to a warehouse where Giovanni Riina is waiting. He had the job of patrolling the streets of the village, identifying the victim and alerting his uncle and the other hitmen.

When Giovanni intercepts him on Via Crispi, Bagarella ordered his nephew: 'Make sure people see you. Go into the piazza; everyone has to remember that you went for a walk this evening.' This is the alibi for the boss's son. Then the other men's cars set off. They pull up alongside Francesco Saporito's Fiat Uno and start firing. They kill him and his wife Giovanna. A ricochet also injured their two-year-old son.

A few minutes later a *carabinieri* patrol catches up with them. They escape for a few kilometres along the alleys of Corleone, then abandon the car and two Kalashnikov clips. Then, clutching their guns, they stop a car, force a boy and his fiancée to get out, and drive off.

During those nights, for three weeks, Giovanni and Salvo Riina don't sleep on Via Scorsone. They are at the home of their cousin Mario Grizzafi, protected by older relatives. They are living in fear.

The *carabinieri* were bugging their phones. A member of the family let slip one word too many.

It's an evening in late January when Antonino Ciaravello calls his fiancée Maria Concetta Riina. She says: 'Problems, right?' Tony replies: 'It's a miracle that Giovanni's alive.' Maria Concetta: 'Fuck, then that's exactly what we were thinking.' Tony *s'annaca*, he boasts to his fiancée: 'Certain people have tried to get in here. Luckily my father worked it out and saved your brothers.'

Only later do they discover that Giuseppe Giammona, who worked in the draper's shop, his sister Giovanna and her husband, Francesco Saporito, had nothing to do with tailing the boss's sons or – apart from a very distant relationship – with old Pino Leggio from Corleone. Or with the Grados from Palermo. They are respectable, law-abiding people; they led a normal life. It was only by chance that night that Francesco Saporito found himself in his station wagon with its lights out behind Giovanni Riina's car on Corso Bentivegna. Just a very unfortunate coincidence.

It took only a suspicion for the death sentence to be passed. It took only the suggestion of Giovanni Riina. Leoluca Bagarella's madness did the rest.

The investigations and three trials will ascertain that the three vitims were 'entirely unconnected' with a plan to kidnap or attempt to murder the sons of Totò Riina.

But Leoluca Bagarella hasn't forgotten those two Palermitans, the one in the Mercedes and the other one in the Alfa 33.

Over the weeks following the deaths in Corleone they go in search of Marcello Grado. They post themselves outside his house in the village of Santa Rosalia and on 2 March they rain bullets down on him. A few days later in a street in Palermo they pick up Gian Matteo Sole and take him to a warehouse on the eastern edge of the city, where they torture him. Leoluca Bagarella wants to make him confess the names of all his accomplices. Gian Matteo also confesses things that he doesn't know. Then they strangle him.

Gian Matteo is innocent as well. He isn't Marcello Grado's brother-in-law. The Mafiosi have got the wrong person: the man they wanted was his brother Massimo. The two men were as alike as two drops of water: both slim, both with the same haircut and the same coal-coloured eyes, the same weasel face and slight fuzz on their upper lip. The two brothers were nicknamed 'the little mice'. They looked like twins.

They know him as a landowner. But Antonio Di Caro is also a 'made man'. The Corleonesi suspect that he is a spy as well, an informer for the *carabinieri* in Agrigento. They have caught too many fugitives in that province over the last few months. And '*il dottore*', as he is called because of his degree in agriculture, probably does his fair share of talking. Leoluca Bagarella is convinced of it. As ever, he makes an irrevocable decision: *il dottore* must die.

He takes Vito Vitale under his wing. And Giovanni Riina. He wants to test 'the boy' in the field. He wants to be present at his nephew's 'baptism': his first homicide. Giovanni has just turned nineteen. And he doesn't disappoint his uncle.

The agricultural businessman Antonio Di Caro was originally from Canicattì, a lush area near Agrigento, where his father Giuseppe was considered a 'patriarch', before falling into disgrace and being killed in 1991. The land that his son had inherited, a terrain of vines and orchards, stretches to the edge of the village of Delia, in the province of Caltanissetta. It is there that *il dottore* had his big farm. And it is there, one morning in 1995 – 22 June – he receives a phone call from a 'friend' in San Giuseppe Jato, inviting him to 'take a walk towards Giardinello'.

Il dottore knows the area. He has been there two or three times to reach agreements with Giovanni Brusca about *'la creatura'*, little Giuseppe Di Matteo, the son of a *pentito* that the Corleonesi had kidnapped, held captive for almost two years and then dissolved in acid. For a number of weeks the Corleonesi put the little boy 'in the care' of Di Caro, who, after transferring the child from one car boot to another at a turn-off on the Palermo–Catania motorway, hid him on his farm.

Leoluca Bagarella's invitation to Giardinello seems normal, one like many others. That afternoon, *il dottore* pays no heed to the committee of honour in an old house among the palm trees and orange groves of the Palermitan countryside far from the sea. Bagarella sits at the head of the table, Vito Vitale near the door, a highly excitable Giovanni Riina at the end of the room. Giovanni is darting frantically from one side to the other, and can't sit still. Every now and again he gives *il dottore* a sidelong glance.

'They made Giovanni do everything; his uncle Bagarella wanted to teach him the trade, show him how to kill *cristiani* (human beings),' Giovanni Brusca will reveal years later when he too becomes a *pentito*. And Brusca also remembers: 'I wasn't there, but they told me afterwards . . . it was Giovanni Riina who first kicked him in the chest and then put the rope around his neck and pulled it while the others complimented him on his work. The son of *zio* Totò had behaved well, he did a good job . . .'

Giovanni supplies the proof that his uncle was looking for. At his first murder he doesn't look away when his victim is dying. He shows character and determination. He doesn't give in. He doesn't feel pity. A 'brave' son, a man of honour, worthy of his father, his uncle, the whole Corleone 'family'.

After being strangled, the corpse of Antonio Di Caro is buried and Giovanni Riina goes back to the village. By now it is dawn on 23 June 1995.

The next day, in Palermo, seven armed agents of the Anti-Mafia Intelligence Directorate surround 'Signor Franco' in Via Malaspina. That is the name by which people in the district know Leoluca Bagarella. The boss behind the massacres, Totò Riina's brother-in-law, has been captured. Once he is in jail the era of bombing that began with Capaci comes to an end.

A few months before his arrest, one morning 'Signor Franco' comes home and finds his wife Vincenzina dead. She has hanged herself out of shame. She could no longer bear being pointed out in Corleone as the sister of Pinuccio Marchese, Totò Riina's loyal driver, who turned *pentito* three years before. Vincenzina has left a letter. Leoluca Bagarella buries her in a secret place, and her grave will never be found.

There are no longer any men of the 'family' in Corleone. Only the boys are still at liberty, the sons and nephews. All the others are prisoners under 41-bis.

But the ending of the 'black novel' of the Corleonesi has not yet been written. A year later, the *carabinieri* burst into the house on Via Scorsone and take away Giovanni, who has been identified as an accessory in three crimes in Corleone, and as a 'material perpetrator' in the murder of Antonio Di Caro, *il dottore* from Canicattì. Six *pentiti* have given his name. He has been trapped by wiretaps.

The investigation into the deeds of the first male son of the boss of the Sicilian Cosa Nostra shows another face of the Corleonesi who came from nowhere, the *viddani*, the common peasants fighting an ancient feud. They haven't been finished off by the arrest of Totò Riina in 1993, or the arrest of Leoluca Bagarella. They have a future. Blood of the same blood, their sons are keeping their Mafia going.

In the 1990s the police and the judiciary come down hard on the faction of Cosa Nostra that has transformed Palermo into Tombstone, a city of graves.

After Leoluca Bagarella they also pick up Giovanni Brusca, and nearly three hundred men of honour. The 'families' of the Corleonesi have been destroyed in a military sense. But their fortune is still almost intact. Many Mafiosi have made the jump; some out of conviction, others out of convenience. They start revealing organisation charts and collusions, talking about compromised politicians, lawyers and magistrates who have allowed Cosa Nostra to amass an extraordinary amount of power over the years, infiltrating themselves into every area of public life.

Not since the days of Giovanni Falcone's first investigation into the affairs of the *cosche* have the Mafia endured such a blow. It looks shambolic now, almost mortally wounded. With Totò Riina's strategy of mass murder, the organisation has found itself on the brink of a precipice. The only figure still at liberty, pulling the strings, is the other big boss of Corleone: Bernardo Provenzano. He is still in hiding.[1]

But for those who are inside there is no escape. For the 'incarcerated ones' it is an unprecendented defeat.

The first trial against Giovanni Riina reaches its conclusion on 23 November 2001. Life. The Appeal trial finishes on 11 December 2003. Life. The Court of Cassation delivers its verdict on 24 January 2005. A life sentence.

---

1 Bernado Provenzano was eventually captured in 2006.

THE FAMILY IN SALVO'S HANDS

The fate of the Mafia of Corleone lies in the hands of Salvo, *u picciriddu*. His father doted on him, even though Giovanni is more like him, at least in terms of his physique and his features. Short, stocky, with a broad face, with the air and the way of talking of a 'peasant' that make him so like Totò Riina as a young man. But his father's eyes gleam when he talks about the other boy, his younger son. He thinks he's less rough, a more subtle thinker, more aware of himself and his own future. He knows he is a true Corleonese. Salvo was proud of his roots. He was the natural successor. And besides, of all the Riinas, he is now the only one at liberty.

But Cosa Nostra's boss of bosses could never imagine Salvo slipping into 'those nooses': police traps, complications, lawyers, trials. Certainly not like that, not with those people. With the Palermitans.

Totò Riina discovers the commotion surrounding his son late in the year 2000 when, in the prison of Ascoli Piceno to which he has been transferred – after seven long years of isolation from the world – he is finally able to read the *Giornale di Sicilia*.

He is far from content that morning when he finishes running through an article at the bottom of the news page reporting some quotes from Salvo's friends in Palermo. They are in inverted commas – conversations intercepted by the *carabinieri* on three mobile phones. Some of them spoke and raved about the litigiousness between the Sicilian 'families', showing certain fears about possible reprisals against the Corleonesi, giving the full names of the men of honour. It immediately becomes obvious to Totò Riina that the source of these words is his own son. It's as if they've opened up Salvo's head to look inside. And they've seen a lot in there. He's furious. It's the first time that *u picciriddu* has 'behaved badly'. He can't believe it.

During the first prison visit, he gives his wife Ninetta a message to take to Corleone: 'Tell Salvo to get rid of all these mobile phones and everything. Has he lost his mind?'

The boy's mother goes back to the village and tells her son about his father's anger. Salvo defends himself, but he doesn't tell Ninetta everything, not least because he doesn't know everything. Salvo doesn't know, for example, that the police have hidden a bug in his Audi. They'd been listening in on him for several months, and will go on doing so for almost two more years.

All the wiretaps end up in the deposition for trial number 13100/100 in the district prosecutor's office in Palermo. It contains the life of Giuseppe Salvatore Riina, known as Salvo, from the beginning of May 2000 to 5 June 2002 – the day when he too will end up in jail; like his father, like his uncle Leoluca Bagarella, like his brother Giovanni.

It's Palermo that *u picciriddu* loathes and adores. It enchants and intimidates him at the same time. He has been taught to mistrust everything beyond the village boundaries of Corleone. He has been inculcated with the idea that you can never turn your back on anyone in that city. They're traitors. They don't respect the rules. They don't have a sense of honour, as the Corleonesi do.

Some mornings Salvo goes down to Palermo before midday. From the fast-flowing sliproad that leads to the Marineo turn-off he can see the sea, the gardens scented with orange blossom, the peak of Montepellegrino and the haze surrounding the sanctuary of Santa Rosalia. Then he enters the city along Via Messina Marine or the other way, by Via Messina Montagne. And he always heads towards the centre. Meanwhile satellites are recording all his movements. The police always know exactly where he is. In Via Magliocco, behind the central branch of the Banco di Sicilia. At the restaurant U Strascinu, on the avenue that runs along the suburb of Uditore. At the Coga bar, on the corner of Viale Lazio and Via delle Alpi. He always held his meetings in the same place. Sometimes they would meet him at a tailor's shop in Via Parisa, a side-street of Via Libertà, the most beautiful street in Palermo.

He often meets a young man a few years older than himself, a certain Salvatore Cusimano, with a clean criminal record. Salvatore has no record himself, but he *knows* everyone. He is 'introducing' Salvo into the Palermo Mafia. He is presenting him to the new heads of the 'families' and the '*mandamenti*', and their relations. That's the task assigned to Salvatore Cusimano: to open all the doors to the son of *zio* Totò. He has to pass on his father's 'contacts' to his young heir – his contacts both within Cosa Nostra and outside it. They always talk in the car, about men of honour, about '*bravi cristiani*', about money, about *pizzo*. About the recent massacres, and the old bosses who want to raise their heads again. About building contracts, and about a small treasure.

Salvo Riina is obsessed by watches, and wanted to buy a Rolex Daytona. He confesses his weakness to a friend: 'I'd settle for a Bulgari – gold though . . . the ones with the crown and it says Bulgari, you know. I – *minchia* – have two watches. You wouldn't believe your eyes – other people could only dream of them . . . and they're all stored away, properly kept . . . I have a big turnip watch in red gold, and a Cartier with a leather stap, one with a red-gold face, one made of normal steel . . . things you never see . . .'

His friend waits until he has finished and tells him the right place to go to find his watches. He says: 'You have to go and see Raul Senapa.'

Salvo asks, 'Who's Senapa?'

Cusimano replies, 'He's got a cousin with his finger in lots of pies.'

'Ah.'

'They're related to the Lucchese family, to the Spadaros – they've always had very good friendships . . .'

Salvo asks again, 'And he only deals in watches and precious stones?'

Cusimano laughs: 'Nooo . . .'

The cousin 'with his finger of lots of pies' is Pieruccio Senapa, a hitman from the Kalsa. The Spadaro family come from the same district. Tommaso, the boss of the 'family', is sitting out the last three years of a twenty-five-year sentence for international drugs trafficking. Every now and again in Palermo Salvo will also see his son 'Francolino', who has just got out of jail as well and who has seen to it that all the restaurants and trattorias take the mozzarella delivered to him every morning from Campania.

In Palermo all they eat now is 'Francolino'-brand buffalo mozzarella.

And he also sees Roberto Enea. Enea's uncles ended up en masse in the maxi-trial. Salvo socialises with the heirs of the other Mafia bosses. He chooses them carefully, and tells his friend Salvatore never again to introduce him to anyone without first 'weighing him up'. He had to be sure about where he came from and 'who he belongs to'. Salvatore tries to argue: 'I just have to look in someone's face; I look him in the eye and I take his photograph.' Totò Riina's son replies: 'I'm sorry for speaking like this, but when one of these *cornuti* turns up and takes all our comfort away, has our properties confiscated, our raw materials and our money . . . before I meet someone you've got to bring me his pedigree. You bring me his pedigree and we'll see. You can't have a coffee with anybody any more.' And then he tells his friend: 'I'm not interested in the crowd – you've got to introduce me to the right people at the right time. I can't trust these *scafazzatti*, these losers . . .'

Salvo is twenty-three years old when he goes around Palermo saying he doesn't want to be approached by anyone without a 'pedigree'. It wasn't just the empty talk of a boy, but the boasts of the favourite son of the boss of bosses. Salvo goes to the city to conquer it, as his father had done twenty-five years before. He's looking for *piccioli*. He's looking for straw men, and he's already found some. He also throws himself into public works, at the port of Palermo.

The motorway at Punta Raisi is brightly lit, and Salvo Riina's Audi is heading swiftly towards the city. It's sunset. At the bend in the road, a few metres before the Capaci turn-off, there is a line of blue floral wreaths. This is the place where the ground opened and Judge Falcone's armoured car was swallowed up.

The son of the Mafioso who ordered the massacre comments on the flowers to his inseparable friend Salvatore Cusimano.

'*Ci appizzanu le corone a stu cosu.*' They're laying wreaths for that guy. Salvatore, who is dozing, wakes up all of a sudden. Salvo Riina growls: 'It was tough. They paid the consequences, but they behaved like men in the end. That stings more than anything. Men.' The young man is referring to his father and his uncle who 'behaved like men in the end'. Salvo shares the choices they made, but regrets what happened later.

They are already in the tunnel of Isola delle Femmine when Totò Riina's son remembers: 'There was too much determination, and then the ball slipped away . . . in '92, in May. That massacre, the other one in July, and then they arrested my father in January . . . Because I don't know what would have happened to him if the state hadn't sawn his horns off . . .' A few seconds of silence, and the dialogue resumes: 'Telling the state: *cca semu nuatri*, we're in charge here. And instead his foot slipped . . . because we cut everybody's horns and told them: here in Sicily we're in charge, maybe you are up there, but we're in charge here.' Salvatore Cusimano tries to cut in: 'The guys who tried to replace him didn't . . .' Salvo doesn't let him finish the sentence: 'He didn't have the guts to take it further . . . a colonel always needs to make decisions, and he has to take responsibility. He can't go: what are you telling me, what's going on? He has to make a decision, and the decision was this: kill them. And they were killed . . . He did horrible things because there were limitations on freedom . . . but they did four or five years; it's not the end of the world. The Palermitans are a bunch of softies . . .'

On those short trips from Corleone and around the suburbs of Palermo, Totò Riina's son never suspects that someone might have put a bug in his car. When would they have done it? How? And where? He and his bodyguards have never taken their eyes off the Audi from the day he bought it. They keep close watch on it even in Corleone. Even on the street that runs below Via Scorsone.

Salvo feels that he was in safety. He talks, he is always talking, to his friend Salvatore. Even about 'pizzo', about extortions. And how to make dirty money disappear: 'Salvato, if you think about what my father did – I tell you, what my father did in the way of pizzo, these days we couldn't do one per cent of that. And I'll tell you why.' Young Riina expatiates at length on comparisons with the past, but demonstrates that he knows how to keep his feet on the ground. And he explains to his friend: 'Today you take 730, 740, you have to declare it, pay a bit of tax – you need to do that with this stupid fucking state . . . and then buy, you can afford to buy something too. If they ask you how you managed to buy that thing? You tell them: I'm earning 50 million, 50,000 euros a year. Unfortunately we need to justify ourselves. But at my house they're all pensioners. So you've got to know . . . you've got to know how to recycle illegal money, and you've got to make it look clean.'

His friend listens, thunderstruck. Salvo climbs into the pulpit to deliver his sermon: 'Otherwise we haven't done anything. If you keep your money under your mattress, it stinks . . . You've got to look legal for appearance's sake; you've got to fill your bags with the illegal stuff . . .'

Sometimes Antonio Bruno, a boy from Corleone, also sits next to him in the Audi. He was the 'godson' of Giovanni, Salvo's brother.

He has no inhibitions about talking to him either, about *pentiti* and politics and Giovanni's legal problems. They call San Giuseppe Jato 'the village of the stool pigeons'. All the collaborators with justice who caught Giovanni Riina for the three murders in Corleone and the strangling of the *dottore* in Canicattì came from there. 'We've got to set fire to San Giuseppe Jato,' Salvo is always saying.

Antonio's question comes promptly: 'What I want to know is why the *pentiti* are worthless now, to people like Berlusconi or Andreotti? What is their work based on?' Salvo repied: '*Minchia*, on all that power they have, all that shitty power, Antonio, let's talk about something else. Let's not talk about such things because I'm fed up with it all. I swear, it disgusts me, being judged by three wasters like that . . .'

Eventually they're joined in the car by another man the police will never identify. He has a strong Corleone accent. Only his name was known: Carmelo.

It's the eve of the 2001 political elections, and Carmelo hopes there will be a new government in Italy: 'The important thing is that the Soviets don't climb to the top.'

Salvo replies: 'They can fuck off straight away . . . Carmelo, a fish rots from the head. We start from Rome and then we see what needs to be done. Once our general headquarters is in Rome, we reassure Rome and then we can start talking. The magistates and everything . . .'

Salvo is starting to get his hands on Palermo. His friends are in contact with a well-known engineer about work in the port. There are docks that need rebuilding; one contract is worth 24 billion old lire, the other 16. The engineer is asking favours of politicians, negotiating with civil servants in the Regional Assembly and officials from the harbour office. He refers to straw men who in turn report each evening to the son of Totò Riina.

But that is only one of many apparently legal activities. Then there are the others. The police are convinced that the young Corleonese has unleashed a platoon of *'esattori'* around the city and that they've already started making extortions.

There is talk of contracts, of businessmen who 'aren't doing what they're told', of businessmen who need 'cutting down'. There's also someone who refuses to pay. He's a tobacconist on Via Pitrè. The *esattori* of Palermo can't get the payments of the *pizzo* out of him. Salvo tells Salvatore Cusimano: 'Give me his full name, the area, what the shop's called, and then let me sort it out. He won't know what's hit him.'

One day Salvo Riina asks the Prefecture of Palermo to release his anti-Mafia certificate.

He needs it to open a commercial enterprise. His official profession – as recorded at the Chamber of Commerce – is 'business agent for agricultural tools and machinery'. But he is going into business with his sister Maria Concetta and his brother-in-law Tony in Agrimar, the dealership in Corleone selling tractors and threshing machines. And he needs that permit. He needs a stamp of good conduct from the state. He presents the demand: 'I have the right and the duty to work honestly to support my family.'

The Prefect Renato Profili denies him his anti-Mafia certificate 'on the grounds of unequivocal closeness to Cosa Nostra'. His father has already accumulated thirteen life sentences. And then the Prefecture – as bureaucratic practice requires – requests information on the 'subject' from the police. The flying squad informs them that 'investigations are under way'. There's a bug in his car revealing all his secrets.

Agrimar opens anyway, with a straw man at its head. During one of his prison visits to Giovanni, he tells him how business is going: 'We've increased our profit by three hundred per cent on last year with the pruning machines . . .' Giovanni makes a joke: 'Better than [Berlusconi's company] Mediaset, who have only gone up by fourteen per cent, and you've gone up by three hundred per cent . . .' And Salvo again: 'Last year we sold four pruning machines and twelve this year; next year it'll be thirty-two, and the year after that, seventy-four. One company: Agrimar. One brand: same.' And before saying goodbye to Giovanni and leaving jail, he tries to boost his morale. 'When you get out of here we'll have to get together, united we could be a volcano . . .'

Salvo Riina also wants to open an agricultural machinery repair shop in Corleone. But there already is one of those in the district of Maddalena, run by Nunzio Vernagallo.

In his interminable chats with Salvatore Cusimano and Antonio Bruno, Salvo lets himself go: 'That bastard Nunzio.' His friend Antonio goes one further, as he guesses the thoughts running through the head of Totò Riina's son: 'We should put a rocket launcher on the edge of the road; they've got these ones that just fire once – you use them and then you throw them away . . .' Salvo drops the subject. Antonio goes on talking about business at Agrimar: 'We need to meet the guys from Anas.' Salvo asks, 'Why?' Antonio replies, startled: 'What do you mean why? To give him those lawnmowers we've got.' Salvo: 'Cuffa's just become the president of the company . . . we've got the president there, the local chief here, the one with the white hair and the moustache.'

The day after that exchange, Salvo receives an unexpected

phone call. There's someone called Franco on the line: 'Franco here. Yesterday I bumped into someone in the restaurant that I think you should meet: he's a mate of mine, his name's Giovanni Assiria.' Salvo never goes to meetings without knowing who's going to be there. He's curious but largely indifferent. He says, 'Giovanni Assiria? Don't know him.' Franco: 'Of course you don't know him, but so what? He runs the forest rangers' fleet, you know?' Salvo replies: 'Don't tell me any more, I'm excited already.'

He sniffs another business deal for his pruning machines and his tractors. The head of the forest rangers' fleet could do a lot for Agrimar in Corleone.

The last time the police listen in on Salvo's voice – before the bug placed in the Audi is deactivated – he's with his mother. And he says to her, 'You're always going on about these things . . . I don't want them, they'll confiscate them from me . . .' Ninetta has doubts, and tries to persuade her son to buy a house: 'I'm sorry, where are we supposed to go?' And Salvo tells her, 'To a rented house, so that then when they confiscate it they confiscate it from the godfather, and what are we supposed to do? That's the modern way, Mamma. You can't buy properties any more.' And Salvo and Ninetta start whispering about a fortune that they've hidden far away from Corleone. In Switzerland.

On 5 June 2002 Giuseppe Salvatore Riina is arrested for Mafia association and extortion. It's a swoop. He and twenty-one other accomplices are locked up in the Ucciardone. The police operation puts Totò Riina's last child out of action. A harsh prison regime for him as well.

At the first trial he is sentenced to fourteen years and eight months in solitary. At the Court of Appeal the sentence drops to eleven years. On 3 July 2007 the Court of Cassation drops the sentence for extortion and also the one for criminal association with a remand order. Salvo's trial for mafia association has to be held again. By now he has spent more than five years in jail, and the term of his preventive detention is about to run out. The last Riina will return to Corleone a free man. Unless the magistrates in Palermo 'force' him to live in exile on the mainland.

As in Palermo the sons of the friends of *u zu* Toto. The youngest son of Ciccio Madonia, Salvino, will take back control of the territory of Resuttana. Benedetto, the youngest of the Graviano brothers, the accessories to the murder of Don Pino Puglisi and the bombs in Milan, Florence and Rome, will go back to Brancaccio. They'll be out in a few months. Not just them, but others too.

The 'young lions' of the Palermitan Mafia will also meet up with old acquaintances and names for a glorious, hated time. Like the Inzerillos, who have fled to America where they are protected by their cousins in Cherry Hills, New Jersey.

THE REPATRIATION OF THE INZERILLOS

The Inzerillos of Passo di Rigano have lived in hiding for two decades and – along with them – the Di Maggios, the Gambinos, the Spatolas, another big 'family' of blood and Mafia, united by marriages between cousins (a tangle of recurring names) and even more by the memory of identical mourning, filled with a desire for revenge that poisons the soul.

As in the Bible – Adam, betrayed; Esau, betrayed; Giuseppe, betrayed; Moses, betrayed; Samson, betrayed; Samuel, betrayed; David, betrayed; Job, betrayed by God himself; and God himself betrayed by mankind – in the history of the Inzerillos it's betrayal that separates life from death, the past from the future. Totuccio Inzerillo is betrayed and killed in 1981. At that time people are betraying the family so as not to be killed – like Franco Inzerillo (*u nivuru*), Totuccio's cousin. He barters his life, his safety, for the death of Pietro, Totuccio's brother. The Corleonesi look for Pietro everywhere, from the mass-killings in the 1980s, to complete the work begun with the little killing spree of Totuccio and his son Giuseppe and his brother Santo, whose corpse was never even found. And another twenty-one Inzerillos: uncles, cousins and nephews.

The Corleonesi know that Pietro is in Philadelphia. They know that he runs a few restaurants and pizzerias. They never find him where he's supposed to be. But *u nivuru* provides the *battuta*, the necessary information. He tells them how and where to find him. On the morning of 15 January 1982 Pietro, Totuccio's brother, is in a car in the car park of the Hilton hotel in Mont Laren, New Jersey, with his head thrown back and a bullet in his head. His balls have been cut off and a bundle of dollar bills stuffed in his mouth. They all wanted to 'eat' too much – the Inzerillos, the Spatolas, the Gambinos, the Di Maggios – fattening themselves up on the heroine trade as if, by some gift of God, the fat of the land was their due and theirs alone, leaving only crumbs for the rest of us. Now they could choke on their money. Let it kill them, because, *u zu* Totò, they're all going to die, from the first to the last, in Sicily, in New Jersey, wherever they're hiding in America. 'Not so much as a seed of theirs must be left on the face of the earth.' That was what *u zu* Totò said, and the new Corleonesi *capimandamento* of Uditore, of Brancaccio, of La Noce, of Torretta and Boccadifalco agreed. That was how it would have been if Riina hadn't had to make a virtue of a necessity, biting his lips with rage.

The five big New York 'families' – the Gambino, Bonanno, Lucchese, Genovese and Colombo families – didn't want the organisation to turn into a death factory. You can't do *bisinissi* with death. All you get from death is hassle and cops and life in jail. They had to split from all that dark stuff if they wanted to continue with the drugs trade in Palermo.

The Commission discuss the request from the Americans and in the end it decrees that the Inzerillo, Di Maggio, Spatola and Gambino families can live on the condition that they leave Sicily for ever and never set foot there again without permission.

A guarantor is found for the agreement. His name is Rosario Naimo (*Saruzzu*). He seals the peace pact, swearing on his own life. In the case of any eventuality, any temporary move, change of residence, the Inzerillos, men, women and *picciriddi*, will turn to *Saruzzu*, who will inform Palermo, and Palermo will grant or deny permission. Theirs is a permanent exile.

So for twenty years that's how things stay. Then, on 31 December 2004, Rosario Inzerillo, the brother of the late Totuccio and Santo, steps off the plane in Fiumicino.

Rosario has been declared 'undesirable' by the government of the United States, and now he's in Italy because of the same fate that befell Francesco, *u truttaturi*, 'the trotter', Pietro's son, also considered undesirable. It's bad news for a lot of 'families', and possibly good news for others. How to behave? Shoot Rosario the first time he goes for a stroll in Mondello, as the rules say they should? As the Commission said they were to do in 1982? Or pretend nothing was up? But can you pretend nothing's up with people who have for twenty years been choking back their rage at not being able to avenge spilled blood with blood? How can you trust their smiles, their apparent calm, their apparently mild resignation? It hasn't escaped the more suspicious men of honour that the Inzerillos – first one, then two, then three – are coming back to Palermo. They've reopened the house at 346 Via Castellana in Passo di Rigano, which has been closed for two decades, and in the morning and the afternoon you can see them all together outside the bakery next door.

There's Francesco *u truttaturi*. And Giuseppe Inzerillo, Santo's son. And Giovanni, born in New York in 1972, an American citizen, Totuccio's only living son. And Tommaso, cousin of Totuccio and brother-in-law of John Gambino. And Matteo Inzerillo, who no one outside the family can place on the family tree. Sometimes you also see Francesco *u nivuru*, as if the betrayal of Pietro had been forgotten. For now or for ever, only time will tell. Along with them, the Spatolas of Uditore, the Di Maggios of Torretta, the Boscos, the Di Maios and a few Gambinos have all reappeared in town. They've come back, that's the blunt truth. The young Inzerillos have come back to the city – the new generation of a Mafia aristocracy and the whole of Sicily, before Salvatore Riina made Cosa Nostra his. More new Mafia blood. Young and fiery like the blood of Giovanni and Salvo Riina from Corleone. Time never passes for the men of honour. It's as fixed as the sun in the sky. Stretching from father to son, from cousin to cousin, from uncle to nephew, is a thick thread that can unite or strangle, that can make the family influential and respected or subjugated and unhappy. Always in the same intricate tangle in which wrongs look like rights and neither can be forgotten, even if a hundred years should pass.

The Inzerillos have been in America long enough to grow, to become men, to get to know the things of the world and the families, to cultivate friendship and business deals. Now, seeing them in Palermo, in the suburb of Passo di Rigano – there are always dozens of them, all together, one beside the other – they look ready to continue their saga, which they think has just been interrupted rather than broken, of the *tragedie* of the past. There is rancour in their eyes, and standing beside them is some old crony from former times, before betrayal became a bitter daily bread.

Cronies like Sandrino Mannino of Boccadifalco; Ciccio Pastoia, the *capomandamento* of Belmonte Mezzagno; Nicola Mandalà, the *capofamiglia* of Villabate; Enzo Brusca, Lorenzino Di Maggio and

Caluzzu Caruso *u merendino*, 'the snack-eater', of Torretta. And most importantly Salvatore Lo Piccolo, the *capofamiglia* of Tommaso Natale. The most dangerous, with a training in Zen. Sly as a devil, he was the godson of Saro Riccobono, the loser, and even now no one in Palermo can exlain how he managed to save his skin during the war, how he managed to float back up as a winner.

Lo Piccolo is the most influential. The most determined to liquidate the past through forgiveness. He also asks Bernardo Provenzano to bury the hatchet. And Binnu doesn't close the door; he leaves it ajar. He lets Rosario Inzerillo stay in Palermo for a while longer. 'Let him celebrate New Year with his family . . .' the Corleonese writes in a *pizzino*[1], and then he tells Antonino Rotolo, the *capomandamento* of Pagliarelli – among the bosses that count, the most hostile to the return of the Inzerillos – that something can be done, something must be done, to heal that wound.

The old man, hidden in Montagna dei Cavalli, suggests: 'Nino, where all this talk about America is concerned, none of the people who made that decision about the Inzerillos are still around. We three are the only ones left to decide: you, me and Lo Piccolo . . .'

Nino Rotolo doesn't take Provenzano's advice well. He comments bitterly to his family: 'Us three? Who else is there? The ones in jail, who have died? There are the guys in jail buried alive with a life sentence, his fellow-villager *u zu* Totò first of all, me with a life sentence because of those bastard cops in the Inzerillo family, and he says there's no one left, that there's just the three of us. Who are the three of us? The two of us, in fact, because I'm not even going to mention that bastard Lo Piccolo. We're nobody . . .' Rotolo holds his breath to control his rage.

---

1   Small slip of paper used by the Sicilian Mafia for high-level communications.

Then he goes on: 'The decision that the Inzerillos must show their faces in Palermo if they don't want a gun being held to their heads was taken by the Commission and no one can change it except the Commission. Unfortunately the Commission can't meet, starting with Totò Riina; they're all in jail or missing. So, the Inzerillos will have to go unless Binnu wants to assume – on his own, though – the responsibility of letting them stay, and then, if things go wrong, we'll know who made the decision and why. And don't tell me the guys in Corleone know how to forgive and forget. They'll kill Giovanni Palazzolo as they swore they would fifty years on. They'll wait for fifty years, and as soon as that *cristiano* appears in Corleone they won't give him a moment's rest.'

Nino Rotolo was also there on the evening of 10 May 1981 when Giuseppe Montalto brought the *battuta*: 'Tomorrow morning, Totuccio Inzerillo will go to his wife at number 50 Via Brunelleschi . . .' He was there the following day, at Via Brunelleschi, when Giuseppe Marchese parked his van beside Totuccio, and Alfetta and Pino Greco blast him with the 'pocket coffees' of his Kalashnikov.

Nino Rotolo can't risk having old and young Inzerillos under his feet, particularly if they're relying on that guy Lo Piccolo, amidst Bernardo Provenzano's ambiguous indifference. The boss of the Pagliarelli feels and sees that things are getting worse. He gets organised. He lives at a residence on Viale Michelangelo. Condemned to life imprisonment, and to house arrest for unlikely 'health reasons'. At any hour of the day and night, cops can turn up at his door, knock and be let in. Who can tell if they're real cops or people dressed up as cops? Rotolo puts up a big floodlight between the gate and the door of his villa. Before opening up – even if it's the chief of police in person, or the commander of the *carabinieri* with his plumed helmet – Rotolo turns on the floodlight, watches a monitor and studies the picture. The face of a *picciotto*, a 'made man', is a face that you would recognise in a million. But are those precautions enough to make him feel safe?

They can't be. He needs to find out what's happening outside, who's doing what and with whom, and take a few steps, and predict each new movement, and do the right things.

The thing to do is to isolate Salvatore Lo Piccolo from the Corleonesi; remind that *sciuminito* – 'idiot' – Bernardo Provenzano that the bastard is *on the other side*, that he was a hitman for Saro Riccobono when 'the war' was on. How can they believe him, how can they trust him? They have to be suspicious, and perhaps they'll have to 'break his horns'. Rotolo sets his informants to work. They tell him that – some time before – they saw him, Lo Piccolo, at the airport in Punta Raisi, with Giovanni Inzerillo, Totuccio's son, the one born in America.

Lo Piccolo explains to Giovanni that someone in Cosa Nostra doesn't want them in Palermo, and Giovanni replies: 'But who doesn't want us? There's nobody there!' And Salvatore Lo Piccolo claps him on the shoulder like a brother and reassures him: 'Don't worry, all good things come to an end . . .'

'All good things come to an end' is more than a warning or a threat. It's a declaration of war. It means that one era has come to an end and a new era is just beginning. That the *tragedie* and mourning of yesterday can't be an immutable fate. For young people like Giovanni Inzerillo a new time – happier and more fruitful – is on the way, Salvatore Lo Piccolo says. It means that anyone who didn't agree to the family coming back to Palermo will either lower their head or lose it.

Nino Rotolo, already worried, has things to be concerned about. He brings together his closest *capimandamento* in a corrugated iron shack near his villa. He turns up with a machine that should interfere with the bugs if there are any. What he doesn't know is that the electronic wizardry they've sold him is useless and the bugs, which are there, record every breath.

Rotolo says, 'We can't sleep soundly, because as soon as we're asleep it's very likely that we're not going to wake up again.

Picciotti, you see that . . . nothing comes to an end, these Inzerillos never forget their dead. There are always anniversaries; they sit down at the table and this one's missing and this one's missing – you can never forget these things . . .'

Nothing came to an end, nothing ever comes to an end in Cosa Nostra. The men of honour live like tireless spiders in their big web where you have to make your own space with tenacity and patience and malicious skill every day, playing it out gradually like a dragnet and superimposing it on other people's space. With their collaboration or their defeat. Supporting or colliding with each other in a circular motion that never leaves anything behind – the living or the dead, betrayal or friendship. It's a struggle that never reaches a state of rest.

All power, even Mafia power – particularly Mafia power – is averse to a state of rest. For men of honour, rest is extermination, mortification. Nino Rotolo knows that very well. He has destroyed all those who, like Stefano Bontate, had deluded themselves that they would be at the top of Cosa Nostra for ever, as untouchable as a royal eagle. Rotolo decides not to stay and wait for the acid rain that he can already smell in the air. Even more poisonous now that a defeated generation has been set aside, and it's the younger ones who are seeking revenge that they've waited twenty years for.

Rotolo says, 'These Inzerillos were children and then they grew up – they're in their thirties now. How can we rest easy? They've got to go. First one, then another, and yet another . . . They've got to go to America. They've got to approach *Saruzzo* Naimo and then, if they come to Italy without permission, first *Saruzzo* will die and then we'll kill them all. How can we rest easy? They've got to go and there's an end to it. No God can help them now . . . We've got to get them off our backs, and that way we'll be able to lift our spirits . . . For the good of everyone, that's what we've got to do. Have you or haven't you understood that Lo Piccolo is already walking arm in arm with the Inzerillos? This story isn't over – it'll never be over . . .'

Inside Cosa Nostra things are always starting over again. Just as he did twenty years before, Nino Rotolo begins a *tragedia*. He wants to, he has to, free himself from Lo Piccolo. He thinks about reminding Provenzano, who once betrayed him, and who will betray him again. He thinks of sending Antonino Cinà to see him in Corleone, or wherever he is, to tell him that Lo Piccolo has taken on Salvatore Biondo, *Varbazza*, 'Goatee', to kill him. And meanwhile he's putting his *picciotti bravi* on alert – the clever ones he's never introduced to anyone as such because, as you know, every family has to hide some of its true strength if it wants to survive when things turn tough.

The boss of Pagliarelli in Palermo throws down a list of the living dead. Surgical interventions. A corpse here, a corpse there, that's what he wants to do. All around Lo Piccolo and the Inzerillos. On a war footing, he's preparing for the final bid to resolve the American question once and for all.

One final bid, to make the Inzerillos understand that only the Commission can decide whether or not they come back to Sicily. That's the rule. Then Rotolo calls in Sandrino Mannino, nephew of the late Totuccio Inzerillo. Sandrino is scared, and who wouldn't be in his shoes? He's afraid that the invitation might conceal a trap. That at the end of the feast he'll find himself with a noose around his neck. Nicola Mandalà, the man who is taking care of Provenzano in hiding, guarantees the boy's safety, going with him to see Rotolo in the villa on Viale Michelangelo. The *capomandamento* of Pagliarelli makes sure Sandrino is sitting comfortably. He sees that he's terrified. He reassures him. He turns on the light to get a better look at him, looks him straight in the eyes.

Rotolo says: 'Nicola's very fond of you, so much so that he persuaded me to come today and that's why you're here. *You're not here because you're you, Sandrino Mannino, you're here because you're him, Nicola Mandalà*. Because you see, you and I are made like this: we're divided by a *vadduni*, a precipice, and there's a river passing below the precipice as well. It was your uncle who dug that *vadduni*, not us . . . You have no responsibility for it. But your uncle Totuccio has come to look for us, even inside our houses, to cut our heads off even though we've never done a thing to him. He did it for power or for money. He looked for us and he found us. We didn't go looking for him. And he created this situation of grief and jail, and it's your uncle's responsibility and that of his *compari* if people have died and been put in jail. And, you know, there's no difference between us, you with your dead people and us with our people in jail for ever. Because what are they? They're the living dead! And there's another difference too, if you like. In your advantage. You still have your property and they've taken everything away from us. I'm telling you that to remind you that you're here, but there can never be an official meeting between us, just a private one, because you're one thing . . . *you are you and we are us.* You were a boy and you didn't create this situation. But your relatives created it, and left it to you. If you're honest with me, I will be grateful and pleased. But be careful, because I notice that you're not being sincere; I might be very displeased and get annoyed because I've brought you into my house, and don't you ever forget it . . . Now you know what the situation is with regard to your relatives from America . . . When that situation existed the Americans came here and an agreement was reached. The agreement was that your relatives had to stay there and answer to *Saruzzo*. They'd all fled to America, but they had to remain traceable and answer to a person who was *Saruzzo* Naimo. You get what I'm saying?'

Sandrino, in a faint voice, replies, 'Yes, I get it . . .' Rotolo goes on: 'When your uncle Rosario Inzerillo was supposed to come here, you told him first because you were worried, because it wasn't something your uncle Rosario had thought of himself. The cops had to bring him because he had to undergo a period of special surveillance, and you were told: it's fine, he can come, there'll be surveillance, and as soon as it's over he's got to go back. But you didn't respect that agreement. So tomorrow, once my house arrest is over, I go out and meet your uncle, your cousin, any Inzerillo and I fire two revolver bullets at you, who's going to take me up on it? Some relative of yours? And bear in mind that if I can shoot, there are a hundred, a thousand people who can do the same, because they're in the same boat as me. So, no one can give your people any guarantees; your relatives have to leave, and they have to tell us where they're going, because we have to keep a check on them. I've finished. If you have something to say to me, you can say it to me.'

Sandrino shifts in his armchair, which feels as if it's made of thorns: 'Many thanks, because no one has ever spoken to me so frankly. What you say is perfectly fair. The things you're saying to me aren't wrong, but you see, I'm on *this side* and there's nothing I can do about it . . .'

Nino Rotolo interrupts him. In an almost fatherly voice he says to Mannino, 'Look, not all those people died because they were cops or because they were bad people. They wanted to do something that hadn't been agreed, but they weren't bad people. I can't say that they were bad people. We did it, we had to do it, because it was their fault. We were all nice and calm in our own homes, and now we're all ruined. Some have people to mourn. Some have people in prison. And we're all in the street. So don't feel guilty, because your relatives weren't bad people. They were bad in their actions, not in their thoughts; because when a person is bad in their actions, in this Cosa Nostra, a person sits down and presents his reasons, and if his reasons are bad, he lowers his head. That's all. It's nothing personal, you know? Your relatives quarrelled with everybody, but it's nothing personal on my part even if they put me on the list of people who were supposed to die. If someone wants you dead there's only one possible end for you . . . Don't worry, I know you're a good person, a good boy, but let me tell you what you've got to do in your position. You have to stay *nna to casedda*, in your little house, without climbing over it, because your name isn't Inzerillo, but you are an Inzerillo. Listen, if there's anything you need, tell me, and if I can help you

I will help you as if I needed you . . . You see, we have a personal relationship. It's not a personal relationship. Because officially I can't receive you . . .'

Nino Rotolo thinks he's understood everything, but he isn't aware of the essential thing: what he fears has already happened. The Inzerillos are already in Palermo. It's true, they weren't given the go-ahead by the Commission to stay. But what they have is way more than a permit from someone like *Saruzzo* Naimo, or the consent of a *capomandamento* from Pagliarelli. Behind them are the people with the power and influence of the cousins in New York and above all the opportunities for new markets that the Americans want to offer on a silver platter to Sicilian Cosa Nostra. Legal and illegal deals.

Rotolo talks; he's always causing *tragedie*, setting traps. He pursues the usual logic. Rotolo hasn't worked out that the deal has already been concluded. That Salvatore Lo Piccolo is the guarantor on this side of the ocean, and on the other, the ambassador of the five 'families' in New York is a man of honour called Frank Calì. In his office at Circus Fruits, between 59th and 60th Street in New York, is the line of guests who have come from Sicily. Cosa Nostra has already ceased to be the monolith governed by the handwritten notes associated with the peasant cunning of old Provenzano or, as in the past, run through with the usual territorial and cultural fracture. On the one side, the peasants and the country villages. On the other, the city-dwellers, the big city, the suburbs.

The Mafia is a bubbling pot, a world in ferment, excited by new opportunities. As if by a conditioned reflex, they are tempted to pick up their pistols to eliminate any contradictions. In some suburbs *ammazzatine* – killing sprees – break out. Nicola Ingarao, the *capofamiglia* of Porta Nuova, doesn't demonstrate the necessary flexibility that the transition requires. They shoot him in the head. His *picciotti* understand that 'good things come to an end'. They too – like others before them – are convinced that they have to seek, without firing a shot, a good compromise to stress the only real motivation that has always fired up the families: *fare i piccioli*, making money. Will they succeed? The outcome of the dispute is completely unpredictable. Over the next few months, war is just as likely to break out in Palermo as peace. Perhaps, in order to understand moods and resentments, we need to go back to Corleone. We should have another chat with Biagio M. If he's still alive.

LUNCH IN CORLEONE

The appointment is arranged for midday, in the main square in Corleone. 'We'll see each other at the place you know, where we met last time,' Biagio says on the phone. Last time.

Last time was almost fifteen years ago. We met Biagio in a bar that had started selling the first bottles of Godfather *amaro*. A homage to Mario Puzo and Marlon Brando. Who knows, perhaps to Totò Riina too. Godfather *amaro* is a d.o.c. product of Corleone, just like its *viddani* Mafiosi. Along with the wheat. Along with the wine of the hills that divide San Giuseppe Jato.

At midday there's no sign of Biagio in the square. His nephew turns up. He says hello and apologises: '*Zio* Biagio isn't feeling so good; he didn't feel up to coming. It's too hot! Let's go and see him in the countryside.'

Under a roasting sun, ten minutes later, we're on the old road that goes down to Marineo.

Biagio M. is sitting in the shade, under the pergola, his chin resting on a knotted stick. He is ill. He has a bad heart, and he hasn't worked in the fields for years. He rarely goes into the village, only for the odd mass on Sunday. At Christmas, at Easter, at New Year's, for consecrated feasts. He hardly sees anyone now. He has locked himself away in a little farm. It was the dream of a life. It's his at last.

We sit down beside him. Biagio asks his nephew to bring

glasses of water and a bottle of anise liqueur. He pours just a few drops. In a flash, a white cloud curdles in the icy water. He says: 'That's how they do it in Palermo; I learned to drink *zammù* from the Palermitans. We Corleonesi, when we want to, are good at adapting to the habits of others.'

It's a good start for the chat we've come to have. We're here to know from Biagio whether the violent character, the peasant culture, the experience of being 'hunted animals' for decades can allow the Corleonesi to adjust to new times. If *u zu* Totò and his men are capable of changing their skin and their ways of thinking. Their model of life, in fact, their self-image, their relationships with others. Their idea of *power*.

We tell Biagio that the death of that man Nicola Ingarao from Porta Nuova, in Palermo – a big shot, but not that big, apparently – made us think that Cosa Nostra might be on the brink of a new Mafia war. We know that not every murder leads to open conflict. A murder can be the necessary instrument for avoiding conflict. It isn't a paradox. It's the cynical, brutal logic of the Mafia: eliminating a hard-headed Mafioso frees up the field and makes a peace agreement possible. If the presence of a boss, in an important *mandamento*, is a point of resistance to innovation, his death makes everything easier. Even Ingarao's death could be explained in that way, couldn't it?

Biagio listens with his lips slightly parted. His eyes are watery and alert, his face wrinkled and motionless. It looks as if he isn't missing a word. We are encouraged to continue the discussion that we put together in long conversations with investigators, magistates, some historians, with a few of those civil servants in the regional administration of Palazzo dei Normanni who know men, vices and mysteries.

From what we have understood, in Sicily today, opportunities for peace are equal to the likelihood of war. Much, if not everything, depends on how the 'America debate' is resolved. Will it be war or peace? Many people have told us that the Mafia 'families' have reached an agreement. What was seen as 'the Inzerillo problem' would soon be resolved.

Inside Cosa Nostra, they have explained to us, it's in everyone's interest to work for unity, in the conviction that the 'families' can only guarantee continuity if they work together. No one wants to make the mistakes of the past again. They have understood that if they want to have a future they have to agree, they have to work together. They want investment prospects. They are looking at the United States, and not only that. Cosa Nosta wants to accumulate money, to move where the proceeds are most likely to be favourable, wherever there's the potential for good opportunities. Certainly, the Sicilian Mafia isn't ignoring the big international drugs trade, but it wants its role to be different from before.

The men of honour on mainland Italy – we say to Biagio, who is drinking his second glass of water and anis – only finance drug cargoes with partnership shares and quotas. Like in tobacco smuggling in the 1950s, you remember? They might make a bit less money, but the profits are safe – far from the long hands of the state.

Biagio nods, but that doesn't mean he approves. These are arguments that he will have heard before. Studying his face it's hard to tell what he thinks.

Then we go on. Imagine two channels, we've been told. They don't coincide, and they can't be superimposed on one another. In one, money is moved. In the other, it's drugs. And the movement of money doesn't coincide in time with the movement of drugs. We have met a number of people in Palermo and Rome who were ready to assure us that Cosa Nostra wants to put its full weight into the financial circuit, abandoning the operation channel to others. The Americans may be essential for this metamorphosis. In order to make certain investments, Cosa Nostra can no longer afford to recycle its profits in identifiable properties on its territory, in buildings and lands, as *u zu* Totò had always done. Salvo, *u picciriddu*, understood that 'illegal has to become original'. He looks for new paths, wherever the proceeds of crime can become clean and anonymous. The route to the United States is only one possibility, they add. There are Sicilian 'families' who could invest major sums in the commercial network in the centre of Manhattan. But there are also American 'families' interested in investing in the network of large-scale distribution in Italy with the protection, support and collaboration of Cosa Nostra.

It's time to sit down at table. Biagio struggles to his feet. We're all in single file, Biagio at the front. The big room on the ground floor is cool and shady, with the shutters closed. A soup tureen in the middle of the round table sends puffs of fragrant steam into the air. The *cavati* (macaroni-style pasta) in tomato sauce and beef ragù are exquisite. We eat in silence for a while. We compliment Biagio on his food, and he waves our remarks away. He hardly eats anything. He holds his empty fork in the air, and asks: 'What else did they tell you?' They talked to us about the possibility of an *'omcidio eccelente'*, an 'excellent murder' that might be the self-proclamation, with a show of strength, of a new Mafia leadership. Wasn't it the same for the Inzerillos? Didn't they kill prosecutor Gaetano Costa in 1980 to tell everyone that their power wasn't burnt out? Well, not many people believe in that solution. Most of them have told us that the hypothesis is unlikely because that strategy of violence now seems to belong to the past. The Mafia are aware of the damage that another challenge to the state might do to them. They're not going to fall into that trap. They want money. And to make money they have to be united, to look for mediation, to forge allegiances. To some government officials, that's what the Sicilian Mafia are trying to do. The choices are homogeneous, and in accord with their interest in the Americans. And, as we know, the Americans disapproved of the killings of Falcone and Borsellino. They only think about business.

*

There's already a *parmigiana di melanzane* on the table, and Biagio whispers: 'Corleone is solid; it's solid in the minds of the men who live there. In every part of Italy and elsewhere things are changing. For better or for worse, but they're changing. Here it's as if everything is frozen in stone. There are a few more lights in the streets, there are colours in the shop windows, there are cars belching out smoke, but to me it all seems like it was fifty years ago, when the estate was here. The *campieri* are still the same. They just aren't doing it in Piano della Scala. They're doing it in the whole country. *They* are still the godfathers, even when they're locked up in a prison somewhere. Even if they're on the run. They have the instinct of rule, of dominion in their blood. They've been brought up to command.'

Biagio asks his nephew: 'Would you always live in Corleone?' His nephew replies: 'I was born here, and I'm getting out as soon as I can. You, *zio*, knew Totò Riina in the fields as a little boy. My father knew Leoluca Bagarella, who looked after the grazing animals. I knew Giovanni and Salvo Riina when they came back to the village. I want to leave this place. Arrogance is passed down through the generations. They are always *up*, we're always *down*. There's no hope of anything new. The state is always a uniform; it's always a van and a road block. We're forced to live either as cops or as Mafiosi. Or worse: surviving as half-cops and half-Mafiosi.' Our old friend in Corleone listens and nods. Then he says to him, 'You know, even here it eventually starts seeming as if times are changing. I've thought so myself: when they arrested Totò Riina in 1993. I went to the bunker courtroom in Palermo to get a closer look at him, I was convinced that that time would be the beginning of the end for him as well. I've told you that before. Unfortunately I would have to say that Corleone is like a city-state; it's a world apart. It's a long way even from Palermo, let alone Italy. Find me a single Corleonese who feels European! Go around and ask everybody, one by one: do you feel European?

They won't even answer you; they'll think you're mad. Corleone isn't Europe and it isn't Africa – it's a bag in between, a diseased bag. It's better not to look into it.' So, Biagio? What could happen? What's Totò Riina going to do? What will he tell his people? Peace or war? Biagio stretches a hand out on the table and picks up a peach from the fruit basket. He takes a knife and slices it slowly. As he carefully peels a quarter, he starts talking about the Mafia in Corleone. 'What do you want me to say? That the sun's going to rise in the other direction? Perhaps the earth has started spinning a different way in Palermo and New York. Not in Corleone. Corleone is still the same village: nothing ever changes here. And *u zu* Totò, his brother-in-law Luchino and all the others who don't know each other and who I know haven't changed either.' He pauses, as if to assess the effect of his words.

'The men of honour have always kept the Corleonesi apart. They hide them from the others, from the people in the other "families". But they also hide them from many people in their own "family". There are still lots of them. Enough to fill four or five buses with fifty seats each. There must be 200 or maybe 250 that nobody knows. All at the service of *u zu* Totò. Whether they're any good at shooting, I have no idea. If they are any good at shooting, they'll do it; they'll never accept the agreement with the Palermitans that everyone's talking about. They're people who are "made differently". You won't find them with those others. They think in the old way: they don't like change; inside they're still peasants. They're conservative Mafiosi. The Palermitans have always been a means to an end, and the Americans might be a way of getting new business, but I don't think so. The *viddani* and their relatives and their children have nothing to do with the Inzerillos or the Gambinos or that guy Frank Calì. They're a different breed. Call them what you like. What did you say? Surgical operations. Twenty years ago, they did one and a half thousand surgical operations, or maybe more. That's the number of people the Corleonesi killed in western Sicily between April 1981 and the autumn of 1983. Wouldn't you call that a Mafia war? Well, call it something else, then: the Corleonesi won't be offended. But I'm sure: if they're strong enough, they'll start shooting again. They won't put up with the Inzerillos who are coming back from America. They won't put up with Lo Piccolo who was and remains a Palermitan traitor as far as they're concerned. Not one of them has ever betrayed. Only the others have betrayed. They have no reason to entrust the fates of the family and their own lives to the hands of men they despise.'

Now Biagio finds the strength to smile bitterly, or perhaps it's resigned common sense. He says, 'Totò Riina is very ill, like me. We're a pair of little old men. We will die soon. But let me tell you that as long as I have a single drop of blood in my veins, *u zio* Totò will never negotiate. He will never strike deals with Palermo. Neither he nor Bagarella nor any of their breed. They're already at war. They're just waiting for a sign, a sign that can only come from one man: from him, from Totò Riina. I could be wrong, but that's what I think. Now if you'll excuse me, I'd like to take a rest.'

Biagio goes back towards the pergola. He sits down on his bench and rests his forehead on his stick. He seems to have a siesta. We go back to a deserted Corleone, in the summer evening. In the square, the stone commemorating Giovanni Falcone and Paolo Borsellino is the luminous trace of another world.

Palermo, 30 July 2007

INDEX

INDEX

INDEX

INDEX

INDEX